T0402468

Economic Complexity and Human Development

This book combines the human development approach with innovation economics to explore the effects that structural economic change has on human development.

While economic diversification can provide valuable new social choices and capabilities, it also tends to lead to more complex decision processes and changes to the set of capabilities required by people to self-determine their future. Within this process of structural transformation, social networks are crucial for accessing information and social support, but networks can also be a root cause of exclusion and inequality reproduction. This implies the need to encourage innovation and economic diversification beyond production expansion, focusing on the promotion of human agency and social inclusion.

This book provides such a modern perspective on development economics, emphasizing the role of social networks, economic diversity and entrepreneurship for social welfare. The author discusses how innovation, social networks, economic dynamics and human development are interlinked, and provides several practical examples of social and micro-entrepreneurship in contexts as diverse as Peruvian rural villages and Brazil's urban areas.

The interdisciplinary perspective put forward in this book illustrates theoretical and methodological methods of exploring the complexity of development in a practical and relevant way. It also provides useful information about structural factors which need to be considered by practitioners when designing pro-poor growth policies. Furthermore, the coverage of the core concepts of innovation, networks and development economics, enriched with multiple examples, makes it a valuable resource for scholars and advanced students of modern development economics.

Dominik Hartmann is Research Fellow at the University of Hohenheim, Germany and a Postdoctoral Fellow at the MIT Media Lab, USA. His work examines the complex relationships between innovation, structural economic change and human development.

Routledge Studies in Development Economics

Economic Complexity and Human Development

How economic diversification and social networks affect human agency and welfare

Dominik Hartmann

LONDON AND NEW YORK

First published 2014
by Routledge
2 Park Square, Milton Park, Abingdon, Oxon OX14 4RN

and by Routledge
711 Third Avenue, New York, NY 10017

Routledge is an imprint of the Taylor & Francis Group, an informa business

British Library Cataloguing in Publication Data
A catalogue record for this book is available from the British Library

Library of Congress Cataloging in Publication Data
Hartmann, Dominik, 1980-
Economic complexity and human development : how economic diversification and social networks affect human agency and welfare / Dominik Hartmann.

pages cm

Includes bibliographical references and index.

1. Development economics–Social aspects. 2. Economic development–Social aspects. 3. Economics–Sociological aspects. I. Title.

HD75.H387 2014

306.3–dc23

2013039823

ISBN: 978-0-415-85891-5 (hbk)
ISBN: 978-0-203-72208-4 (ebk)

D100

Typeset in Times New Roman
by Sunrise Setting Ltd, Paignton, UK

Contents

Figures

Tables

Preface

This book constitutes my doctoral thesis in economics at the University of Hohenheim. But more than a title, it is the final outcome of a research journey of seven years, which has taken me from Germany to Spain, Peru, Brazil, Netherlands, England and Turkey, collecting information and seeking advice on the relations between economic development and human development. This research endeavour aims to contribute to the creation of bridges between structural change and human development research and examine the variety of methods that allow us to explore and research the complex relations between social networks, economic diversity and human development. It is highly sceptical of two-dimensional categorizations, such as black-and-white thinking, which simplify a multidimensional and complex world.

The main motivation behind this book resulted from an internship in agricultural development projects at a Peruvian non-governmental organization (NGO), in the autumn of 2005. The NGO brought farmers together to create associations and produce and distribute value added, durable agricultural goods. I was given the task of elaborating, in cooperation with the farmers, a marketing plan for their products. The experienced project managers of my NGO deliberately sought to promote the commercialization and business aspect of their project, as they considered it a critical factor in promoting sustainable development in less developed regions. When evaluating his personal success after thirty years in development projects, one project manager said: 'Well, I think we have contributed to a higher and better production of local goods. We have also contributed to capacity building, democracy and human rights; yet often it has also felt like we have taken one step forwards and two steps backwards. I think one core problem has been selling the products that we had improved and creating a sustained income source'.

I learned from this experience that social development is a crucial part of development; however, it must also go hand in hand with economic and business development. This requires interdisciplinary approaches that take the complex relations between economic and human development into account. Another lesson I learned from working in this project was that business development itself is strongly related to promoting human agency, skills, innovation and social capital. I thought that the efficiency of production and the income of the farmers could have been significantly increased if they could have supplied their basic products or work to bigger companies in more advanced sectors and distribution systems. Most clients would certainly have appreciated that sort of social choice, which would have enabled them to obtain paid employment instead of struggling with their small agricultural businesses. The NGO did excellent work on the local level, although I began to wonder if a more concerted structural policy by the government and private sector companies would have facilitated the establishment of competitive companies able to benefit from economies of scale and establish national and global distribution chains.

My experiences with the NGO deepened my interest in learning about the relations between business development, structural change and social welfare. When I returned to the University of Augsburg in Germany, I wrote my Master's thesis on 'Systems of Innovation and Competence Building in Latin America'. This led me to the work of several researchers, who suggested introducing the understandings of Amartya Sen and the human capability approach when applying the innovation system approach to developing countries (Arocena and Sutz 2005; Johnson *et al.* 2003; United Nations Development Programme (UNDP) 2001). This helped me to became aware of three things. First, the learning and problem-solving capabilities of the entire population must be improved in order to create prolific regional, sectoral and national innovation systems. Second, endogenous development and external knowledge transfers must complement each other. Third, innovation should not merely be considered as a tool for improving human development, but more as being essentially intertwined with human agency and development. This convinced me that innovation is a key driver of both social and economic development, but equally, as with economic growth, I do not consider it the ultimate goal. The goal is human agency, freedom and well-being, for their own sakes, not merely as an offshoot of the expansion of production or the installation of new technologies.

This led me to consider several questions. What are the effects of innovation-driven structural change on human development? What are the interrelations between diverse types of entrepreneurship and human agency? And what role does social network play in people's choices and capabilities? These questions gave birth to the basic motivation behind this book, which is intended to help disentangle the complex relations between innovation, structural change and human development.

Searching for information and advice led me to many different places to research, study and work. I first completed a Master's in International Economics and Development at the Universidad Complutense de Madrid; then for my doctoral studies in innovation economics I went to the University of Bremen, the Federal University of Rio de Janeiro and the University of Hohenheim; and for case and empirical studies I travelled to the Centre for Studies and Promotion of Development (DESCO) in Peru, to the Microfinance Institute Estrela in Patos, Brazil and to the Centre of Innovation Studies at the Eindhoven University of Technology. I am very grateful for the ideas and advice from many people on this research journey. I finally finished my PhD thesis at the Chair of Innovation Economics of the University of Hohenheim and defended it in March 2012.

In summary, this book is the result of a research journey which aims to contribute to an emergent strand of research and policymaking that analyses the complex relations between innovation, structural change and human development and seeks to design economic policies that do not merely raise economic production, but rather raise the welfare and agency of the people.

Acknowledgements

I am grateful to the many people who have helped and inspired me during this research journey, and in particular I would like to thank the following. First of all, I would like to express my gratitude to my PhD supervisor Andreas Pyka, from the University of Hohenheim. I have worked with him since my graduate studies in Augsburg in 2003; in all that time he has always believed in me, given me expert advice and the freedom to follow my ideas. He instilled my interest in the importance of innovation, networks and economic diversification for development. My appreciation is extended to Atilio Arata, Alberto Rubina and my colleagues from DESCO, Arequipa and Lima, for giving me enthusiasm for development: the chapter in this book on social capital and human development was improved significantly by a joint empirical study on social capital and innovation in rural regions of Peru. My professors and friends from the Master in International Economics and Development at the Universidad Complutense de Madrid (UCM), to whom I am indebted, I want to thank for teaching me a critical and creative perspective on development. Furthermore I wish to acknowledge with much appreciation the dedicated work of Edinalda Lima and my former colleagues from the microfinance Estrela Institute in Paraiba, Brazil. The chapter on entrepreneurship and human development was inspired by the highly motivated and competent team of the Estrela Institute. My respect and gratitude goes also to Koen Frenken and the researchers at the Technical University of Eindhoven, who provided very useful advice and ideas for my doctoral thesis in general and the chapter on economic diversification and human development in particular. With respect to this chapter, I would also like to extend my thanks to Pier Paolo Saviotti and Andrew Stirling, whose ideas on diversity deeply affected this work. I would like to offer my thanks also to the participants of the many conferences, workshops and summer schools I have attended. All of them gave me significant insights and advice – most importantly, the participants at the Human Development and Capability Conferences in Lima 2009 and The Hague 2011, the Schumpeter ISS conference in Rio de Janeiro 2007 and the DIMETIC European doctoral schools at BETA Strasbourg and UNU-MERIT in 2011. I am also grateful for the coordination of the Mercator IPC fellowship program, in particular Daniel Grütjen and Onur Sazak, at the Istanbul Policy Center, who supported me in the revision for this Routledge publication. A special thanks is due to the invaluable support of

David Hendrix who has twice critically read through the entire manuscript and encouraged me to give more examples and keep the language self-explanatory for the interested but not specialised reader. My appreciation goes to Carlota Perez for her seminal work on technological revolutions and waves of development and allowing me to use her figure on the 'panorama of the changing context of the twentieth century'. I am indebted to Donna Kelley and the international GEM consortia for permitting me the use of empirical figures on total early stage and necessity-based entrepreneurship from the Global Entrepreneurship Monitor 2010 Global Report. The empirical study on systems of innovation and development in Latin America (in Chapter 2) draws upon a joint publication with Andreas Pyka and Horst Hanusch in the journal *Structural Change and Economic Dynamics* in 2010; I want to thank Elsevier for allowing me to use several excerpts and tables of this work. I am also grateful to the professors Harald Hagemann and Alexander Gerybadze, who formed part of the PhD board in my thesis defence to become a doctor of economics at the University of Hohenheim.

There are countless friends, colleagues and family members who I would also like to take this opportunity to acknowledge and thank warmly. I thank all those who have kindly helped me in various ways, with whom I have had many intensive discussions and who read through various parts of this thesis, in particular: Fernando del Rio, Giorgio Triulzi, Stefan Mendritzki, Laura Pawson, Guadalupe Calderon, Michael Fendt, Florian Keller, Stefan Gschossmann, Anita Hernanz Ruiz, Markus Wallner, Tobias Buchmann, Evangelos Bourelos, Monika Faulstich, Lai Ping Lee and George Dyson. Finally, and most importantly of all, I wish to thank my parents, my sister and my wife for their endless love and support.

Dominik Hartmann
Augsburg, 19 July 2013

Abbreviations

BNDES	Brazilian National Development Bank
BoP	Base of the Pyramid
CIS	Community Innovation Survey
CNSE	Comprehensive Neo-Schumpeterian Economics
DESCO	Centre for Studies and Promotion of Development in Peru
GCI	Global Competitiveness Index
GDP PPP	Gross Domestic Product at Purchasing Power Parity
Globelics	The Global Network for the Economics of Learning, Innovation, and Competence Building Systems
HDCA	The Human Development and Capability Approach
HDI	Human Development Index
HHI	Hirschman-Herfindahl Index
ICT	Information and Communication Technology
ILO	International Labour Organization
INEI	Instituto Nacional de Estadística e Informática de Perú
IPC	Istanbul Policy Center
ISI	Import Substitution Industrialization
ISS	International Joseph A. Schumpeter Society
LASA	Latin American Structuralist Approach (or School)
MFI	Micro-Finance Institution
MNE	Multinational Enterprise
MPI	Multidimensional Poverty Index
NBER	The National Bureau of Economic Research – USA
NC	Network Cohesion
ND	Network Density
NGO	Non-Governmental Organization
NIS	National Innovation System
OECD	Organisation for Economic Co-operation and Development
R&D	Research and Development
RCA	Revealed Comparative Advantage
SENASA	Peruvian National State Agency for Agricultural Health
SITC	Standard International Trade Classification
SME	Small and Medium Enterprise

SNA	Social Network Analysis
STEPS	Social, Technological and Environmental Pathways to Sustainability
STI	Science, Technology and Innovation
UNDP	United Nations Development Programme
UNU-MERIT	The United Nations University – Maastricht Economic and Social Research Institute on Innovation and Technology

1 Introduction

Economic complexity and human development

Economic diversification and social networks affect the social choices and human agency of people in a multitude of positive, negative and ambiguous ways. Having limited social contacts and few occupational choices tends to limit the opportunities people have in choosing and determining their own lives. Even assuming that people had the same level of education and health, an eighteen-year-old person living in a city with an advanced economy (for example which produces cars, software and multiple services), tends to have more social choices and opportunities for lifelong capability upgrading compared to a person living in an local economy showing a low-level of economic complexity with a few disconnected economic sectors, small-scale agriculture, informal mining and some garment-trading activities. Improving the educational level of and the health services available to people living in an economy with a low-level of complexity and productive capabilities is an important factor, but on its own is not enough to achieve a sustained convergence of the development and social choice capabilities of these two different economies. The type and quality of the occupational choices in an economy, as well as the type of personal networks, are essential for the agency and life quality of the people. Yet high levels of economic diversity and large social networks can also lead to difficult decision processes and the high opportunity costs of activities which were not chosen by the individuals may result in a negative impact on their quality of life.

Development policies must furthermore consider the fact that economies, their agents, relations, goals and choices are not static, but due to the introduction of economic and social innovation, change over time and differ between various regions and countries. Because of market failures and negative polarization effects, governments need to create an institutional framework and incentive structures that encourage (a) the connectedness of people to diverse social networks and (b) the emergence of sectors that deliberately promote not just economic growth but also human agency and welfare. In addition, sound policy-making needs to recognize that the capabilities people require to become full members of their society and be able to determine their own lives change over time. Whereas physical strength may have been crucial at one point, Internet literacy is increasingly important in the modern age to be (considered) a full member of the society. Indeed, modern approaches in development economics consider development as a set of complex and dynamic processes with multiple directions, goals and causal relations between diverse agents (e.g. Social, Technological and Environmental Pathways to Sustainability (STEPS) centre 2010; Stirling 2010).

Recently, the terms innovation, social networks, diversity, entrepreneurship and also life quality, human development and happiness have gained relative importance alongside traditional topics such as capital accumulation and economic growth. The approach elaborated in this book contributes to the modern perspective on development, which highlights the complex and dynamic character of development, by (a) showing theoretical and methodological possibilities on how to combine the complementary perspectives of the human capability approach, innovation and structural change economics; and (b) asking how innovation-driven economic diversification and social networks affect human agency and welfare. It considers development as a process of structural changes, which from a human development perspective should lead to the expansion of human capabilities and agency (Chapter 3). It also shows through the discussion of the complex relations between diversification and human development (in Chapter 4), social networks, innovation and human development (in Chapter 5) as well as (social) entrepreneurship and human development (in Chapter 6) that structural economic change and human development are highly interrelated forces of development. A sustained expansion of human development requires the joint action of human development, innovation and structural change policies (Chapter 7).

Over the last few decades, the human development approach has become the dominant approach of the United Nations Development Programme (UNDP) and has also become an approach applied by thousands of development agencies worldwide. In other words, it affects the lives of millions of people through projects aiming to address basic needs and empower people. Human development refers to the capabilities of people to actively make decisions and to participate in the development of their societies (Sen 1999; UNDP 1990). It is for this reason that minimum standards in education, health, shelter, income and other dimensions are necessary to empower people. Yet there are still many people (1.3 billion in 2008, according to the World Bank 2013) around the world who are living on less than US$1.25 a day, and too many people are deprived of their basic human rights and access to the decent healthcare and education that would allow them to live healthy, long and full lives. The United Nations and an increasing number of non-governmental organizations (NGOs) and social entrepreneurs aim to address the needs of these people. At the same time, cutting-edge approaches in economic development emphasize the need for economic diversification to bring about economic competitiveness and growth (e.g. Hausmann and Rodrik 2003; Rodrik 2004; Saviotti and Pyka 2004; Frenken *et al.* 2007; Hidalgo *et al.* 2007). This approach sees economic development as a recombinant process, in which economies' technological and productive capabilities are formed through prolific interaction, cooperation and competition between diverse agents from the public and private sectors. Innovation and development economists argue that prolific innovation systems and dynamic entrepreneurs are necessary to generate, implement and diffuse new products, processes, inputs, markets and organizations

(Schumpeter 1912; Freeman 1987). As innovations are often new recombinations and alterations of existing competences, a diversity of ideas and knowledge spurs the recombinant growth of new technologies and ultimately leads to the emergence of new sectors (Jacobs 1969). Governments and companies across the world aim to upgrade their technological capabilities to diversify into higher value added sectors, achieving economic competitiveness and providing more and better occupational choices. Key words of this approach include 'innovation', 'entrepreneurship', 'innovation networks' and 'high-tech clusters'.

This book argues that merely focusing on economic diversification or on human development is not enough to promote sustained social progress and a more equal distribution of capabilities and outcomes across the world. Both approaches are needed, because they can complement and reinforce each other. Whereas economic growth does not automatically trickle down to the poor, neither is an emphasis on human capabilities alone enough to create the economic demand for such capabilities. The establishment of higher value added sectors, providing more and better jobs for the poor, needs both economic policies to create the institutional framework and subsidies required to trigger learning processes as well as human development policies which are needed for a better educated, healthy and creative labour force. Furthermore, the productive structure and level of economic diversification of a country profoundly influence the types of occupational choices available and the contribution that economic growth makes to human agency and welfare. Creativity and demand-driven innovation and structural change are almost impossible without a well-educated and healthy population. However, sustained endogenous investment in human development is difficult to realize without simultaneous investment in economic competitiveness and diversification. Social innovations, such as microfinance, can indeed be powerful mechanisms for providing the poor with the means to help themselves, but they are not enough to allow the formation of globally competitive, small and medium enterprises; a well-educated, healthy and creative workforce that has better access to better jobs is also required. All of this simply means that human and economic development policies are complementary forces. It is, therefore, very important that we gain a better understanding of the linkages between human development and the structures and dynamics of socioeconomic systems if we are to design prolific development policies in the real world.

The idea that the forces of human development and economic growth are not in opposition but rather complement each other is certainly not entirely new. It is worth noting that the UNDP human development index (HDI) is composed of three equal parts: life expectancy, education and income (UNDP 1990, 2010). Some of the leading researchers in the human capability approach discuss how economic growth and opportunities can improve human freedom (e.g. Sen 1999; Ranis *et al.* 2000; Ocampo and Vallejo 2012). There are also new initiatives coming from the innovation and structural change research community, who deliberately take the human capability approach into account (e.g. STEPS centre, Globelics). Recently, interesting approaches have appeared which scrutinize the effects of productivity growth and structural change or the effects of social capital on human development (e.g. Ranis *et al.* 2000; Ibrahim 2006; Ocampo and Vallejo 2012; Capriati 2013). Nevertheless, there is still a need for more work on increasing the level of interdisciplinary cooperation between human development and leading innovation approaches, by taking into account the findings of each other. Alkire (2010), for example, has shown that in twenty years of UN Human Development Reports, 'the terms work and employment only appear under the names creativity and productivity and only for five years' (Alkire 2010, p. 14). At the Global Network for Economics of Learning, Innovation and Competence Building System there are still comparatively few works which deliberately focus on and enter into the concepts employed by the human development approach (e.g. Johnson *et al.* 2003; Arocena and Sutz 2005; Cozzen and Kaplinsky 2009; Capriati 2013). It can be argued that the difficulties in establishing interdisciplinary approaches are not due to a lack of interest on either side. Rather, it is due to a series of complex issues. One of these is a natural tendency for researchers to continue working in their core field of expertise. The complexity of interdisciplinary work and the difficulties of publishing such work in leading journals can also lead to scientists conforming to the established or dominant approaches within their research community approaches. This book aims to contribute ideas on how bot research communities can learn from each other to shed new light on the complex relations between economic growth and human development. It attempts to do so by disentangling the positive, negative and ambiguous effects of economic diversification and social networks on human agency and welfare, and presents a set of different methods that enable more comprehensive engagement with the relations between economic diversity, social networks and human development.

This book is structured as follows. Chapter 2 discusses the core ideas and concepts of the different approaches in development economics that are essential to understanding the work presented here: (a) the neoclassical economic growth paradigm; (b) the innovation and structural change paradigm; and (c) the human development approach. Focus is placed on the last two approaches; however, the first must be taken into account, as both the innovation as well as the human development approach developed partly out of a critique of the neoclassical approach. To demonstrate the need for interdisciplinary approaches, a short empirical study of Latin America shows that none of the approaches (i.e. human development, innovation or economic efficiency) were individually able to provide a fully comprehensive picture of the strengths and bottlenecks of development. Whereas some countries and regions in Latin America suffer from serious levels of poverty, violence and unfreedom, the main challenges for further improvement in other countries and regions may be more related to the lack of technological capabilities or economic efficiency.

Having laid out the main terms, ideas and concepts of the innovation economics and human development approach, and having shown the empirical shortcomings of each specialised approach, Chapter 3 then presents the 'Sen meets Schumpeter' paradigm. This approach aims to disentangle and analyse some of the complex relations between individuals' capabilities and the structures and dynamics of the socioeconomic systems that people live under, to broaden the information base which economic policies can make use of to deliberately promote not just economic growth but also human development. In addition, complexity thinking is used – as a third approach – in an attempt to create bridges between the different approaches. Complexity approaches emphasize agents, networks and diversity as key features of complex systems. Neo-Schumpeterian approaches take these features explicitly into account to study the novelties that are created through entrepreneurship and the interaction of diverse agents in complex systems. A main driver of diversification (of sectors, ideas etc.) processes is innovation, which itself is driven by entrepreneurship and interactive learning between diverse agents of the economy. Within the so-called 'Sen meets Schumpeter' approach we recognize that social networks, entrepreneurship and economic diversification are not just core features of structural economic change; they also directly affect human agency and the welfare of individuals.

These three structural features and drivers of economic systems can contribute to understanding the complex relations between economic growth and human development and help to design innovation and structural change policies that do not just facilitate economic growth, but deliberately empower and increase people's social choices. This perspective places human development at the core of development, yet also claims that structural change and innovation policies, which take network structures and the value of different types of entrepreneurial choices and network structures into account, can be important factors in improving people's agency and welfare. Based on this approach, the subsequent chapters present theoretical and empirical means that help to disentangle the positive, negative and ambiguous effects that economic diversification (Chapter 4), social networks (Chapter 5) and entrepreneurship (Chapter 6) can have on human agency and welfare, as well as what structural change policies need to take into account and how they need to be designed to deliberately provide valuable new social choices and facilitate people's capabilities and their well-being (Chapter 7).

Chapter 4 argues that economic diversification can expand the social choices of individuals (e.g. their occupational choices) and influences which capabilities are demanded in an economy. Diversification, furthermore, can prevent the emergence of rigid top-down networks in an economy and favour more democratic regimes through better distribution of economic power. Nevertheless, at very high levels of economic diversification, people may be paralysed by the increasing complexity of decision processes and thus well-being can be negatively affected. Consequently an emphasis is required on promoting real new choices (rather than, for instance, choosing between a massive number of very similar products) as well as improving people's capabilities of dealing with complexity through appropriate education systems. A cross-sectional analysis of over 121 countries confirms that economic diversity has a significant positive effect on human development. Export data from over 772 product categories was used to calculate different measurements of diversity and their impact on income per capita and on the HDI. The results are highly significant for all the diversity measures applied: entropy and the Hirschman-Herfindahl index (HHI) revealed comparative advantages and average product ubiquity on the different levels of disaggregation

(1-, 2- and 4-digit level) in the Standard International Trade classification (SITC). The analysis confirms the hypothesis that economic diversification affects human development and economic growth in different ways. Unrelated and related economic variety have a marginally increasing positive effect on income; related variety and product proliferation have a marginally decreasing positive effect on human development.

Chapter 5 studies in more detail how social networks affect people's capabilities of becoming active agents of development. Social networks have a major effect on the diversity of information and help that people can access (Woolcock and Narayan 2000; Borgatti *et al.* 2009). Networks strongly impact the choices (e.g. occupations, life styles, nutrition, etc.) that people are aware of and the entrepreneurial actions and learning processes that they engage in. People's capabilities and functioning (i.e abilities and achievements) are not merely based on their individual skills, national institutions (such as laws and regulation) or the provision of social services (e.g. schools and healthcare centres), but also on their direct networks as individuals, such as through their parents, friends and colleagues. A case study shows how the capabilities of peasants to innovate in a small agricultural valley in Peru are even more dependent on their embeddedness in social networks than on their formal education.

Chapter 6 studies the relations between entrepreneurship and human agency in more detail. Entrepreneurship does not necessarily indicate the presence of human agency and freedom if the individuals involved are forced into engaging in entrepreneurial action owing to a lack of other occupational choices (often in an under-diversified economy). New concepts such as entrepreneurship as a functioning (Gries and Naude 2010) or social entrepreneurship (Yunus 2007), however, show new ways of interpreting and evaluating entrepreneurship. They do not merely focus on the contribution of entrepreneurship to the expansion of economic production, but rather evaluate the contribution of entrepreneurial actions to human capabilities and agency of the entrepreneurs as well as the society as a whole. The chapter will present a qualitative case study based in north-east Brazil that shows how social innovations, such as microfinance, can contribute to people's human agency. Nevertheless, comparatively weak network structures in the support system prevent further improvements in human agency and welfare.

Chapter 7 deals with the question of how to make structural change policies work for human development. Following the basic ideas of Rodrik (2004), it is shown that appropriate institutions must be designed and industrial policies must necessarily be put in place (covering areas such as information, coordination and technology externalities) to overcome market failures, and to trigger self-discovery processes and economic diversification (Hausmann and Rodrik 2003). The chapter goes on to explore the need for structural change, network and human development policies to overcome intrinsic inequality reproduction stemming from the effects of polarization (Myrdal 1957; Hirschman 1958). To promote a high standard of social welfare, policy makers must find, in cooperation with the actors involved, an appropriate balance between seemingly contrary forces such as specialization and diversification, related and unrelated variety growth, regional and national policy-making or cooperation and competition. Indeed these terms are not necessarily contrary; they can, in fact, be complementary forces of development. As such, it is crucial to involve in an open and prolific manner social policy makers, civil society and sectors central to the improvement of human development (such as education, health and regional development agencies) in the industrial policy-making process, to promote mutual understanding between the different interests and needs of the different groups and promote interactive learning and innovation.

Chapter 8 summarizes what has been presented in the book and gives a research outlook as to how further theoretical emphasis on occupational choices as well as new methods such as agent-based modelling and the use of big data can contribute to an understanding of the relations between economic complexity, structural change and human development. The empirical examples in the book reveal how a variety of different methods can be applied to explore the relations between economic growth and human development. Of course, much more research is necessary to obtain a more comprehensive picture of the complex relations between structural change, economic complexity and human development. It is shown, however, that there are multiple theoretical and empirical ways in which it may be possible to further explore and research the complex relations between economic growth and social welfare, by combining the human development approach with approaches from complexity research, innovation economics and development economics. This book aims to help the emergent research community, revealing how economic and human development policies can reinforce and complement each other.

2 Development paradigms

What is development? In which directions could and should societies develop? What are the drivers of development? There are no simple answers to any of these questions. Multiple opinions and arguments have been advanced and discussed by philosophers, scientists, politicians and members of society in general. Different answers have shaped the evolution of societies, the direction and types of techno- logical progress as well as our value systems, the modes of economic production and the relationship between humans and nature. This chapter outlines three main paradigms that over the last century have dominated the thinking about develop- ment in industrialized countries:

- the *economic growth* paradigm, highlighting the role of capital accumulation and aggregated production;
- the *innovation paradigm*, highlighting the importance of novelty, interactive and cumulative knowledge and qualitative change;
- the *human development* paradigm, focusing on individual freedom and well- being, highlighting distributional justice, quality of life and self-determination.

In practice all three approaches influence and are connected to the value systems of virtually all industrialized societies. However, there is a debate about the pri- ority and weight that should be provided to each development paradigm. This book does not aim to constitute a comprehensive critique of this understanding of development (for an example, see Rist 1996), but focuses instead on the relations between the three components in order to formulate policies that facilitate struc- tural change for human development.

2.1 The economic growth paradigm

Since the Industrial Revolution, the term 'development' has been closely connected to the expansion of production, income and consumption. This is sub- stantiated by the empirical observation that the Industrial Revolution led to an explosion in production and a steep rise in the standard of living, both of which, until then, were unprecedented in the history of humanity (Maddison, 2003). It also led to a great divergence in income between different areas of the world.

Table 2.1 compares the evolution of the per capita income between China and the Western European countries and their historical offspring between 1400 and 1989 (based on Maddison 1991). We can see how western Europe along with USA, Canada and Australia rapidly grew in the second part of the nineteenth century and the twentieth century, whereas the economic production in other regions such as China stagnated until the last decades of the twentieth century.

Before the Industrial Revolution spread from England to other European states and North America, the increases and declines of absolute production figures have been closely related to the population growth or decline. In many regions, the basic way of living and production has been relatively similar for several centuries. This drastically changed with the arrival of the Industrial Revolution. The fact that modern economic growth rates were greater than population growth (Kuznets 1966) allowed for an enormous expansion of occupational and consumption choices. Large numbers of new jobs and professions were created and people found themselves with an increasing number of choices in terms of food, housing, health and leisure. Such growth allowed the state to raise an unprecedented amount in taxation, which could be reinvested into public goods such as infrastructure, education and the establishment of social security systems. For this reason, it is quite natural that the term 'development' has been strongly connected with economic growth. Consequently, economists and politicians dealt less with the theoretical and philosophical question 'what is development?', and more often with 'how to promote economic growth?' While ideas of justice and the ethical distribution of income played a role in development economics (e.g. Marx 1867; Rawls 1971), economic growth has increasingly been identified by the most influential approaches to development as the core factor in raising the standard of living. This can be seen in the way that governments that favour free-market forces and those that foster state-led development (including communist countries) have put strong emphasis on the expansion of production. Since Adam Smith (1776) identified the division of labour and trade as key factors for the wealth of nations, economists have tried to identify and explain the key drivers of economic growth. Economists, sociologists and historians such as David Ricardo, Karl Marx and Joseph Schumpeter came up with a variety of explanations,

Table 2.1 Divergent growth rates of China and 'Western' industrialized economies between 1400 and 1990

Evolution of GDP per cápita (in US$ from 1985)	*1400*	*1820*	*1950*	*1989*	*Growth between 1400 and 1989[a]*
China	500	500	454	2,361	372%
Western European economies (and the historical offspring USA, Canada and Australia)	430	1,034	4,902	14,413	3,252%

Source: Adapted from Maddison (1991, p. 10).

Note
a Growth rates added.

including factors such as international trade, technological progress or institutional changes. For a long time the three production factors – capital, labour and land – have been considered as the dominant growth driver (Malthus 1803; Marx 1867; Solow 1956). This is natural, because the picture of growth is strongly connected with visible changes such as: (a) the creation of new factories, industry and capital; (b) the construction of railways, streets and buildings; (c) new jobs and a growing population density in megacities: and/or (d) the exploitation of new resources and lands. While this approach is still influential in government policy (as well as being taught in introductory economics across the world), the focus today is increasingly turning towards institutional and technological progress as the main growth drivers (Romer 1986, 1990; Fagerberg *et al.* 2005; Acemoglu 2009). Theorizing about the role of technological progress has played an important role throughout the history of economic thinking, and can be seen in theorists from Smith (1776) to Marx (1867) and Schumpeter (1912, 1939, 1943). However, technology has been considered an exogenous factor and was not endogenously explained within the most influential mainstream growth models dating from the 1950s until the early 1990s.

The growth models of Robert Solow (1956, 1957) are probably the most widespread growth models taught in universities around the world and form the basis for mainstream macroeconomics. Solow's growth accounting approach (1957) considers that total production is dependent on three factors: capital (K), labour (L) and the total factor productivity (A). On the basis of a set of assumptions, the model predicts a (conditional) convergence in the income of different countries, as long as free-market forces are in place. Arguably the most important and critical assumptions are the following.

1   The production factors capital, labour and land are homogeneous across different countries. This means that there are, for instance, no differences in the age and skills of labourers in different regions.
2   There are diminishing returns to the single factors of capital and labour. For example, given a constant number of ten workers, the first textile machine has a stronger effect on the production expansion than the 100th machine, owing to the rate of depreciation and capacity of the labourer to use them.
3   Technology is freely available and all economic agents and countries have produce at the technology frontier.
4   All agents are fully informed (e.g. of prices, scarcities, technologies) and act rationally: in other words, agents always choose the best technology, the most efficient workers and the best and cheapest products.
5   The total factor productivity (in the model) is only related to the capital growth as labour is considered to be fairly constant.

These assumptions lead to the situation that all countries conditionally converge in the model to an optimal capital stock, as long as free-market forces are in place and the assumptions are fulfilled. If all countries guarantee free-market forces, trade and rational economic behaviour, then the best possible outcome will be achieved and the income of the countries will converge, up to some natural level of inequality, which can for example be due to different natural resource endowment and geographical conditions of the countries. Subsequent strands of research, such as the polarization theory (e.g. Perroux 1955; Myrdal 1957; Lasuén 1973), the endogenous growth theory (Romer 1986, 1990; Rebelo 1991; Krugman (1991a, 1991b) and Neo-Schumpeterian economics (Hanusch and Pyka 2007b), have empirically and theoretically shown that many of the assumptions of Solow and other neoclassical deductive models do not properly resemble the complexity and dynamics of the real world. Recent approaches stress further crucial factors, such as knowledge externalities, agglomeration and cumulative effects, which can lead to economic divergence. This book will explain the ideas of some of the contemporary approaches, focusing on innovation and economic diversification; however, it is beyond the aim and scope of this book to enter into the details of all the various models of mainstream economic growth literature. The interested reader can refer to the models of Romer (1986, 1990), Rebelo (1991), Krugman (1991a, 1991b), Barro and Sala-i-Martin (1991) and Ray (1998) for an overview on growth models and development economics.

It can be argued that the economic growth paradigm takes for granted that production and income expansion are the core dimensions (or at least the best proxy measures) of development. The focus of this paradigm is not so much on the qualitative question 'what is development?' but rather on 'how can economic growth be stimulated?', and 'why does the economy of one country grow faster than another?' as well as considering circumstances under which income convergence or divergence can be expected. Income and production is basically considered to be development. It has been assumed and shown in deductive models that market forces would lead to a Pareto optimal distribution of income and that an increase in the overall production leads to trickle-down effects, as well as to an increase in the overall social welfare of the population. The subsequent innovation and structural change paradigm also originates from literature that aims to promote economic growth. However, knowledge creation, innovation, entrepreneurship and changes in the composition of the economic system become further goals of development.

2.2 Innovation and structural change

Change, progress and innovation have become the key words of policy makers, publicity and business managers since the end of the twentieth century. Companies aim to represent themselves as technology leaders that produce high value added, innovative products for consumers. Governments aim to subsidize future-oriented sectors such as bio- and nano-technologies or ICT. The EU's Lisbon Strategy has set a goal to become the most competitive knowledge-based economy in the world. China puts strong emphasis on technology upgrading, and in increasing its patent portfolio aims to become a technology leader. India's economic catch-up is strongly related to the software industry.

One reason for the increased emphasis on innovation is a change in the type and nature of the competitive advantages and organization of economic activities in the last decades of the twentieth century. In the decades after the Second World War, mass production technologies, electronics and economies of scale could reach their full potential, which allowed for mass consumption and facilitated multiplier effects in the rich countries. Owing to standardization and economies of scale, producers could provide the consumer with a variety of products such as cars or domestic appliances at affordable prices. With the advances of information and communication technologies, a further significant decrease of transportation costs, increased purchasing power and ultimately globalization, the nature of competition in the rich world has increasingly changed from price competition towards an innovation and design competition. Furthermore, the organization of production has become more specialized and complex. Virtually no company is capable of being aware of all the available technologies, or is able to be competitive in all specialized activities, such as use of database systems and accounting techniques, production of electronic relays and components, and specialized research in materials. Whereas many companies have formerly internalized most R&D, production and distribution activities within their companies, they are now increasingly working in complex value chains and networks of suppliers and distributors. Car producers, for example Mercedes, work with a multitude of specialized component suppliers, research labs and consultancies. The productive capabilities and competitive advantages of companies, regions and countries often depends upon the ability to create a prolific network with a great variety of specialized private and public institutions learning, cooperating and competing with each other. Changes in the nature of today's economy and competition, together with the increased focus on innovation, have led to a broad acceptance in economic policy and business management that knowledge, innovation and structural change play a key role in economic competitiveness and growth. Decision makers all around the world are deliberately investing in innovation so that they can compete and survive in global markets. Clusters, business incubators, subsidies for the promotion of key technologies and other innovation-related activities and policies are spreading across the world. Through human capital and knowledge spillovers, technology and innovation have also found their way into mainstream economic growth models (see for instance Romer 1986, 1990). However, this book will focus more on innovation and Neo-Schumpeterian economics as a specialized discipline which provides new theoretical perspectives and methods to help understand the creation, implementation, imitation and diffusion of knowledge and technologies. In the following section the theories and concepts of Schumpeter, innovation economics and the Latin American Structuralist School (LASA) will be explained in more detail.

2.2.1 Innovation and creative destruction

Joseph Alois Schumpeter can be considered the father of modern innovation economics. He showed that development is a historical process of structural changes driven by innovation and defined innovation as new combinations leading to new products, processes, organizations, inputs and markets (Schumpeter 1912, 1939, 1943). In his theory of economic development, either entrepreneurs (Schumpeter 1912) or R&D labs (Schumpeter 1943) introduce these new combinations, thereby triggering profound changes in the economic structure and creating business cycles (Schumpeter 1939). In Schumpeter's original theory of economic development (1912) the abilities and initiative of entrepreneurs, which generally draw upon the discoveries of scientists and inventors, create entirely new opportunities for investment, growth and employment. The profits made from these innovations are then the decisive impulse for new surges in growth, acting as a signal to swarms of imitators (Freeman 1982, p. 2). It is important to note that not every imitator can make big profits. When the bandwagon starts rolling, some people fall off, profits are gradually competed away until recession sets in and the whole process may be followed by a depression before growth starts again, with a new wave of technical innovation and organizational and social change (Freeman 1982, p. 2). Hence, according to Schumpeter (1912), the innovation process can be divided into four dimensions: invention, innovation, diffusion and imitation. In Schumpeter's analysis, the invention stage or the basic innovation has less impact on the economy than the diffusion and imitation stages. The macroeconomic effects of any basic innovation are scarcely perceptible for at least the first few years, or even longer. What matters in terms of economic growth, investment and employment is not the moment of the basic innovation itself, but rather its diffusion, the swarming process when imitators begin to realize the profitable potential of the new product or process and start to invest heavily in that technology (Freeman 1982, p. 5). Examples of technologies and innovations that radically changed the economy and society are steam power, electricity, and ICT. They caused a wave of new products and services and changed society in the first and second Industrial Revolution and during the current move towards an information society.

Within the field of Neo-Schumpeterian economics, a large number of studies have been made on entrepreneurship, innovation, knowledge spillovers and networks, business cycles and structural change (e.g. Freeman 1982, 1987; Dosi *et al.* 1988; Klepper 1997; Audretsch and Thurik 2000; Perez 2002, 2007; Fagerberg *et al.* 2005; Hanusch and Pyka 2007a, 2007b). An important feature of Schumpeterian analysis is the consideration that structural changes might be driven by the capabilities of single individuals (Schumpeter 1912) and/or (the research labs of) big enterprises (Schumpeter 1943). The emphasis on single agents stands in contrast to the common perspective of most approaches in economics, where the (representative) agents are determined by the system. Other interesting features of Neo-Schumpeterian economics are the consideration of historic development processes and the emphasis on the interaction of heterogeneous agents (Hanusch and Pyka 2007a, 2007b). Generally speaking: 'Neo-Schumpeterian economics deals with dynamic processes causing qualitative transformation of economies driven by the introduction of various and multifaceted forms of novelties and the related co-evolutionary processes' (Hanusch and Pyka 2007a, p. 280).

Qualitative change, punctuated equilibrium (considering the idea of permanent and disruptive changes) and pattern formation are core topics of interest in the Neo-Schumpeterian analysis of economic development (see Hanusch and Pyka 2007a, 2007b). While the concept of structural change mainly refers to a change in the number and balance of sectors, the Neo-Schumpeterian concept of qualitative change is broader, as it also considers changes on more disaggregated levels (e.g. the organizational structure between and within the enterprises of a sector), as well as changes in domains that are not strictly economic, such as education or regulation. Qualitative change is considered to be basically driven by innovation; making fertile relations and coordination between the industrial, the financial and the public sectors, all necessary to exploit and deploy the full power of innovation for economic and human development (Perez 2002, 2007; Hanusch and Pyka 2007a, 2007c, 2007d; Hartmann *et al.* 2010).

An influential contribution to the understanding of the cyclical long-term transformation of economies and co-evolutionary institutional changes has been made by Carlota Perez (1983, 2002). She illustrates how technological revolutions and strong surges of development typically follow a sequence of steps in the core countries of the technological revolution, for example going from a technological breakthrough towards a hype in the financial sector to financial bubble explosions. At the turning point a decoupling of the new emerging technological paradigm and the existent socioeconomic system can often be seen, and substantive social and institutional changes are necessary to allow the technologies to spread more broadly across the society. The new paradigm, though, eventually becomes complacent, saturated and stagnating, which can lead again to a socioeconomic crisis that requires the emergence of a new technological revolution and techno-economic paradigm. Perez (2002) makes a distinction between five technological revolutions between the 1770s and the 2000s.

1   The Industrial Revolution, starting in Britain with the historical milestone of Arkwright's mill opening in Cromford in 1771.
2   The age of steam and railways, which literally took off with the test of the Rocket steam engine for the Liverpool-Manchester railway in 1829.
3   The age of steel, electricity and heavy engineering, which can be related to the opening of the Carnegie Bessemer steel plant in Pittsburgh, Pennsylvania in 1875 and led to the industrial forging ahead of USA and Germany.
4   The age of oil, the automobile and mass production, which began when the first Model T come out of the Ford plant in Detroit, Michigan in 1908.
5   The age of information and telecommunications, starting when the breakthrough of the creation of the Intel microprocessor was announced in Santa Clara, California, in 1975.

Each of these techno-economic paradigms seems to follow recurrent phases of irruption, frenzy, synergy and maturity. Figure 2.1 shows the panorama of the changing context of the twentieth century according to Carlota Perez (2011).

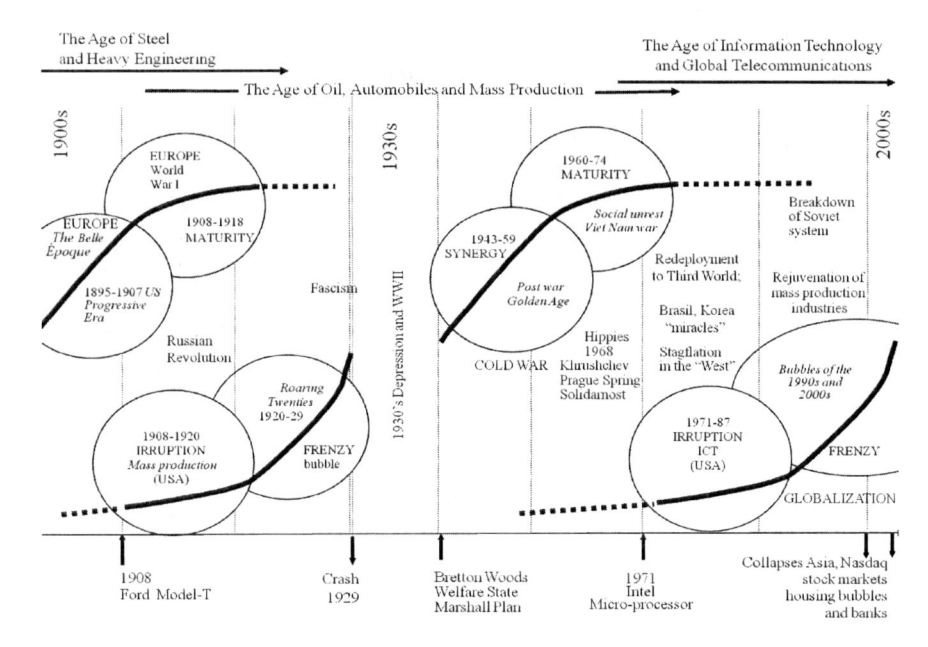

Figure 2.1 Carlota Perez' analysis of technological revolutions and waves of development in the twentieth century

Source: Perez, C (2011).

It becomes obvious how technological revolutions, financial bubbles and social transformations are related to each other, leading to a cyclical evolution of irruption, frenzy, synergy, maturity and crises. In the maturity phase of the age of steel and heavy engineering, the socio-political split exploded during the First World War and the Russian Revolution. It was during this period that also the age of mass production, automobile and oil started. After the First World War it unfolded its full power. The Roaring Twenties, however, then led to polarization of the rich and poor and the financial crash in 1929. The rise of fascist governments unfortunately went together with the use of mass production technologies to provide weapons for total war. New institutional arrangements after the Second World War, such as the Marshall Plan, Bretton Woods and modern welfare states, allowed the synergy of new technologies: the institutional setting led to coherent growth with increasing positive externalities, production and employment expansion in the post-war golden age. When entering the maturity stage, the new paradigm once again encountered crisis, symbolized by the hippie movement and social unrest in 1968, the Vietnam War and stagflation in the West. It was at this moment that technological breakthroughs allowed the emergence of the new age of information and telecommunications, which after the frenzy phases led to bubble explosions in the 2000s. These bubble bursts now require new institutional arrangements to allow the information technologies to unfold their full potential and spread across the world, lifting social welfare in both developed and developing countries.

The inspiring analysis of Perez on the dynamics and bubbles of golden ages has recently been complemented by an expansion of the research on creative destruction and economic diversification processes that lead to a change in the composition of socioeconomic systems (e.g. Saviotti 1996; Frenken *et al.* 1999; Saviotti and Pyka 2004; Hausmann *et al.* 2011). Creative destruction processes are driven by selection, variation and adaptation processes in which new sectors emerge and the balance and composition of the economic system changes. Whereas new sectors emerge some other sectors decrease in importance or even become obsolete. In total, however, the number of sectors and their complexity tends to increase, because innovation allows higher levels of specialization and productivity, leading to more consumption and choices of occupation, and typically not all sectors become obsolete, but many can decrease in relative importance. For example, light bulbs have largely replaced candles and the Internet is now increasingly replacing printed newspapers. But we still have candles and newspapers continue to be a main source of news. As Saviotti (1996) based on Pasinetti (1981, 1983) pointed out, selection and creative destruction makes some products, capabilities and sectors obsolete, but in the long run the system needs to diversify over time to overcome the problems on the demand side.

The question that then arises is: in which ways and in which directions do countries diversify? Empirical studies show strong path dependencies in the diversification process. Countries and regions typically diversify their production structures into related activities (e.g. Frenken *et al.* 2007; Hidalgo *et al.* 2007; Saviotti and Frenken 2008). This means, for example, that a region that specializes in cotton farming may diversify into textile production and fashion design, but may not necessarily jump straight from cotton production into the chemical or aerospace industry. This is natural as most new capabilities build upon previous capabilities and experiences. Innovation is certainly a key driver of diversification (Schumpeter 1912; Saviotti 1996; Saviotti and Pyka 2004; Klinger and Lederman 2006). However, there are different types of innovation, such as product, process, or radical and incremental innovations, which lead to different types of economic diversification, such as related or unrelated variety growth (Frenken *et al.* 2007; Saviotti and Frenken 2008). Related variety refers to diversification into similar sectors (such as from cars to trucks). Unrelated variety growth refers to diversification into entirely new sectors (such as introducing and establishing a software industry in a former agricultural region). Most innovative activities in processes, products and services are of an incremental nature and lead to the diversification of the economy into similar, related products (e.g. new car models or the new generation of smartphones). However, for long-term economic development, radical innovations (such as steam power, electricity or the Internet) leading to profound structural changes and unrelated variety growth is even more decisive than incremental innovations (Schumpeter 1912; Perez 2002; Saviotti and Frenken 2008). Radical innovations (such as the first steam machine, automobile or personal computer) bring the system out of equilibrium, promote economic growth and lead to business cycles (Schumpeter 1912).

2.2.2 Innovation and the Latin American Structuralist School

Combining insights from Marx, Schumpeter and Keynes, the so-called development pioneers (e.g. Rosenstein-Rodan 1943; Nurkse 1953; Myrdal 1957; Hirschman 1958) focused on the effects of innovation and structural transformation in bringing about long-term development. The related Latin American Structuralist School (e.g. Prebisch 1949, 1959; Furtado 1961; Fajnzylber 1990) suggested that structural transformation with equity should be a key objective of development policies (the Economic Commission for Latin America and the Caribbean (ECLAC) 2008). They aimed to promote the economic diversification of developing countries in more value added sectors and reduce the negative effect of dependent integration in the global economy. Applying Schumpeterian ideas to the southern hemisphere, several Latin American scholars revealed structural obstacles to innovation and development in the periphery of the global economy, such as dependent integration into the global markets as primary goods supplier, technological asymmetries and structural heterogeneity, lack of interactive learning and weak policy orientation towards innovation (e.g. Fajnzylber 1990; Cassiolato *et al.* 2003; Arocena and Sutz 2005; Cimoli 2005; Katz 2007). The Schumpeterian idea of innovation-driven endogenous development and structural change has certainly been an essential theoretical source for the Latin American Structuralist Approach (LASA). Technological and structural changes have been considered as main drivers of economic growth. Since the 1950s LASA has emphasized the diversity, non-linearity and uniqueness of historical development paths, the importance of endogenous production transformation, the role and impact of centre and periphery in the world economic system (e.g. regarding technological dynamism and terms of trade) and the need for strategic government intervention to overcome structural obstacles to development (e.g. Prebisch 1949, 1964; Furtado 1958, 1961; Fajnzylber 1990; ECLAC 2008). The Prebisch-Singer thesis (of the long-term deterioration of the terms of trade for primary products in the periphery of the world economy) led, in the period from the 1950s to the 1970s, to strong public intervention and industrialization through import substitution policies in many Latin American countries. The purpose was to promote endogenous industrialization processes and make the domestic economic systems independent from the global capitalist system, which was seen as systemically creating dependency and underdevelopment on the periphery (Prebisch 1964). However, the small internal markets of many Latin American economies, government failures, inefficiencies and last but not least, stagflation in the 1970s, led to a huge economic crisis for almost all Latin American countries in the 1980s (Krueger 1985; Bustelo 1999). The neoliberal 'counterrevolution' (Toye 1987) and the dominance of monetary approaches throughout the 1980s and 1990s arguably stabilized the macroeconomic situation of most Latin American economies but also led to a widening in the gap between rich and poor. Indeed these approaches did not provide significantly higher growth rates than the former import substitution industrialization (ISI) approaches (Rodrik 2004) and led to a certain de-industrialization and deterioration of the future orientation of the production structure of Latin America (Katz 2007).

In the 1990s, LASA re-examined the former approaches by taking into account the need for markets of certain sizes to implement economies of scale, certain government failures and profound changes of international production organization at the end of the second millennium (Di Filippo 1998). However, LASA sustains its focus on the rich understanding of development as processes of structural change, non-linear and unique historical development trajectories and the specificities of institutional setups and socioeconomic structures. It continues to analyse the impact of the global markets on the development paths in the periphery, but considers the complex intra and intersectoral linkages of the global economy (ECLAC 2008). LASA argues for the need for strategic government policies to promote a more future-oriented domestic production structure, but also considers the power of adequately opened markets and the benefits of economies of scale, international knowledge spillovers and learning opportunities (ECLAC 2008). Innovation and a future vision of the production structure are seen as essential for promoting economic growth and tackling social problems in the long run (Fajnzylber 1990; ECLAC 2008).

2.2.3 Systems of innovation

Based on the theories of Schumpeter and also inspired by research in developing countries, the system of innovation approach (Freeman 1987; Lundvall 1992) emerged at the end of 1980s. It has become an important concept in economic policy-making and has underpinned the theoretical background of the EU growth strategy since 2000. The basic idea is that innovation is not a linear process, starting from knowledge generation and invention by scientists and proceeding straight to production and distribution by private companies in a straightforward linear manner, but rather it is an interactive process, with multiple backwards and forwards linkages in which multiple persons from public and private institutions, such as public and private research institutions, supplier, consumer and knowledge transfer institutions, are involved (Freeman 1987). Freeman showed how Japan has achieved its technological competitiveness through its networks of public and private institutions promoting innovation in a concerted manner. Since the end of the 1980s, the term 'national innovation system' (NIS) has gained a lot of attention in the academic world. Christopher Freeman defined an innovation system as '…the network of institutions in the public and private sectors whose activities and interactions initiate, import, modify and diffuse new technologies' (Freeman 1987, p. 1). Several basic elements of the NIS approach appear in this short definition, indicating a systemic approach to action and interactions between different institutions at different stages of the innovation process. An essential feature of innovation is its interactive and collective character.

Bengt-Åke Lundvall proposed a broad definition of NIS as '…all parts and aspects of the economic structure and the institutional set up affecting learning as well as searching and exploring' (Lundvall 1992, p. 12). There are many other definitions of NIS (e.g. Patel and Pavitt 1994; Nelson 1993; Metcalfe 1995; OECD 1997; Edquist 1997), but the essence is captured rather well in the definitions given by Freeman and Lundvall.

As argued by Heidenreich (2005), the basic elements of every NIS definition consist mainly of: (a) the central importance of institutions; (b) the systemic inter-actions and networks between different actors; (c) the recognition of the different stages of the innovation process; and finally (d) a certain conceptual ambiguity. This last characteristic can be considered the major weakness as well as the major strength of the NIS approach (Johnson *et al.* 2003). The conceptual ambiguity pro-vides the concept with a high degree of flexibility to adapt to the specific case or country under scrutiny, but also leads to a certain difficulty in comparing between different cases. Trying to give a better explanation for complex real world phenom-ena, the systemic approach of NIS research considers the importance of manifold interactions and learning processes between the different economic, social and political institutions. The specific history, culture, customs and social interaction structures that exist between the members of a country influence the country's economic performance and capacity to innovate. The diversity of different histori-cal paths, cultures, agents, institutions and networks in different countries implies the need for a flexible definition of innovation systems. To be successfully imple-mented, the NIS approach must be adapted to the specific determinants and path dependencies of each country or region (e.g. Cassiolato *et al.* 2003; Tödtling and Trippl 2005). As mentioned above, this can make the innovation system approach very rich and flexible, but also quite poor, when merely stating that there is not enough cooperation and interactive learning in a region or country, but not stating how the cooperation could be improved.

2.2.4 *Measurement of innovation*

For a considerable length of time, the focus of innovation measurement in eco-nomics was on technical progress as an input factor for economic growth on the aggregated macro level, rather than on the complex determinants and drivers of innovation on the industry, company, regional or even individual level. Technical progress has been typically measured or inferred by labour and/or total factor pro-ductivity (Abramowitz 1956; Solow 1957). However, as a result of the increasing importance of the knowledge-based economy and the rise of the new economies such as ICT, bio- and nano-technology, more scientific and political emphasis has recently been put on the measurement and analysis of innovation and the knowl-edge-based society in terms of its complexity of different factors and outcomes (OECD 1997, 2005; Chen and Dahlman 2005; Eurostat 2008). Consequently over the last two decades, a wide variety of indicators and measurement taxonomies has been applied. Common methods of measuring innovation include counting patents and innovations, measuring R&D expenditures, describing innovation in detail in case and industry studies, and/or using innovation questionnaires (OECD 2005; Swann 2009). Each of these indicators has its strengths and weaknesses.

- *R&D expenditures* are a key input of innovation. However, innovation expenditures are often considered of strategic importance by companies and therefore are not made public. Furthermore, small companies in particular do not have the figures for their innovation expenditures, as they are accounted as part of regular business expenditures (Swann 2009).
- The main advantage of *patents* is their availability and the detailed information they contain concerning inventors, applicants, technical features, citations and technology classes. However, only a small percentage of patents have any economic value. Patents are often used strategically to impede the entry of competitors rather than to innovate. Different industries have different propensities and interests that affect their ability to patent and thereby lay open their knowledge. Furthermore, there is much debate as to whether patents can be seen as an innovation output proxy or should just be considered as an innovation input factor (OECD 2009).
- *Innovation surveys* can provide rich information on different types of innovation and the innovative behaviour of companies (e.g. Eurostat 2008). The Community Innovation Survey (CIS) asks detailed questions about the innovative behaviour and performance of firms in different countries in Europe. The questions basically ask if the company has made product or process innovation or cooperates in R&D collaborations, and can therefore be biased and are dependent on the respondents self-perception and knowledge about their own and other companies. For instance, people from different departments within the same company may provide different answers. In medium to large companies respondents are unlikely to be able to overlook every activity and department in the company.
- *Case and industry studies* can consider the particularities of technologies and industries, their historical evolution, presumed key actors and network relations. However, case studies are often very time-consuming and often their findings cannot be generalized, since each case tends to be unique. This makes it also very difficult to compare the findings of different case studies.
- Innovation can also be measured by the *number of new product sales* (or occasionally expert commissions) of the most important new products, processes and organization techniques. This can provide insights into the emergence of innovation over time and across regions, countries and industries (e.g. Harris 1988). However, it leaves itself open to a wide range of different subjective interpretations and judgements of the role and importance of different incremental or radical innovations.

After taking all these various factors into consideration, the conclusion is that measuring innovation is an extremely difficult task. This is because innovation is a complex and interactive phenomenon that involves a varied set of agents such as inventors, entrepreneurs, finance institutions and banks and their interactions (Freeman 1987; Lundvall 1988; Pyka 1999; Hanusch and Pyka 2007b). Nevertheless, measurement is crucial in being able to compare different cases, reveal strengths and weakness, consider different types of innovation inputs and outputs, reveal causal relations and design institutional framework and policy measures to improve the interactive learning and innovation outcomes of different agents in complex innovation processes.

It is possible to categorize different types of innovation, such as radical or incremental innovation in products, processes, inputs, marketing, or business organization. Furthermore, innovation is not the same as invention or knowledge, but is the successful introduction of new products, processes, or services into the market or the production process (Swann 2009). But knowledge, R&D and invention are drivers of innovation. To understand innovation and provide useful suggestions for decision makers, simply counting new products and services, for example, is not enough. It is also important to analyse and theorize how innovation can be generated, implemented, imitated or diffused (OECD 1997). There is consequently a trend towards the measurement of innovation systems and the development of composite indicators (Fagerberg and Shrolec 2006; Balzat and Pyka 2006; Hollanders *et al.* 2009; UNU-MERIT 2010). The European Innovation Scoreboard (UNU-MERIT 2010) distinguishes between innovation inputs (such as human resources, finance, firm investments, linkages, throughputs and entrepreneurship) and innovation outputs (such as the number of firms that introduced different types of innovation, and their economic effects in terms of employment, exports and sales). Furthermore, taxonomies are being developed that consider the more general underlying socioeconomic factors affecting a country's capacity to generate, imitate or diffuse technologies. For this reason, variables such as the level of inequality, good governance, social capital, the economic structure and/or geographic factors are included in the measurement taxonomies (Godinho *et al.* 2004; Fagerberg and Shrolec 2006; Hartmann *et al.* 2010; Castelacci and Natera 2011). Advances have also been made in the measurement of regional innovation networks and sectoral linkages (Giuliani and Bell 2005; Cantner and Graf 2006; Neffke and Svensson 2008).

2.3 Human development

In 1990, the UNDP presented the Human Development Index (HDI), a simple composite development indicator, taking education, life expectancy and income into account. This provided the means for policy makers and researchers around the world to compare the development of their countries beyond the basic comparison of being income rich or poor. As Table 2.2 shows, it reveals that some income-rich countries performed less well in the human development ranking than in the measures based merely on income, whereas some income-poor countries got a higher position in the development rankings, owing to relatively high levels of life expectancy and an improved access to education.

Table 2.2 Positions of countries in the GDP and human development ranking

Country	Change in position when HDI is applied instead of GDP	Human development rank in 2007	GDP rank in 2007	Human Development Index in 2007	GDP per capita in 2007 (PPP[a] US$)
Cuba	+44	51	95	0.863	6,876
France	+17	8	25	0.961	33,674
Japan	+16	10	26	0.960	33,632
Canada	+14	4	18	0.966	35,812
Spain	+12	15	27	0.955	31,560
Italy	+11	18	29	0.951	30,353
China	+10	92	102	0.772	5,383
Brazil	+4	75	79	0.813	9,567
Norway	+4	1	5	0.971	53,433
Germany	+2	22	24	0.947	34,401
United Kingdom	−1	21	20	0.947	35,130
United States	−4	13	9	0.956	45,592
India	−6	134	128	0.612	2,753
Luxembourg	−9	11	2	0.960	79,485
Russian Federation	−16	71	55	0.817	14,690
Turkey	−16	79	63	0.806	12,955
Nigeria	−17	158	141	0.511	1,969
Saudi Arabia	−19	59	40	0.843	22,935
South Africa	−51	129	78	0.683	9,757

Source: Human development data and charts (2013).

Note
a Purchasing Power Parity.

This simple but powerful indicator illustrates a more complex concept which focuses on the people instead of the aggregated production. The first human development report started with the words:

> People are the Real Wealth of Nations. The basic objective of development is to create an enabling environment for people to live long, healthy and creative lives. This may appear to be a simple truth. But it is often forgotten in the immediate concern with the accumulation of commodities and financial wealth.
>
> (UNDP 1990)

The human development and capability approach (HDCA) is a people-centred development approach. It views development as a process by the people, of the people and for the people (UNDP 1991; Alkire 2010). Development is not considered as mere economic growth, but rather as '...a process of enlarging people's choices and the level of their achieved well-being' (UNDP, 1990). This means that inequality is no longer considered merely in terms of economic income, but also in terms of the inequality and deprivation of the capabilities of people to actively participate in society and decide upon their own lives. The approach emerged as a critique of approaches that view development merely as economic growth, neglecting the poverty, deprivation and unfreedom of a significant part of the population in developing countries.

Since the 1970s, there has increasingly been the perception among development practitioners that the efforts put into industrialization and economic growth have not led to a significant reduction in poverty and inequalities in development countries. These efforts have failed to provide the poor sections of the population with basic requirements such as water, electricity, healthcare and basic education. In some areas social indicators have worsened even while the overall GDP has shown considerable growth rates. Responding to this gap between economic growth and improvements in the life quality of many people, the development community has increasingly put emphasis on attending to the basic needs of the people as primary goals of development policies (ILO 1976; Steward 1979; Streeten 1979; Streeten *et al.* 1981). The purpose of development was seen as the reduction of mass deprivation and giving all individuals the opportunity to live a full life (Streeten 1979). It was considered insufficient for development policy to focus only on economic growth, without considering the life quality of the people and their capacity to live a full life. Meeting people's basic needs was seen as the priority of development policy: an emphasis on basic education, nutrition, sanitation and healthcare would not only contribute directly to the alleviation of poverty, but also would directly and indirectly improve the productivity and economic growth of countries by increasing resources and using them efficiently (Streeten *et al.* 1981).

In 1990, Mahbub ul Haq, Amartya Sen, Paul Streeten and Keith Griffin, a group of leading development scholars focusing on social welfare and life quality, presented the HDI (UNDP 1990). They combined GDP per capita with life expectancy and levels of education to draw a broader and more comprehensive picture of development, focusing on social choices and life quality. Whereas former development approaches focused almost exclusively on efficiency and growth, the human development concept proposes a switch towards an agent-based perspective, distributive justice, well-being, empowerment, freedom and quality of life (UNDP 1990; Nussbaum and Sen 1993; Sen 1999; Robeyns 2005; Nussbaum 2001; Alkire 2010; UNDP 2010). Human development has been defined as a process that enlarges people's choices and enhances human capabilities (the range of things people can do) and freedoms, enabling people to live long and healthy lives, have access to knowledge and a decent standard of living, and to participate in the life of their community and the decisions affecting their lives (UNDP 1990). The focus of this approach is on '...advancing the richness of human life, rather than the richness of the economy in which human beings live, which is only part of it' (Sen, 1998b). Increasing the freedoms that give humans the capabilities, opportunities and choices to assist and contribute actively to development are at the same time the primary goal and the fundamental means of development (Sen 1999). Key terms of the human development and capability approach are capabilities and functionings. 'Functionings' refer to what people do and what they actually are in a very concrete sense (e.g. having a good job, being healthy, having self-respect), whereas capabilities indicate the basic freedoms and abilities (e.g. being able to choose to live healthily, to study, to vote) that people need to achieve these functionings. In other words, capabilities refer to the freedoms that people need to be active agents in their lives and to decide for themselves what is best for them. In this way, the human capability approach provides a new perspective which incorporates the belief that the poor have the power, intelligence and determination to help themselves when they are given the basic opportunities and freedoms to do so (Yunus 2007). In this vein, Sen (1999) identifies: (a) political freedom; (b) economic facilities; (c) social opportunities; (d) guarantees of transparency; and (e) protective security as instrumental freedoms required to make people agents rather than patients of development. Whereas the external factors are important, Sen views the expansion of individuals' freedoms and agency as the core means and goals of development. People should not merely be seen as poor patients who need paternalistic help, but rather as agents who can help and decide for themselves, once they have the basic capabilities to do so. As Sen (1999, p. 11) puts it:

> In terms of the medieval distinction between 'the patient' and 'the agent', this freedom-centred understanding of economics and of the process of development is very much an agent-oriented view. With adequate social opportunities, individuals can shape their own destiny and help each other. They need not be seen primarily as passive recipients of the benefits of cunning development programs.

2.3.1 *Amartya Sen and the human capability approach*

The 1998 Nobel Prize winner in Economic Sciences, Amartya Sen, is a leading intellectual of the human development and capability approach. During his many decades of research and professorship at Harvard and Cambridge University, he has been very influential and has successfully promoted his people-centred approach to development in the leading research communities in economics, social choice and welfare theory, and development studies. In asking the incisive question 'equality of what?' (Sen 1979, 1995), he contributed to the elaboration of human development and capability measures (Sen 1985a, 1985b; UNDP 1990), elaborated principles of justice, rationality and human freedom (Nussbaum and Sen 1993; Sen 1999, 2002, 2009), laid the theoretical groundwork for partial comparability within social choice and welfare theory (Sen 1970a, 1970b, 1982, 1996, 1998a; Arrow *et al.* 1997, 2008) and made crucial contributions to gender, poverty and famine research (Sen 1981, 1999; Dreze and Sen 1989, 2002). Furthermore, he coined the essential key words and concepts of the human development and capability community, such as capabilities, functionings, choices, agency, process and opportunity freedom (Sen 1985b, 1999). Sen's contributions to social choice theory, welfare economics and human development thinking, while too extensive to be fully elaborated here, are summarized below.

Sen's work is grounded in social choice theory, economic philosophy and welfare economics (Sen, 1970a, 1970b, 1995, 1998a, Arrow *et al.* 1997, 2008). Deeply influenced by theories of justice and ethical foundations of economic behaviour (Smith 1759, 1776; Mill 1859; Aristotle cited in Barker 1958; Rawls 1971), Sen (1970a, 1970b, 1985a, 1985b, 1999), he revolutionized social choice theory by showing the possibility of enlarging the informational base in welfare economics from the mere comparison of aggregated utilities towards partial comparability and ruling out worst options in a variety of dimensions affecting human life, such as health, nutrition and education. Accordingly, Sen opened up the possibility of scientifically valued research about distributional issues, which had been hitherto neglected (Sen 1970a, 1970b; Rawls 1971), by introducing the total-sum maximization of the utilitarian approach to welfare economics (Edgeworth 1881; Marshall 1890; Pigou 1920).

Before Sen's work, welfare economics had run into a dead end, believing that it is not possible to make scientifically based interpersonal comparison of utilities in economics (Robbins 1938), because different people may derive different levels of happiness from different types and quantities of things (or even from the same things). The assumption of diminishing return – that a person who has already something (e.g. a religious education, or access to wine) may derive less happiness from further such things (more religious education, more access to wine) than a person who has less – does not necessarily hold true. Following this argument, it was held that economics should, therefore leave normative judgements about the value of different options to the specialized field of political philosophy. A constructive critique that presented a huge challenge to welfare economics was made by one of its main contributors: Kenneth Arrow (1950, 1951, 1963). He showed within an axiomatic framework that it is not possible to make a perfect preference ranking of individual values in a society that is consistent with the assumptions of non-dictatorship, universality, independence of irrelevant alternatives and Pareto efficiency (Arrow 1963). This means that already under these basic assumptions it is not possible to make a consistent aggregation of individual values and hence the existence of consistent majority rules to promote policies for the 'common good' does not seem to be possible.

The practical implication of Robbins' critique (1938) and Arrow's impossibility theorem (1963) is that any political action for the common good is highly problematic. It furthermore means that welfare economics must question itself and may do better to limit itself to a comparison of the aggregated utilities. The welfare of countries may reach a maximum value simply if market forces can freely unfold and the rule of Pareto efficiency is fulfilled. From a theoretical perspective too, there was a sharp reduction of the possibilities by which social choice theory and welfare economics could compare the distribution of welfare in different domains. Sen provided a pathway out of the dead end caused by the utilitarian approach, excessive focus on Pareto efficiency and the impossibility of interpersonal comparisons (Robbins 1938). He showed mathematically ways of enlarging the informational base by including ethical needs, by allowing partial comparisons in different domains and ruling out worst options (Sen 1970a, 1970b, 1998a). While it may not be possible to have a perfect preference ranking of all domains in society, nevertheless most people in a democratic would want to live in society where no one dies of hunger or lives in inhumane conditions and slavery; especially when individuals imagine (e.g. in the sense of Rawls's 1971 veil of ignorance) that this deprived condition could constitute one's own life or one's own family. This allows an expansion of the information used in social welfare theory gained from mere aggregated utilities of entire societies to include the discussion of minimums standards where the worst options which may hamper the capabilities of the people to shape their own lives and be agents of development are ruled out.

Sen also argued that it is not just the ownership of commodities or resources that matters for the welfare and agency of people, but also the interpersonal differences involved in converting them into the capability to live well (Sen 1970b, 1998a, 1999). Hence it is not just the possession and distribution of outcomes (e.g. commodities) that matters, but also the freedoms of individuals to achieve them first-hand and the capabilities to make them work (Sen 1999). Sen furthermore criticized the utilitarian tradition for simply focusing on interpersonal comparisons of mental states, pleasures and desires (leading to the Robbins critique in his 1938 paper). The comparison of mental states can be misleading and mask diverse forms of substantial deprivation and corresponding desire adaptation (Sen 1998a). For example, a woman in a society with gender inequality may adapt her ambitions to a lower level and be happy with her achievements, but she essentially continues to be deprived (Sen 1999). Therefore, Sen argues, more dimensions should be considered to analyse individual advantages and deprivations. Sen furthermore showed that viable collective choices are proximate to the impossibility situation drawn by Arrow (1950, 1951, 1963). During the introduction of assumptions (such as universality or Pareto efficiency), just one step before impossibility there is often a possibility for social choice (Sen 1998a).

In sum, arguably the core contribution of Amartya Sen was to show that partial interpersonal comparisons of individual advantages and quality of life can be made to discover substantive deprivation and rule out the worst options. He forced an important change of perspective by arguing that it is not just the possession and distribution of outcomes that are crucial, but also the freedoms of individuals to achieve them first-hand and the capabilities to make them work (Sen 1999). This is where the distinctions between process and opportunity freedom and between capabilities and functionings come into play. By functionings, Sen means the beings and doings that people have reason to value, such as being nourished, being well-sheltered, being educated, having income and a decent job (Kuklys 2005; Alkire 2010). Functionings are the achievements of individuals in different aspects of life and determine their well-being and quality of life (Nussbaum and Sen 1993; Binder and Coad 2010a, 2010b). Hence not only commodities but also many other aspects of human life, such as education, health, and human rights, lead to an individual's well-being (UNDP 1990; Sen 1999); thus the approach is essentially multidimensional. The functionings can be described as a vector of functionings b (Sen 1985b; Kuklys 2005 cited in Binder and Coad 2010b):

$$b = f_i(c(x) \,|\, z_i, z_e, z_s),$$

where $x \in X$ is a vector of commodities out of all the possible commodities and resources. Commodities, here, refers not merely to economic products, but also to many other services and non-market goods. The translation of the commodities into functionings depends on the conversion function c, which maps the commodities on a vector of characteristics (Lancaster 1966; Anand *et al.* 2009). The conversion further depends on individual (z_i), social (z_s) and environmental (z_e) factors (Kuklys 2005 cited in Binder and Coad 2010b). Examples of these conversion factors can be intelligence, gender, or disabilities (in the case of individual conversion factors), legal frameworks or density (for the social factors), and geographical conditions and pollution (for environmental factors): see Binder and Coad (2010b). Capabilities are the set of functionings f_i that a person is able to achieve (Anand *et al.* 2009). Each person i has a capability set Q_i. The capabilities of the individuals i to achieve the set of functionings b_i are constrained by the total set of commodities X_i and the conversion factors z_k (Binder and Coad 2010b):

$$Q_i(X_i) = \{b_i | b_i = f_i(c(x) \,|\, z_i, z_e, z_s), \forall f_i \in F_i \wedge \forall x_i \in X_i\}.$$

This also means that individuals' capabilities are determined by the set of functionings from which they can choose (Sen 1985b; Gries and Naude 2010). A central intellectual contribution of the human capability approach can then be found in the way it does not focus merely on the outcomes. It also focuses on the process freedom and the entitlement of people to chose their own life, in the sense that it considers the capabilities individuals possesses and the choices they make in trying to achieve certain functionings (decent work and levels of health), if they wish to achieve them (e.g. through a healthy lifestyle and studying) – rather than merely counting the achieved commodities and functionings. For this reason, the human development and capability community makes a theoretical distinction between two different sides of human development: 'One is the formation of human capabilities, such as improved health or knowledge. The other is the use that people make of their acquired capabilities, for work or leisure' (UNDP 1990, p. 10). The freedoms and abilities to choose are recognized by the term 'capabilities'; the outcomes and realized choices by the term 'functionings'. Naturally, in practice capabilities and functionings are often interwoven and cannot clearly be distinguished empirically (e.g. Binder and Coad 2010a, 2010b). For example, health and education can be both a capability and a functioning. However, the essential theoretical understanding lies in recognizing that it is not only outcomes (functionings), but also people's freedom to choose, act and participate that are important. This means that issues such as democracy and principles of justice (which relate to poverty reduction, equity, efficiency, participation, responsibility, sustainability and human rights, for example) are also of crucial importance (Alkire 2010).

2.3.2 Measurement of the quality of life and human agency

Since the introduction of the Human Development Index (HDI) in 1990 (UNDP 1990), the discussion around the measurement of people-oriented development has expanded. Today, we can draw on education, income and life expectancy data for virtually all nations and even regions in the world. The measurement of development is critical for the advancement of socioeconomic development for several reasons.

First, discussions about which indicators should be included and how they should be weighted can lead to knowledge exchange and social progress. Accordingly, an ongoing debate about the measurement of social progress and welfare can contribute to democratic advancement and adaptation processes in the direction of socially desired goals. In the process of discussing the goals and methods, new knowledge can be explored and shared, leading to an accumulative and interactive learning process. Democratic discussion should foster the flexibility of this process, also allowing the change and diversification of directions and the introduction of new knowledge.

Second, during the measurement process (developing taxonomies, raising data and analysing the results) problem areas, hidden structural relations and causal relations can be discovered that need further quantitative and qualitative exploration.

Third, ranking and visualizing trends and development, based on data, provide policy makers, development practitioners and society in general with the opportunity to compare and illustrate areas in which advances have been made, as well as strengths and weaknesses. This can facilitate the process of discussion, advancement, agreements and change.

The human capability approach and its application in development programmes would have probably never been so successful without the HDI providing simple and comparable rankings that put emphasis not just on income, but also on life expectancy and education. Whereas the academic concepts of capabilities and functionings are inspiring, in practice this simple ranking plays an important and easily understandable role which does not requires much expert knowledge. If an income-rich country suddenly appears in its position behind a less income-rich country, owing to a lower performance in life expectancy and general education, the rich country may feel competitive pressure to improve its development and also in other areas, such as education or life expectancy and health. It reveals in a clear and straightforward manner the advances, strengths and weaknesses of countries in different dimensions of development. Before this data was available (e.g. via household survey data), most researchers could only observe (and sometimes assume) qualitative differences but not empirically prove them on a larger scale. Many researchers chose to work (or could only work) on topics where data is available. If the only available data is on capital, labour and the aggregated production (instead of including other social dimensions), it can be difficult to obtain appropriate knowledge and agreement about the necessary actions in other socioeconomic domains. Instead, working with existing data (e.g. capital and income data) and corresponding topics (capital accumulation and income growth) tends to be common. Because of (or perhaps despite) all the criticisms of specific quantitative indicators and taxonomies, increased measurement capabilities have made a significant contribution to the discussion of the direction and process of development.

The main centre of interest for human development and capability indicators is the measurement of human agency, freedom and the well-being of people. There is a huge debate between proponents of fairly objective measures of human agency and development such as education, income and life expectancy and the supporters of more subjective measures of well-being and the quality of life, such as community and family life, a good work-life balance, or even life satisfaction (e.g. Diener and Suh 1999; Economist Intelligence Unit 2005; Stiglitz *et al.* 2009; Alkire 2010; UNDP 2010). Despite their differences, they have something in common: they focus on social progress and development for people and not just merely on income, capital or (total factor) productivity expansion as the main goals of development. Table 2.3 provides a list of composite indicators which have been developed by different theorists to measure life quality, well-being and social progress. It becomes obvious that many people around the world are interested in the measurement, comparison, evolution and understanding of quality of life, well-being, human agency and social progress. There are several international initiatives such as the HDI, the OECD well-being indicators and the Gallup Healthways Well-Being Index, but there are also several national initiatives, such as Bhutan's Gross National Happiness Index, Great Britain's Well-Being Index and Germany's National Welfare Index. While mainstream economies may focus on growth as the main indicator of progress, this is not entirely true for global society. There is a great deal of discussion around quality of life, especially in developed countries, but also increasingly in emerging and developing countries. Table 2.3 presents a list of different approaches to measure well-being and quality of life. It becomes obvious that national statistics institutes and modern development taxonomies do not just focus on income and consumption, but are also interested in a varied set of other issues such as education, health and infrastructure. It becomes furthermore obvious that taking qualitative and non-economic aspects into account for development is no longer a niche, but is rather a widespread perspective on development.

Table 2.3 List of human development, well-being and quality of life measures

International well-being and quality of life measures

Measure	Reference / webpage
Human Development Index (HDI)	UNDP 1990, 2010
Inequality adjusted HDI	UNDP 2010
Multidimensional Poverty Index (MPI)	UNDP 2010; Alkire and Foster 2007
Commission on the Measurement of Economic Performance and Social Progress	Stiglitz *et al.* 2009; http://www. stiglitz-sen-fitoussi.fr/en/index.htm
OECD well-being indicators	www.oecd.org/dataoecd/4/31/ 47917288. pdf
EIU quality of life index	Economist 2005
Mercer's Quality of Living Reports	www.mercer.com
Physical Quality of Life Index (PQLI)	Morris 1980
Gallup-Healthways Well-Being Index	www.well-beingindex.com
The Genuine Progress Indicators	www.gpiatlantic.org
Voices of the Poor	World Bank 1999b; Narayan *et al.* 2000
Living Standards Measurement survey	http://econ.worldbank.org
Popsicle Index	http://solari.com/articles/ popsicle_index/
Happy Planet Index	www.happyplanetindex.org

National well-being and quality of life measures

Bhutan Gross National Happiness Index	www.grossnationalhappiness.com
General Well-Being Index (GB)	www.well-beingindex.com
Nationaler Wohlfahrtsindex (DE)	Diefenbacher und Zieschank 2009
Measures of Australia's Progress	http://www.abs.gov.au/about/progress
Canadian Index of Well-Being	www.ciw.ca/en
Measuring Ireland's Progress	www.cso.ie/

Measures of individual well-being and agency

The Development of Capability Indicators	Anand *et al.* 2009
Literature in psychology	Kahnemann *et al.* 2003

Within these taxonomies a large range of different aspects of human life are considered. Table 2.4 presents four different exemplary taxonomies, ranging from more objective measures of development (such as the HDI), over multiple variable composite indicators (such as the Economists's quality of life index, or the social progress taxonomy of Stiglitz *et al.* 2009) to more subjective measures of well-being (such as life satisfaction survey).

The power of the HDI clearly lies in its simplicity. It is a simple indicator composed of three equally weighted factors: life expectancy, education and income; three dimensions of development which, when combined, few people would criticize as not being important for themselves or their country. Furthermore, data on life expectancy, education (measured by literacy rates and

Table 2.4 Objective and subjective measures of the quality of life

Human Development Index	Social progress	Quality of life	Life satisfaction surveys
Income	Material living standards	Material wealth	On the whole are you satisfied?
Life Expectancy	Health	Health	Very satisfied
Education	Education	Job Security	Fairly
	Insecurity (economic and physical)	Political stability and security	Not very
	Political voice and governance	Political freedom	Not at all
	Social connections and relationships	Family life	
	Environment	Community life	
	Personal activities including work	Climate and geography	
	Subjective measure of quality of life	Gender equality	

Objective measures	————————————————➔	Subjective measures

Sources: Human Development Index (UNDP 1990); Social Progress (Stiglitz *et al.* 2009); Quality of life (Economist Intelligence Unit 2005); life satisfaction (Oswald 1997).

school enrolment) and income per capita are available for almost all countries in the world, as well as across considerable periods of time. The extent of objectivity in measures such as life expectancy or years of schooling is higher than it is in life satisfaction or happiness. Recent approaches to social progress and quality of life tend to be multidimensional, and include social and institutional indicators such as community and family life, work-life balance, political and economic insecurity and gender equality, as well as environmental sustainability and subjective measures of development. However, it is difficult to weigh the importance of these factors, because they may be estimated differently by different individuals, countries and cultures and may change over time. Critical voices within the human development community argue that life satisfaction and subjective happiness measures by themselves have serious shortcomings in measuring the capabilities, agency and deprivation of people and may not always be helpful when working to provide ethically acceptable justice and equality of opportunities (Sen 1985b, 1999). Imagine the situation of an illiterate African woman with a life expectancy of approximately thirty-eight years, stating that she is fairly satisfied with her life. Then compare this with a master's student with a life expectancy of eighty years, who also states that she is fairly satisfied with her life. The second woman has a much longer and healthier life, she has many more options available to her, such as the ability to learn, chose and the option to have many more experiences. However, most importantly, she is much more the agent of her own life than the first woman. Studies have revealed that after giving illiterate women education and providing them with the capability to read and write, they also adapt their expectations accordingly, through having access to information and thereby also developing more ambitious plans for their future and that of their children. This demonstrates that the mere question of whether someone is happy or generally satisfied with the life they lead might not take objective deprivations in the freedom and agency of people into account.

It is worth noting that virtually all measures of well-being, quality of life and human capabilities include income. This is reasonable, as even though income might not be the ultimate goal of development, a certain minimum income is fundamental to be an active member of society and not be deprived of the freedom of economic choices. Being economically poor means (within market economies) not being able to deal, for instance, with serious health problems or providing children with proper education and basic school supplies, or more generally of being deprived of most activities available to the 'common citizen' of the home country. Whilst accepting the critique of income not being the sole goal of development, we should not 'throw the baby out with the bath water'. Income is certainly not the only element of importance, but continues to be a significant element of economic freedom and human agency. Several studies (e.g. Economist Intelligence Unit 2005) have shown that a minimum threshold of income is necessary for well-being; if people do not earn a certain amount of money they tend to be less satisfied with their life than people who can consider themselves as middle class or full members of the society. The positive effects of income on happiness, however, level out at high levels of income. Rich people (in relative and absolute terms) are not necessarily happier than people from the middle class. It depends on a wide range of further factors such as health, work-life balance, marriage and family. In any case, it is obvious that life satisfaction and happiness, as well as human agency and freedom, are highly relative concepts. For this reason, one goal of the Human Development and Capability Association is the promotion of certain minimum standards and the reduction of ethically unacceptable levels of inequality. This implies the need to promote the measurement of poverty to reveal the level and patterns of deprivation, unfreedom and inequality within countries and across the world. Recently the Multidimensional Poverty Index (MPI) has placed emphasis on the conditions and life quality of the most deprived and vulnerable citizens (Alkire and Foster 2007; Alkire and Santos 2010). The MPI is made up of the same three factors as the HDI; however, it also considers the typical types of multidimensional deprivations which poor people in developing countries suffer from. Table 2.5 presents the components of the acute multidimensional poverty index suggested by Alkire and Santos (2010).

The Human Development Report 2010 (UNDP 2010) revealed that in the 104 countries considered in the sample, about 1.75 billion people live in multidimensional poverty, showing very low values in at least 30 per cent of the proposed indicators. This controversial debate is ongoing, and measurement will always have to adapt to the changes in the development goals and new forms of relative deprivations (such as digital divide). To sustain the societal debate,

Table 2.5 Components of the multidimensional poverty index

Health (1/3)	*Education (1/3)*	*Standard of living (1/3)*
Child mortality: if any child has died in the family (1/6)	**Years of schooling:** if no household member has completed five years of schooling (1/6)	**Electricity:** having no electricity
Nutrition: if any adult or child in the family is malnourished (1/6)	**Child enrolment:** if any school-aged child drops out of school in the first eight school years	**Drinking water:** according to the Millennium Development Goals (MDG) definitions
		Sanitation: according to the MDG definitions
		Flooring: dirt, sand or dung indicate poverty
		Cooking fuel: wood, charcoal or dung indicate poverty
		Assets: poverty, when the household does not own more than one of the assets: radio, TV, telephone, bicycle, motorbike

Source: Adapted from Alkire and Santos (2010, p. 4).

however, the availability and translation of data into knowledge is an essential task which informs society, researchers and policy makers.

2.3.3 Main critiques

The human capability approach has received three main critiques: (a) there is a certain difficulty in translating the qualitative richness of the capability approach into empirical measures; (b) it is an individualistic approach that might not consider systemic aspects of development; and (c) in its emphasis on life quality the approach may underestimate the importance of economic competitiveness and growth as a means of development.

While quite straightforward from a qualitative and theoretical perspective, the distinction of capabilities and functionings in measurement issues is quite challenging (Kuklys 2005; Anand *et al.* 2009). For example, Binder and Coad (2010a, 2010b) show that there are complex relations and adaptive processes between different types of well-being, such as education and health. Amartya Sen himself reiterated that several dimensions of well-being, such as health or education, can be both a functioning and a capability (e.g. Sen 1999). However, this does not undermine the theoretical and ethical understanding that process and outcome freedoms, capabilities and functionings matter.

Another critique regarding the measurement of human development is that the aggregation and weighting of elements in joint measures might be arbitrary. So far, the HDI is the only widely accepted measure of human capabilities; however, education, life expectancy and income are not comprehensive measures, but omit many other dimensions of human development and capabilities, such as political freedom or self-esteem. From a practical measurement perspective, the aggregations of capabilities and functionings within a joint measure such as the HDI is certainly not perfect and should be further advanced, but they can still provide a useful proxy for human development. In the predictable future, no single empirical measure will be able to capture the whole complexity of capabilities, functionings and evolution of human beings and societies. However, indicators such as the HDI or the MPI are useful proxy indicators that allow policy makers and the society to debate for minimum standards and inequalities in diverse realms of the human life.

The second common critique to the human development approach is the individualistic and therefore limited nature of the human development approach. While this critique might has some merit, it is important to understand the way in which the human development approach considers individualism as well as the individual within a system. It is true that the human development community clearly postulates ethical individualism, in the sense that the well-being of individuals is considered as being the ultimate goal of development (Robeyns 2008, cited in Alkire 2010). However, the human development approach does not support ontological and methodological individualism in the sense that societies can simply be explained by the sum of their individuals and their properties (Robeyns 2008, cited in Alkire 2010). Many works by the human development community focus on a varied set of systemic issues, such as global resources, gender, religion, democracy and group capabilities. A prime example of this is to be found in the annual Human Development Reports from 1990 to 2010, in which UNDP worked through a great variety of individual, social, political and economic topics (Alkire 2010; UNDP 2010). In his book *Identity and Violence*, Sen (2006) draws attention to the heterogeneity of human individuals and identities, and the participation of individuals in multiple groups and identities. Judging persons merely by their religion, or another dimension, does not correspond to the heterogeneity of group affiliations and categories influencing the unique identity of each individual. Recently some human development researchers also introduced the concept of group capabilities (Steward 2005; Ibrahim 2006) and external capabilities (Foster and Handy 2008). This shows how several researchers have carefully considered problems of individualism or attempted a more systematic approach. This book aims to contribute to this discussion by discussing various positive and negative effects of social networks and economic diversification on human development (see for example Chapter 4 and Chapter 5).

2.3.4 *Human development and economic development*

Due to its focus on well-being and human rights, technological innovation and economic development have not been the core focus and interest of the human development community. This does not mean that knowledge, consumption and production are not considered as important elements for the well-being of individuals. Notably, income and knowledge are two of the three constitutional pillars of the HDI (UNDP 1990, 2010). The relation and differentiation between economic growth and human development is a topic passionately discussed in the human development community. Amartya Sen emphasizes the interconnectedness of different dimensions of instrumental freedoms in the social, political and economic space (Sen 1999). He argues that economic unfreedom can also lead to unfreedom in the social and political arena. For example, in his famous account about Kader Mia, he illustrates (during the Nobel Prize Lecture in 2011) how a lack of economic opportunities and occupational choices can lead to unfreedom and even death:

> One afternoon in Dhaka, a man came through the gate screaming pitifully and bleeding profusely. The wounded person, who had been knifed in the back, was a Muslim daily labourer, called Kader Mia. He had come for some work in a neighbouring house – for a tiny reward – and had been knifed on the street by some communal thugs in our largely Hindu area. As he was being taken to the hospital by my father, he went on saying that his wife had told him not to go into a hostile area during the communal riots. But he had to go out in search of work and earning because his family had nothing to eat. The penalty of that economic unfreedom turned out to be death, which occurred later on in the hospital. The experience was devastating for me, and suddenly made me aware of the dangers of narrowly defined identities, and also of the divisiveness that can lie buried in communitarian politics. It also alerted me to the remarkable fact that economic unfreedom, in the form of extreme poverty, can make a person a helpless prey in the violation of other kinds of freedom: Kader Mia need not have come to a hostile area in search of income in those troubled times if his family could have managed without it.
>
> (Sen 1998b, 1999)

This example shows how the lack of economic choices can lead to human unfreedom. If Kader Mia had had other occupational choices or enough savings during those troubled times, he would not have died. The main emphasis of the human development community, though, is not so much on economic sectors and employment, but rather on the human freedom and the well-being of the people. It is worth noting that in twenty years of United Nations Human Development Reports '…the terms work and employment only appear under the names creativity and productivity and only for five years' (Alkire 2010, p. 14). Being productive and being creative are not considered as priority dimensions of human development. From a human development perspective this is arguably true, as there is a series of basic capabilities to be accomplished first, such as education, health, security and agency (Streeten *et al.* 1981). Nevertheless, it should not be forgotten that professional life and the division of labour have always played an essential role in any human society, from the first settlements to the present day. Money, trading, income and a decent job are core aspects of daily life, desires and preoccupations, and are even more crucial to the poor. Amsden (2010) argued that grass-roots methods of poverty alleviation will fail until they also result in job creation.

It is not enough to expand people's capabilities; long-run poverty reduction also requires determined investment in the creation of paid employment and self-employment above starvation wages. Development policy and anti-poverty programmes often neglect the critical dimension of employment. It is wrong to assume that the supply of capabilities would also imply (via a Say-type law) the existence of economic demands for these capabilities. An increase in basic capabilities (e.g. by government programmes providing basic shelter, education and health services) is important, but might not automatically come along with the creation of more and better jobs and a long-term (income) poverty reduction. The availability of education may not necessarily match the demands and possibilities of the labour market; the poor may still be forced into self-employment with potentially low economic gains, or have to work many hours at very low wages. Furthermore, without the creation of good occupational choices, the highly educated and skilled may try to emigrate. This can lead to brain drain and further unequal economic and technological development between countries. Countries need these educated people to promote endogenous economic, technological and institutional development. They are required to build up well-organized and competitive enterprises able to compete in global markets and to create sustainable and well-paid jobs at home. Nevertheless it is wrong to assume that the mere expansion of capabilities (education, health, democracy and infrastructure) is enough. Industrial and employment policies are needed to create the incentives, institutional environment and economies of scale to allow (especially small and medium sized) enterprises in developing countries to grow, innovate and be competitive in the global markets (Rodrik 2004). The promotion of innovation, business competitiveness and economic diversification continues to be crucial in the long run to the creation of more and better jobs and the expansion of economic and human development. This is where innovation economics comes into play, because innovation is a main driver of economic development, diversification and the creation of jobs. Several studies from different economic disciplines have indicated that innovation and technological progress are the core drivers of structural changes, the creation of new and better jobs and long-term economic development (Marx 1867; Schumpeter 1912, 1939, 1943; Abramowitz, 1956). Economic development is not enough by itself, but can be a powerful driver of human development.

2.3.5 *Human development and innovation*

New technologies have been key to improving the life expectancy, income, education and social choices of people. As the Human Development Report 2001 pointed out, '…the 20th century's unprecedented gains in advancing human development and eradicating poverty came largely from technological breakthroughs' (UNDP 2001, p. 2). Advances in medicine, such as penicillin or Malaria prevention, or technological progress in agriculture and food production, have been essential to the advance the health and nutrition of the population. In the words of Lipsey *et al.* (2005, p. 5):

People living in the first decade of the twentieth century did not know modern dental and medical equipment, penicillin, bypass operations, safe births, control of genetically transmitted diseases, personal computers, compact discs, television sets, automobiles, opportunities for fast and cheap worldwide travel, affordable universities, central heating, air conditioning ... technological change has transformed the quality of our lives.

Despite the positive impacts of technological progress, many innovations (such as war technologies) have affected groups in different positive, negative and ambiguous ways. Many new products and services originating in the Silicon Valley, which have gone on to improve the capabilities of people across the world, may never have been developed without former R&D expenditure to produce electronic weapons during the cold war. The ICT revolution has provided a massive amount of new opportunity, but also led to even higher inequality between different people, regions and countries. Several studies illustrate that there are there are multiple complex relations between innovation, well-being, inequality and the agency of individuals (UNDP 2001; Johnson *et al.* 2003; Arocena and Sutz 2005; Perez 2007; Miller *et al.* 2008; Srinivas and Sutz 2008; Cozzen and Kaplinsky 2009). Innovation impacts on human development through a varied set of channels.

- *Technical and organizational progress* in critical technologies affect human development, e.g. new medicines, distance learning, agriculture etc. (UNDP, 2001).
- *Economic diversification* brings with it more choices for employment and consumption (see Chapter 4).
- *Structural change* (e.g. Pasinetti 1981, 1983; Saviotti 1996) and *creative destruction processes* (Schumpeter 1912) lead to changing capability requirements as well as positively and negatively affecting groups.
- *Co-evolutionary institutional changes* (e.g. better access to information, network society, development of the financial sector) change people's rights and agency (e.g. Benkler 2006).

The importance of innovation to human development becomes clear when we consider the role of innovation in economic history (e.g. Schumpeter 1939; Perez 2007). Various technological innovations (e.g. steel, steam power or use of electricity), organizational innovations (e.g. Taylorism, Fordism and Toyotism) as well as social innovations (e.g. the French Revolution, new institutional arrangements, new social security systems, microcredits) certainly have had strong impacts on actors' social choices, their freedom to live and behave as they desire and their capabilities to achieve certain life standards. For example, industrialization led to difficult adaptation processes, whereby some freedoms were suppressed and others were expanded. Many workers were exploited in the industrial production machine and had to live in inhumane conditions. On the other hand, many people achieved a higher level of income, better access to education and new choices and opportunities within the expanding cities. Nascent workers movements and syndicates were the basis for bringing about many progressive social policies and rights for individuals. Industrialization has led to both higher general levels of human freedom (in the sense of an expanding set of social choices) but also to an expansion of inequality in freedoms between the actors. The same is happening with the information and communication revolution which has opened up completely new possibilities for the poor, but also poses the threat of a potential digital divide. On the one hand, it has facilitated information and knowledge flows over large distances, allowed new forms of social and economic organization, and has opened up a large set of new opportunities (e.g. education through distance learning, health services etc.); on the other hand it has created a new threat for the poor in the form of a digital divide and created new economic monopolies and oligopolies. Thus, the question arises of how to reduce the negative implications of these creative destruction processes and how to foster the positive ones.

Recently, increased focus has been put on social innovations, such as those found in the microcredit revolution, which can empower people to become active agents of development (Bornstein 2004; Yunus 2007). Furthermore, by focusing on frugal innovation (promoting emphasis on simple usage and the core features of products) companies can segment markets and also attend to the demand and acquisitive power of the poorest strata of the population, as well as learning from the poor and including them in local production and research facilities. In sum, innovation and technology is affecting human development in multiple direct and indirect ways. The human development community's perspective on technology has emphasized how specific innovations (e.g. vaccines or microcredits) can improve human development, and has also concentrated on the ethics aspects and the appropriate design of technologies (e.g. Oosterlaaken and Hoven 2012; Oosterlaken 2013). This is an important task, but how innovation emerges and how it affects human development and social choices indirectly through economic development and capability adaptation processes must also be examined. Employment and consumption are central dimensions of human life and well-being, especially for the poor. For this reason, innovation-driven economic diversification is vital for human development. The human development community could learn from innovation economics about the emergence and economic impact of innovation, and innovation economics from the human development approach about the dimensions of development by, of and for the people. This joint learning process could also help to disentangle the complex relations between human development and economic growth.

2.4 Modern integral development approaches

Modern development approaches and the corresponding means of measurement increasingly consider the complexity of linkages, causalities and interdependences between different social, economic, political and ecological dimensions. Extreme positions of either market and state as the ultimate planner or 'invisible hand' of the economy have shifted towards a more intermediate position, drawing on the need for both forces to work complementarily with one another. Comprehensive taxonomies have been presented in different fields of research, such as those developed by the comprehensive Neo-Schumpeterian approach (Hanusch and Pyka 2007a, 2007c, 2007d), the systems of innovation and development approach (Cassiolato *et al.* 2003; Lundvall *et al.* 2011), the Global Competitiveness Index of the World Economic Forum or the taxonomy proposed by Stiglitz, Sen and Fitoussi (2009) in the Commission on the Measurement of Economic Performance and Social Progress. Modern development approaches have moved beyond all previous discussions on the market and state as either/or solutions. Instead they move towards promoting complementary action, coordination and interaction between the market and state; facilitating on the one hand the strengths of market forces, and on the other promoting the interaction between the different agents of society. This is necessary to address properly the need for regulation and strategic interventions by the state and to create the institutional framework, facilitating innovation, economic development and social welfare (e.g. Sen 1999; World Bank 2003; Rodrik 2004). After decades of ISI policies and government intervention between the 1950s and the 1970s, followed by the subsequent so-called neoliberal 'counterrevolution' in the last two decades of the twentieth century, recent development approaches argue in favour of an intermediate position between market and state (e.g. Rodrik 2004). Furthermore, recent approaches consider various complex factors: the strategic need to promote fertile cooperation patterns between the different agents of the economy (Cassiolato *et al.* 2003); the ethical and economic need to provide the people with the capabilities to be active agents (UNDP 1990); and the importance of promoting the institutional setup and strategic policy processes necessary to overcome failings in coordination and information about potential new sectors and enable economic diversification through self-discovery mechanisms, including finding out which activities work and which do not (Hausmann and Rodrik 2003; Rodrik 2004). Three recent approaches in economics considering the role of multiple influence factors and their interrelatedness are briefly discussed in the following sections.

2.4.1 Comprehensive Neo-Schumpeterian economics

Hanusch and Pyka (2007a) show that the innovation principle can be seen as the Schumpeterian complement of the price mechanism. Companies do not merely compete for lower prices, but also (especially in the long run) for innovations and the introduction of new goods, services, marketing methods and organization models. By focusing on innovation in all economic realms, the Comprehensive Neo-Schumpeterian Economics (CNSE) approach challenges the short-term orientation of modern capital market approaches, as well as the market-failure-based approaches to an economic theory of the welfare state.

When considering the future orientation and qualitative composition of an economy, complexity issues combined with true uncertainty (about the optimal choices) enter economic theory and demand a new methodology. The prerequisites of long-term prolific economic development and growth depend not only on entrepreneurship, but also crucially depend on the long-term orientation of capital markets faced with strong uncertainty, and a public sector willing to cope with the strong uncertainties and increasing complexities that confront modern economies (Hanusch and Pyka 2007a; Hartmann *et al.* 2010). In other words, CNSE argues that innovation and uncertainty matter not just for industrial dynamics (on which most research has so far focused), but are also crucial for future-oriented financial markets and the public sector. The lack of a future orientation in only one of these economic areas could be a bottleneck that hampers all dynamic development processes, balanced growth and prolific development potential. The empirical application of this approach to industrialized European and OECD countries has shown that there is no one single optimal design; different institutional designs can be found. These different designs (e.g. the Scandinavian model, the Mediterranean model or the Central European model) co-exist and also change over time (Hanusch and Pyka 2007c, 2007d). To apply CNSE to developing countries, specific strengths, weaknesses and structural differences have to be considered (Hartmann *et al.* 2010). For instance, development economics and global competitiveness research help to provide insights into the specific conditions and the range of problems in less developed countries. Several authors show the high cross-fertilization potential between innovation economics and complementary approaches from development economics (Johnson *et al.* 2003; Arocena and Sutz 2005; Cassiolato and Lastres 2008; ECLAC 2008). Accordingly, the adaptation of CNSE to the specific conditions and challenges of developing countries has to take into account the inability of a large percentage of the population to participate proactively in innovation and development, as well as the serious structural problems relating to economic efficiency and providing the economic opportunities for endogenous learning-by-solving processes (see also Arocena and Sutz 2005). Thus, when applying CNSE to developing countries, the efficiency and future orientation of their economic structure must receive greater attention, as should the enlargement of the capabilities of all actors so that they can contribute to innovation and the development of their countries and regions. Nonetheless, we are still lacking a CNSE development approach able to combine the understandings of all three approaches (knowledge, market and state), consider evolutionary change and make individual actors the centre of interest.

2.4.2 Systems of innovation and development

An interesting effort to analyse innovation systems in developing countries has been undertaken by the Global Network for Systems of Learning, Innovation and Competence Building Systems (Globelics). Globelics has sought to engage in a deeper understanding of the interplay between innovation, learning and inequality. Researchers such as Johnson *et al.* (2003), Arocena and Sutz (2005), Cassiolato and Lastres (2008) and Lundvall *et al.* (2011) have contributed to the potential for cross-fertilization between development and innovation economics. For example Arocena and Sutz (2005) identified a fertile area for intersection between Sen's capability approach and the innovation system approach by emphasizing that learning-by-solving requires a steady flow of opportunities to solve non-trivial problems. In a similar vein, Evers *et al.* (2006) pointed to the knowledge trap that emerges if the importing of knowledge and technology does not foster endogenous learning processes and the creation of non-knowledge, or in other words the awareness of ignorance and of which further problems need or should be solved. Each problem-solving process and research activity intrinsically leads to the creation of knowledge of what we do not know and what still has to be improved or further analysed. A lack of non-trivial technological problem-solving opportunities seriously hampers the capacity for endogenous capability upgrading and innovation (Arocena and Sutz 2005). Srinivas and Sutz (2008) claim that local and national efforts are needed to promote local capacities for endogenous problem-solving and innovation. A better understanding of scarcity induced innovation, however, is required.

> To innovate or to solve problems in a technological universe characterized by scarcity requires the development of a series of skills – learnt by doing, by searching, by interacting and by solving – that are idiosyncratic: term them capacities to innovate in scarcity conditions.
>
> (Srinivas and Sutz 2008, p. 135)

These innovative capabilities must be understood before appropriate policies can be designed. Arocena and Sutz (2005) argued that a combination of both capabilities and opportunities is necessary to open up the way for evolutionary learning in underdeveloped settings. A good formal education is not enough if people do not have opportunities to apply and enlarge their capabilities through learning processes (Arocena and Sutz 2005). It is crucial that we understand that it is not just the lack of skills or capabilities of the agents (e.g. provided and fostered by education, health services etc.), but also the lack of opportunities (access to finance, information flows, a variety of economic activities) that prevents many people in developing countries from advancing through learning-by-doing, solving processes and entrepreneurial action. Johnson *et al.* (2003) argued that a parallel emphasis on basic needs and innovation is necessary for the long-term development of national systems of innovation and competence building. Couto Soares and Cassiolato (2008) claimed that innovation and social policies need to be integrated to promote socially oriented innovation. Palliative interventions to tackle extreme poverty might not be enough to overcome the systemic reproduction of inequalities. Long-term development requires a fertile national innovation system (and science, technology and innovation (STI) policies) oriented towards people's social needs.

Naturally, innovation is not the only factor impacting on inequality and poverty, but often it may have decisive feedback loops. Cozzen and Kaplinsky (2009) have shown that the causalities between innovation, poverty and inequality are not unidirectional, but multi-layered and complex. There is no straightforward answer to the questions of whether one causes the other, or they are just coincidental and/or co-evolved. Sometimes innovation reflects and reinforces inequalities and sometimes it undermines them. More in-depth analysis of the linkages between the different types of inequalities (e.g. horizontal or vertical inequalities), of innovation (e.g. process, product, functional and chain innovation) and of competence building is necessary (Cozzen and Kaplinsky 2009). For this reason, inequality research and innovation research can and should learn from each other. Furthermore there is increasing academic interest in the creation of indicators of innovation and well-being (Miller *et al.* 2008). However, several co-evolutionary and adaptive processes within and between different types of capabilities (Anand *et al.* 2009; Binder and Coad 2010a, 2010b) and types of innovation and innovation processes (Schumpeter 1912; Fagerberg *et al.* 2005; OECD 2005; Hanusch and Pyka 2007b) make the interrelations between innovation, inequality and well-being very complex (Miller *et al.* 2008; Cozzen and Kaplinsky 2009). For instance, a new technology or product (e.g. in ICT) could make some competences and products decline, or even become obsolete and hence people lose their jobs; on the other hand new jobs may be created in new sectors, providing people with new choices. The effects may also not be static, but change over time; new demands on the skills of the people and companies may lead to stress and large initial inequalities, but then become more widespread, improving the overall educational level. In the same way, the initial effects of more choices through the creation of new sectors, life style, social security and leisure possibilities can be very positive, but without a proper selection and simplification can lead at some point to stress, ignorance within complexity and choices overload (see also Chapter 4). In turn this can trigger the creation of adaptation processes and better choices, such as more user-friendly product designs or services. Hence positive and negative effects may change over time and might not be equally distributed across different people, groups and countries. To promote the positive and reduce the negative effects, the different agents of an innovation system need to constantly interact with each other, to (a) promote the future orientation of their economies, but also (b) prevent exclusion and very high levels of inequality and (c) develop mechanisms that constantly improve the capabilities of people to actively participate in the innovation and development process of their countries.

2.4.3 *Modern economic competitiveness approaches*

Mainstream economics research has also switched from monocausal analysis of development (emphasizing single factors such as capital accumulation) to a more integral and complex type of analysis (considering a varied set of factors): see World Bank (2003) and Lopez-Claros *et al.* (2006a, 2006b). Growth has been identified as a necessary but not sufficient element for development (UNDP 1990; World Bank 2003). For example, in the World Development Report 2003 (World Bank 2003), economists from the World Bank argued that ensuring sustainable development requires that attention should be paid not to economic growth alone, but also to environmental and social issues. Unless the transformation of society and the management of the environment unite with economic growth, growth itself will be jeopardized in the long term. Even the mainstream economic measures of competitiveness (being developed by neoclassical scholars, who have been so often blamed for their unrealistic world model) consider now a variety of elements, including a series of institutional, social and political domains. For example the Global Competitiveness Index (GCI), developed by Sala-i-Martin (Sala-i-Martin and Artadi 2004) to measure the competitiveness of countries, takes the following factors into account: (a) the fulfilment of basic requirements (e.g. infrastructure, macroeconomic stability, health and primary education); (b) efficiency enhancers (e.g. higher education and training, technological readiness); and (c) innovation and sophistication indicators as key indicators of competitiveness (e.g. in Lopez-Claros *et al.* 2006b).

Despite the substantial differences between the Neo-Schumpeterian, the human development and the neoclassical approaches behind the GCI index, the necessity of obtaining good values or at least minimum standards in these three dimensions is common sense. Humanity has an ethical responsibility to make human agency and welfare a focus of development policies; however, traditional key concepts in economics, such as market efficiency, macroeconomic stability, capital accumulation and economic growth, also remain important factors in economic development. Economic growth does not necessarily bring with it poverty reduction (or higher levels of freedom), but without economic growth, it seems be also very difficult to provide more and better occupational choices.

2.5 Empirical example: Revealing different bottlenecks for development in Latin America

To shed some light on the complexity of development and study to what degree (a) efficiency based economic growth, (b) innovation and structural change, as well as (c) human development are overlapping factors or depict different dimensions in the development patterns of countries, Hartmann *et al.* (2010) studied the systems of development and innovation in Latin America. Taxonomies for measuring innovation systems (Godinho *et al.* 2004; Balzat and Pyka 2006; UNU-MERIT and EC-JRC 2006; Fagerberg and Shrolec 2006) were combined with insights from the human capability approach (Sen 1999) as well as more mainstream economic competitiveness measures (e.g. López-Claros *et al.* 2006b). This approach allowed the illustration and combination of different perspectives on development and at the same time showed how none of them alone provides a comprehensive picture of development, neither the mainstream economic emphasis on the efficiency and openness of the economy, nor the Neo-Schumpeterian focus on knowledge and innovation, or the human development and capability focus on freedom and well-being.

A future-oriented economic structure, freedom of the actors and knowledge and innovation are argued to be mutually interconnected and reinforcing factors of development. The agents have to be free and need cognitive capabilities and economic opportunities to be able to develop as people and thereby become agents of qualitative entrepreneurship and innovation. This approach was applied to Latin American economies using a composed data set of 44 indicators of freedom, knowledge and economic structure for the period 2000–2005 (see Hartmann *et al.* 2010). A confirmative factor analysis using Cronbach's alpha shows that all three factors are interrelated. Cronbach's alpha is constructed by computing the mean of all possible split-half coefficients, which are estimated by dividing the test into two shares with a random distribution of the items and measuring the correlation between the two shares using the Spearman-Brown method (Schnell *et al.* 2005). Cronbach's alpha can be formalized as presented in equation (2.1).

$$\alpha = \frac{n}{n-1}\left(1 - \frac{\sum \sigma_i^2}{\sigma_x^2}\right)$$

n = Number of items
σ_i^2 = Varience of item i (2.1)
σ_x^2 = Total test varience

The alpha can have a value between 0 and 1, a commonly used threshold value for acceptable reliability – i.e. the alpha value is 0.7 or higher (Hair *et al.* 1995). Further information on the data and the calculation of Cronbach's alpha can be viewed in Hartmann *et al.* (2010). A high level of intercorrelation between the factors freedom, knowledge and economic structure was found, with a high alpha value of 0.918. The elimination of one of the factors leads to lower, but still high alpha values (see Table 2.6). Each factor (objective class) is highly correlated with each of the other two factors (objective classes).

In the case of Latin America, then, the theoretical hypothesis that freedom, knowledge and economic structure are highly intercorrelated factors can be empirically confirmed. The high alpha values indicate that these three indicators seem to measure a common latent dimension (we may call this 'future-oriented development'), yet the three dimensions are not the same and qualitatively require different political interventions.

In the next step, an average linkage cluster algorithm was applied to identify the similarities and dissimilarities and comparative strengths and weaknesses of twenty Latin American countries, comprising 97 per cent of the Latin American population. Cluster analysis techniques test a sample for the degree of structural commonalities between the units of analysis (Jobson 1992; Hair *et al.* 1995; Backhaus *et al.* 2006). Its outcome is a categorization of the analysed units, so that the coherence of each cluster, as well as the heterogeneity between different

Table 2.6 Interrelationship of development dimensions

Constructs (development dimensions)	Alpha, when construct deleted	Cronbach's alpha value value for all three constructs
Freedom	0.845	
Economic structure	0.894	0.918
Knowledge	0.904	

Source: Hartmann *et al.* (2010).

clusters, is maximized (Jobson 1992). For this purpose, the distance values between the countries were determined on the basis of the characteristics of each country. In particular, squared Euclidean distances were used. The distance between the indicators of two countries i and j is calculated as follows:

$$d(i,j) = \sum_{k=1}^{m}(a_{ik} - a_{jk})^2$$

Here a_{ik} represents the parameter values of the characteristic $k = 1,...,m$ for country $i = 1,...,n$. Thus the entire quantitative data matrix is $A = (a_{ik})_{n \times m}$. A hierarchical average linkage cluster algorithm is applied because it is not overly influenced by single cases and neighbours (compared with other algorithms), and it is not particularly susceptible to distortions should outliers that are very different from all other cases appear (see Backhaus *et al.* 2006). Inter-cluster diversity is calculated as follows:

$$v(K, L) = \frac{1}{|K| \cdot |L|} \sum_{\substack{i \in k, \\ j \in L}} d(i, j)$$

Both distinct classes K and L (i.e. $K \neq L$) belong to the entire classification K. Since no analysis of a given, ex ante predetermined classification of countries is intended, an agglomerative classification is used that starts with single country clusters and entails a stepwise concentration of countries according to their degree of structural similarity. The selected clustering method yields an exhaustive as well as a disjunctive classification. This means that every country is assigned to one cluster ($U_{K \in K}$ $K = N$), with N being the total number of analysed objects) and no country can be part of two different classes ($K, L \in K$, $K \neq L$, so that $K \cap L = \varnothing$). To identify the optimal number of clusters (for the remaining cases), the so-called elbow criterion is applied. This measure is determined by analysing the change in the heterogeneity index over the course of the different agglomeration steps of the cluster algorithm. The elbow criterion appears when further merging steps lead to a sharp rise in the heterogeneity coefficient, i.e. a strong loss in the coherence of the different clusters and thus a strong quality reduction for the entire classification. The idea of the elbow criterion is to find the optimal cluster number that can provide the best trade-off between intra-cluster homogeneity and at the same time inter-cluster heterogeneity. Finally, to reveal the (relative) structural weaknesses, the performance of the different country clusters in terms of the development indicators freedom, knowledge and economy is measured by the mean square values of the corresponding item values. Each item was N (0, 1) standardized beforehand. Table 2.7 shows the resultant cluster profiles of the eight-cluster solution.

The analysis reveals that while in some countries knowledge is the main bottleneck for future-oriented development, other countries suffer from having inefficient economic structures or large parts of their population being excluded

Table 2.7 Patterns of development in Latin America[a]

Cluster profiles	Freedom (UNDP perspective)[b]	Knowledge (Neo-Schumpeterian perspective)[b]	Economic structure and efficiency (mainstream economics perspective)[b]
A: Chile	1.83	1.44	**1.13**
B: Costa Rica	**0.58**	0.81	0.68
C: Uruguay	0.74	0.54	**–0.12**
D: Argentina, Brazil	**0.14**	0.81	**0.18**
E: Mexico, Panama, Trinidad and Tobago	0.36	**0.18**	0.69
F: Colombia, El Salvador	0.17	**–0.29**	0.03
G: Peru, Venezuela	**–0.31**	–0.11	**–0.37**
H: Dom. Republic, Ecuador	–0.46	**–0.61**	–0.21
I: Bolivia, Guatemala, Honduras, Nicaragua, Paraguay	–0.69	**–0.75**	–0.64

Source: Adapted from Hartmann *et al.* (2010).

Notes
a Relative weaknesses of corresponding countries/cluster group are shown in bold.
b UNDP perspective', 'Neo-Schumpeterian perspective' and 'mainstream economics perspective' added to the original table of Hartmann *et al.* (2010).

from economic life. For example, while Uruguay performs comparatively well in terms of human freedom and low absolute poverty levels, the economic inefficiencies and lack of future orientation of the economy hamper the overall developmental potential; or, while Mexico, Panama, and Trinidad and Tobago have quite open economies with a considerable amount of manufactured exports, advances have to be made in the dimensions of human freedom and knowledge to facilitate higher levels of social welfare. Argentina and Brazil, in contrast, show comparatively good aggregated levels of knowledge in terms of R&D expenditures and some technologically advanced sectors; however, these countries struggle with considerable social problems such as corruption, crime and high levels of inequality, which negatively affect human freedom, well-being and economic efficiency. As many Latin American authors, such as Furtado (1958, 1961), have shown, the heterogeneity of socioeconomic structures and comparative strengths and weaknesses are even more accentuated within national borders, on the regional and local levels, between social classes and between different economic sectors. Nevertheless, the message of the analysis is straightforward. Each of the three approaches alone (mainstream economics, human development or innovation economics) may overlook structural bottlenecks preventing development in other economic or social domains. The policy which focuses on just one of the three objective classes may not lead to qualitative change because the interrelatedness of social stability, freedom of the actors, innovative capacity and economic structure and dynamics may be neglected:

- focusing on the knowledge factor alone will not allow for the socioeconomic imbalances and economic inefficiencies in developing countries to be dealt with;
- concentrating only on expanding the capabilities, human rights, social choices and freedoms of all actors, the main purpose of human development goals, may underestimate the importance of (strategic) technological competitiveness and economic efficiency; and
- concentrating purely on economic efficiency and openness neglects the importance of strategic alignment towards technological and sectoral competence building as well as the unfreedom and inability of large parts of the population to participate in and benefit from the innovation and development process.

However, this empirical analysis has some shortcomings that need to be explored further. First, there is even greater heterogeneity within the Latin American countries on the regional and sectoral level (Furtado 1958, 1961; Cimoli 2005; Lopez-Claros *et al.* 2006a; Katz 2007). Second, we need to have a better understanding of the micro behaviour (e.g. of entrepreneurs) and meso-structures (such as the sectoral structures and dynamics) to develop proper development policies (Dopfer *et al.* 2004).

2.6 Chapter conclusion

None of the development paradigms presented above (economic growth, innovation and human development) are individually able to provide a comprehensive understanding of future-oriented sustainable development. Different objectives, assumptions, key fields of interest and different research methods lead to different results and policies. It can be argued that they are most likely complementary perspectives, providing different insights on the complexity of the real world. The question should not be so much which approach is right or wrong, but rather what weight does society give to the different goals and what can the different approaches learn from each other?

Regarding the priorities and weights assigned to the different approaches, the economic growth paradigm continues to be the dominant perspective. In the global media, the adjectives 'poor' or 'developing' are often used almost as synonyms for persons with low incomes and countries with a low average production. In mainstream economics, the core focus has been on macroeconomic models, aiming to explain production growth by the means of aggregated production factors such as capital, labour or the total factor productivity. Nevertheless, since the 1990s, the terms innovation and human development have grown in importance. Innovation and technological progress is increasingly seen as the key driver of economic growth and is sometimes considered a goal in itself. Focus of the innovation paradigm is on the generation, implementation and diffusion of knowledge and technologies, entrepreneurship and R&D that trigger innovation as well the changes in the composition and diversity of the socioeconomic system owing to innovation. Apart from technology and innovation, an increasing focus of development economics is put on human development. This concept aims to address the needs of the poor, empower them and provide them with the means and choices to become active citizens of society and decide upon their own lives. This approach, however, is also closely related to another type of thinking, in which income is not seen as the core goal of development, but rather the emphasis is put on the well-being and life quality of the individuals. A rough generalization is that the growth paradigm focuses on the aggregated production of economies on the macro level, the innovation paradigm on the structures and dynamics of the economy on the meso level (how novelties are introduced and diffused and how they change the composition of the socioeconomic system), and the human development paradigm focuses on the capabilities and well-being of the individuals on the micro-level. Hence, despite setting different development goals and drivers, in many cases they might not be opposing, but rather complementary forces of development. The question should not so much being on 'either/or' but on the 'and', as well as on how they are connected with each other. The following chapter presents the 'Sen meets Schumpeter' approach as an attempt to gain new insights in the relations between structural economic change and human development.

3 Towards a 'Sen meets Schumpeter' approach

A better understanding of the complex relations between structural change and human development could provide the democratic debate (between the civil society, scientists, companies and politicians) with information on how to design structural change policies that enhance human agency and welfare. To contribute to this task, the 'Sen meets Schumpeter' approach, outlined in this chapter, presents possibilities and challenges which combine Schumpeter's understanding of economic development as structural change with Amartya Sen's understanding of development as the expansion of human capabilities and freedom.

Through the UNDP, Sen and other authors on social choice, human development and inequality have promoted the idea that the expansion of human agency, well-being and capabilities are the means and ends of development (Sen 1999). This has positively affected the lives of millions of people around the world, through development initiatives aiming to provide the poor with education, healthcare, basic shelter, access to finance and gender equality. One key shortcoming of the approach from an evolutionary economics perspective, however, is its weak emphasis on structural and technological aspects of economic systems; such as social network dynamics, technological progress and the structural changes in the variety and balance of economic activities that affect the economic competitiveness and occupational choices in the places where people are living. Structural economic change matters; innovation-driven socioeconomic change has decisive influences on the capabilities of the actors to become active agents in the development processes. For instance, the variety of economic sectors in a country and the access to information and finance networks determine occupational choices and learning opportunities. An evolutionary theory of welfare must take into account the fact that economic diversification and social network dynamics can contribute to human development but also lead to the reproduction of inequality in various dimensions such as income, occupational choices, education and political power. This requires an interdisciplinary approach, taking both human capabilities and freedom as well as structural and dynamic features of economic development into account.

From the beginning of the twenty-first century several researchers from different fields have begun combining the insights of Amartya Sen and Joseph Schumpeter to provide a more comprehensive picture on the evolutionary character of development (Binder 2010; Schubert 2012), the agency and learning capabilities of people (e.g. Arocena and Sutz 2005) and the establishment of prolific innovation systems in developing countries (e.g. Johnson *et al.* 2003). This book attempts to contribute to this emerging evolutionary approach to welfare economics, or the 'Sen meets Schumpeter' approach, by using complexity thinking to bridge between human capabilities and inequality research and innovation and structural change research. This chapter is structured as follows. Section 3.1 briefly discusses the complementarity of Sen and Schumpeter's perceptions of development. Section 3.2 reviews the strengths and challenges of existing approaches, combining insights from innovation economics and the human capabilities approach. Section 3.3 argues that complexity thinking can help to create bridges by studying the relations between social networks, human agency and economic diversification, and includes examples of theoretical fields to which such an evolutionary and complexity considering approach to welfare economics can contribute.

3.1 Complementarity of Sen and Schumpeter's perceptions of development

As discussed in Chapter 2, the question 'what is development?' can be answered in many different ways. Since its emergence in the 1950s, development economics and development studies have discussed multiple goals and means of development. While some approaches have emphasized economic production and income generation, others have claimed that well-being and freedom of the people is the true wealth of nations, or have regarded knowledge accumulation, novelty and technological progress almost as development goals themselves.

The research results and policy recommendations of the different research communities have been influenced by different perspectives and normative goals. For instance, while some consider equality as a core goal, others aim to maximise aggregated outcome. These underlying goals can lead to very different assumptions and ways on how to study development, which factors and causal relations are considered and which policy implications are drawn. The results and recommendations of each specialised research community, even if in most cases sensible from the chosen perspective, of course are unable alone to deal with the enormous complexity of possible goals, heterogeneous agents and multiple causal relations within complex societies and economies.

It is important to be aware that development can be defined in multiple nominal categories (such as individual freedom, social cohesion, ecological sustainability, novelty, happiness or knowledge generation) that might only be partially comparable and depend on value judgements about the priority of each development goal (see Chapter 2). It is important for societal progress to discuss what values a society does and should have; therefore it is also essential to be aware of the normative foundation chosen. Unfortunately, economists can easily forget the normative foundations of their research (e.g. maximising utility or studying income distributions), omitting a core dimension of the complexity of human behaviour and economic development. To explore the complexity of development and promote a constructive debate, an awareness of the assumptions, acceptance of diversity and humility of each approach is necessary. It is essential to encourage and be open to diverse perspectives because this process contributes to knowledge accumulation and a richer understanding of complexity. Humility is necessary to be able to listen to and learn from each other in a constructive way. Of course, some approaches and normative goals appear to be the diametric opposite of others and thus there can be difficulty in combining them within one single framework. By considering the issues in less divisive ways (e.g. state versus market, business competitiveness versus human well-being), many perspectives and development goals can be shown to be more complementary, or at least overlap in some important and informative ways, than at first sight seems to be the case.

This does indeed seem to be the case with the Neo-Schumpeterian and human development perspectives. These two approaches may focus on different goals and drivers of development, and they may also naturally argue for the higher importance and weight of each goal and driver. Nevertheless they are not necessarily opposing views but can provide complementary insights to the evolution and distribution of inequality over time. Of course there are differences regarding the priorities of developmental goals and topics under study; nevertheless in substance they can be viewed as basically complementary. Both approaches have a huge impact on development policies and practice. It must be noted also that while it is only since the start of the twenty-first century that connections and relations between the approaches have been explored, in practice they are often already applied jointly, such as in the case of social innovations and entrepreneurship, or NGOs that aim on promoting economic competitiveness and provide new occupational choices in less developed regions (which are meant to empower the people and provide them with more social choices and life quality).

3.2 Contributions and challenges of linking approaches

It is crucial at this juncture to consider how the economic focus on innovation and the ethical need for human development can be brought together. The innate logic is that the business world and advanced economies put emphasis on innovation and economic competitiveness, whereas social scientists and development researchers aim to promote global justice and human well-being. However, it seems necessary to bring these camps together to tackle systemic inequality reproduction, prevent social instability and create widespread social and economic welfare. Without economic development, it seems difficult for income-poor countries to establish widespread social security and a welfare system. At the same time, without a well-educated, healthy and creative population, it seems difficult to promote innovation and maintain long-run economic development. Consequently in recent decades, new approaches have been emerging that aim to bring the two camps together and try to understand the complex relations between innovation, economic and human development, deliberately considering ideas from both Amartya Sen and Joseph Schumpeter. Probably the most important are:

- social entrepreneurship (e.g. Bornstein 2004; Yunus 2007);
- making technology work for human development (e.g. UNDP 2001; Oosterlaken and Hoven 2012; Oosterlaken 2013);
- systems of innovation and development (Johnson *et al.* 2003; Arocena and Sutz 2005; Lundvall *et al.* 2011; Capriati 2013); and
- evolutionary welfare economics (Binder 2010; Schubert 2012).

The first two rather practice-oriented approaches have affected the lives of millions of people around the world; the last two are promising approaches for gaining a better understanding of the relations between innovation economic and human development and therefore creating more systemic policies that bring innovation, economic growth and human development together. Some core strengths and weaknesses of these new approaches are discussed in the next section.

3.2.1 Contributions

Perhaps the best example of where the thinking of Sen and Schumpeter are realised in practice is in the area of social entrepreneurship. Social entrepreneurs aim at introducing social innovations such as microfinance or new organisation of activities (education, health, democracy) that empower people and contribute to their human capabilities and societal welfare. The idea of social entrepreneurship has attracted the attention of many policy makers, academicians and entrepreneurs around the world, as demonstrated by the existence of organisations such as Ashoka, the Skoll Foundation and the Schwab Foundation for Social Entrepreneurship that support social entrepreneurs. Probably the most famous social entrepreneur is Muhammad Yunus (along with the Grameen Bank) who was behind the microfinance revolution, providing poor people in developing countries with the relatively small amount of financial means they need to get their own businesses started (Yunus 2007). Global companies and management journals highlight innovations from which companies and people in developing countries can benefit and local innovators can become empowered. New concepts such as social businesses, reverse innovation and frugal innovation, which aim to learn from and empower clients from less developed regions, have also received much attention (Hart 2010). Increasingly, global innovation processes originate from the findings in developing markets, and huge companies create products adapted to less developed settings. Chapter 6 will examine the concept of social entrepreneurship (which intrinsically combines innovation and human development) in more detail.

Another approach that can make substantial contributions to human agency and welfare is deliberately taking human development expansion into technology design (Oosterlaken and Hoven 2012; Oosterlaken 2013). This has the goal of making technology work for the poor (UNDP 2001). Famous examples and initiatives are the US$100 computer for the poor, and the creation of medicines for diseases widespread in developing countries.

It is important that the poor in developing countries become not only the recipients of technologies developed in the North, but also have the capabilities to actively contribute to the innovation processes, shape technologies according to their needs and build up their own innovation capabilities to solve problems and innovate (Juma *et al.* 2001; Srinivas and Sutz 2008). This later perspective links with initiatives to combine the innovation system approach with Sen's human capabilities approach (e.g. Johnson *et al.* 2003; Arocena and Sutz 2005; Capriati 2013). The emphasis is on the promotion of learning capabilities as a crucial factor for the freedom of the people. Several researchers from Globelics emphasize that in establishing prolific innovation system in developing countries, as well as high-tech R&D and technology, focus must be placed on basic needs and human capability to promote learning and innovation capabilities. For this reason, prolific institutions are required to promote interactive learning and innovation for both economic competitiveness and human development.

Another valuable approach has been made by a group of researchers from the Max-Planck Institute for Evolutionary Economics, who aim to introduce a dynamic perspective into welfare economics which takes into account the fact that preferences and needs of people substantially change over time (Binder 2010; Schubert 2012). They show, for instance, how different human capabilities, such as education and health, co-evolve over time (Binder and Coad 2010a, 2010b) and how innovation should address changing consumer needs (Schubert 2012). All of these approaches make essential contributions in bringing innovation and human development together. They all take different but valuable perspectives, but of course they also have their shortcomings and weaknesses, and can, therefore, learn from each other.

3.2.2 *Challenges*

Despite the fact that within each specialised field there is a growing number of people working on issues combining innovation and human development, it is not that uncommon for researchers from one approach to be unaware that researchers from another approach are working on similar topics. Unfortunately there seems to be insufficient direct interaction between the innovation economics and human development research communities, interaction such as the leading scholars of one approach participating in the conferences of the other, or the production of joint publications. There are several reasons why integration of and interaction between the approaches is difficult. First of all, each specialised research community has different core goals and scientific terminologies that can paradigmatically lead researchers in different directions to address different concerns. By definition, the core of innovation economics involves innovation and technological capabilities of companies, whereas the core of the human development approach is on inequality of the capabilities and well-being of people. There is also an additional communication problem caused by specialized language and concepts, which can be misunderstood, misinterpreted, or not understood at all. A typical example of a term which can easily be misunderstood or misinterpreted is each approach's use of the word 'capabilities'. In innovation economics it refers to skills and technological capabilities, but in the human development approach it refers to the abilities and freedom to choose. It must be emphasized that the main subjects in human development approaches are people, their life quality and choices, whereas in innovation and structural economic change approaches the focus is rather on companies, universities and economic policies. There is certainly an overlap, but naturally the interrelations between innovation, structural change and human development are complementary, rather than core topics within the specialised fields.

This leads to a difficult question: should a 'Sen meets Schumpeter' approach be embedded within an existing research community (e.g. innovation systems, human development or welfare economics) or should it should form its own interdisciplinary research community and workshops with good ties to all fields, to prevent to natural gravitation towards the core focus of each specialised approach on either innovation and economic development on the one hand, and human capabilities and well-being on the other? Forming such a research community might also provide the possibility of a 'Sen meets Schumpeter' approach evolving from a niche approach within their individual fields to form a higher, aggregated discussion, contributing to the understanding of the complex relations between economic and human development. While being a widespread phenomenon in the real world, where ideas of innovation, income, jobs, well-being and inequality often go hand in hand in complex societal, political and economic debate, there are significant degrees of specialization within different approaches to development. Arguably, the 'Sen meets Schumpeter' approach and initiatives such as STEPS, Globelics, evolutionary welfare economics, or technology and design for human development all provide inspiring new ideas and can contribute to the task of bridging the ideas of innovation economics and the human development approach; nevertheless, it seems necessary to form more joint working groups, journals and conferences. Despite all of the potential integration problems, there is great potential for integration facilitating new theoretical insights, which are all the more important for being highly relevant in practice, such as in promoting productive local development projects or designing industrial policies that bring economic growth and human development together. There is a need to develop a better understanding and promote public discussion on how economic and human development policies can complement each other and how they are not necessarily contradictory – for example, by creating pathways that take public discussions away from the idea that austerity, macroeconomic and economic efficiency on the one hand are diametrically different from discussions about human rights, poverty and lost generation on the other, towards how and which innovation and structural economic reform promoting new sectors can contribute to economic growth, job creation and human development.

3.3 Using complexity thinking to create bridges: Networks, diversity and inequality

This section aims to shed some light on the complex relations between human development and economic development by combining the insights of the approaches above with complexity thinking, to investigate how economic diversification and social networks affect human agency and welfare. Accordingly, it continues along the lines of a critique by Alice Amsden in the *Journal of Human Development and Capabilities* (2010), which postulates that the supply of human capabilities does not necessarily mean (via a Say-type law) that there will automatically be a demand for them. Without the creation of economic demand and opportunities, the long-run expansion of human capabilities in a region may be undermined by a lack of jobs, consequent emigration and decrease in its economic competitiveness. Hence, the economic system also needs to create the occupational choices and demand for such capabilities. Innovation and industrial policies must complement and go hand in hand with human development policies. Merely claiming that governments should invest in human development and innovation systems might not help to create policies within the typical financial constraints governments face.

What also matters is how the different elements of complex socioeconomic systems, such as the economic structures and dynamics created through innovation, affect social choices, agency and well-being. So too does the question of how human development contributes to innovation and structural change. People's capabilities and social choices are embedded in evolutionary economic systems and social network structures. Over time, new sectors emerge and perish, leading to a variety of new choices, as well as constantly changing demands for human skills and capabilities. The economic diversity of the place where people live and the social networks that people access have a deep impact on their agency, capabilities and choices and vice versa. Even assuming uniform availability of formal education and health conditions after childhood, the agency, capabilities and life choices of an individual living in a poor agricultural village would be hugely different from those of a person living in a large city with numerous sectors. The economic system where a person is living deeply affects the diversity of social choices that person can make. Most importantly, however, the economic structure changes over time, due to the interaction and learning processes of the multiple heterogeneous agents involved. This is where complexity thinking can help to create bridges between the ethical individualism of the human development approaches and the focus on meso-dynamics and structural economic changes of the Neo-Schumpeterian economics, to jointly contribute to a more dynamic theory on the evolution and distribution of inequality.

Complexity approaches (e.g. Arthur 1994, 1999; Pyka *et al.* 2007; Pyka and Fagiolo 2007; Hausmann *et al.* 2011) put emphasis on the interactions between heterogeneous elements, leading to hidden properties that are hardly observable from either the individual properties of the elements or the aggregated outcomes, but rather emerge from the interactions between these elements. Complexity thinking puts emphasis on networks, diversity and feedback mechanisms between micro, meso and macro structures, entering deeply into the relations between the actions and interactions of heterogeneous elements within complex systems. The understanding of heterogeneous agents, multiple interaction and diverse outcomes are applied in this book to analyse the relations between (a) social networks and human capabilities; (b) economic diversity and human development; and (c) entrepreneurship and human agency within a 'Sen meets Schumpeter' framework. The focus is less on the mathematical and computational formulation of complexity, but rather on how complexity thinking can help to reveal the multiple positive, negative and ambiguous relations between human agency, social networks and economic diversification. Table 3.1 shows how three key elements of complexity – heterogeneous elements, networks and diversity – are applied to explore the relations between human development and evolutionary economic systems.

Table 3.1 Applying complexity thinking to bridge the development approaches of Sen and Schumpeter

Elements of complex systems	*'Sen meets Schumpeter' approach*
Heterogeneous agents ⟶	Entrepreneurship and human development
Multiple interactions ⟶	Social networks and human development
Diversity of choices / ⟶ outcomes	Economic diversity and human development

Goals
• Exploring the relations between economic complexity and human development   • Study how economic diversity, social networks and human agency affect each other   • Develop policies that bring economic and human development together

This approach can be helpful, because it allows an understanding of how the interaction of heterogeneous individuals (having different capabilities and functionings) leads to structural dynamics and innovation in the systems (new choices, network structures and access to instrumental freedom) and aggregate outcomes (such as economic diversity and the distribution of functionings) which themselves feed back into the action and interactions of the individuals. It creates bridges between human development, innovation and economic growth approaches in the more problematic and complex areas, such as how economic production factors work together to create economic development or how human capabilities become translated into functionings. This may help to contribute to evolutionary welfare economics and the design of pro-poor growth strategies. During the course of this book, emphasis will be placed on the following key pillars:

• the heterogeneity of the actors and their capabilities, in contrast to simplistic approaches assuming fully informed and rational agents;

- consideration and analysis of social networks and economic diversification as crucial constituent elements of evolutionary socioeconomic systems and determinants of the capabilities and choices of individuals;
- a broad perspective on entrepreneurship and innovation, including the study of social entrepreneurship and innovation promoting human agency; and
- the complementing of traditional statistical and case study research methods with modern approaches from complexity research and network analysis.

The purpose of examining these points is to reveal the complex feedbacks between economic complexity and human development, which in turn helps to design innovation and structural change policies that deliberately aim to promote human agency and create a positive virtuous circle between economic development and social welfare.

3.3.1 Heterogeneity and a bottom-up approach

A common ground for the integration and mutual learning of the human development and the Neo-Schumpeterian approach can be found in the way that both highlight the heterogeneity and agency of people. Both lines of research stress the diversity of individuals (e.g. Simon 1957; Saviotti 1996; Sen 2006). Amartya Sen and other scholars of social choice, basic needs and human development introduced a qualitative change to social welfare theory by enabling interpersonal comparisons of well-being and focusing more on freedom, rather than considering aggregated economic growth alone (e.g. Streeten *et al.* 1981; Nussbaum and Sen 1993; Sen 1998a, 1999). This change paved the way for a major shift in development thinking by:

- putting the agents at the centre of development policies and treating them as agents rather than patients of the development process (UNDP 1990);
- moving beyond the neoclassical representative agent in a theoretically innovative as well as in a sustained empirical, mathematical and ethical way; and
- considering human diversity (e.g. in Sen 2006) and focusing on the heterogeneous capabilities and opportunities of people to participate in, contribute to and benefit from the development processes (Sen 1999).

Sen's capability approach provides a promising theoretical bridge to the agent-based approaches of Neo-Schumpeterian economics, in which the capabilities and opportunities of agents to introduce new combinations into the system are of fundamental importance for their individual success and the development of the overall system. The emphasis on the heterogeneity of the actors is a substantial pillar of Neo-Schumpeterian economics (Dopfer 2005; Hanusch and Pyka 2007a). Because Neo-Schumpeterian economics views innovation as a collective phenomenon stemming from the interactions of heterogeneous agents, the heterogeneity of the agents is a key source of novelty (e.g. Saviotti 1996). Learning processes and innovation cannot be fully explained by means of the neoclassical representative agent within a general equilibrium framework. Research in cognitive psychology and experimental economics (Kagel and Roth 1995; Plott and Smith 1998) shows that a series of neoclassical assumptions, such as the ubiquitous presence of representative utility-maximising rational agents, are at odds with empirically observed patterns of behaviour and interactions on the micro level (Pyka and Fagiolo 2007). Neo-Schumpeterian economics gives the learning and the cognition of the agents a central theoretical place. Heterogeneous and bounded rational actors engage in learning-by-doing and learning by trial and error in uncertain and constantly changing environments. Agents are essentially heterogeneous and bounded rational beings, meaning that they have limited information, make mistakes and engage in trial and error processes (Dosi *et al.* 2005). If the agents already knew everything they needed to know, there would be no room for true learning processes and innovation (Pyka and Fagiolo 2007). Without a minimum willingness to cope with true uncertainty (Knight 1921), innovation processes can hardly be understood (Pyka and Fagiolo 2007). In reality, innovation and creative destruction deeply affect the capabilities and choices of individuals. Both the set of possible choices and required capabilities might substantially change over time.

3.3.2 A broad approach of entrepreneurship and innovation

Several authors argue for the need for a broad concept of innovation (e.g. Mytelka 2000; Cassiolato *et al.* 2003; Lundvall 2007; Hanusch and Pyka 2007a). Even though innovation is most visible at the industry level, it occurs at all levels and in all domains of socioeconomic systems. It is not found merely in industry, but is also important in the public and financial sectors of the economic system and in many cases is the result the interplay of innovations in all three domains (Hanusch and Pyka 2007a).

It is worth noting that innovation, in a broad sense, does not necessarily mean new high-tech products, such as those involving nanotechnology, biotechnology or ICT, but rather refers to the introduction of new combinations and novelties leading to a systemic restructuring and qualitative change in any dimension of a socioeconomic system (i.e. the global, national or local level). This can occur within high-tech enterprises, regions and sectors, as well as on the local level, such as in communities in the Amazon, in small enterprises in Eurasia, or in social organizations anywhere around the world. For this reason, we generally understand the term innovation to mean *the introduction of novelties or new combinations into the system which leads to a qualitative change of the status quo.*

In addition, we assume that virtually every human being of working age has the potential for entrepreneurial action, in contrast to the heroic image of the Schumpeterian entrepreneur, which draws the picture of unique outstanding innovator-entrepreneurs who possess the skills and means to introduce radical innovations on a global scale. There may be people with more motivation, intelligence and luck than others, but this cannot be defined beforehand and therefore every individual is assumed to have the opportunity to engage in entrepreneurial action and assist actively in the development process. Naturally, there will always be a significant number of persons in a population who do not want to engage in entrepreneurial action. However, it is important to realize that there is a major difference between not wanting to do something and lacking the basic freedom to do it. All over the world we can find examples of entrepreneurial action in all ethnical groups and social classes, from the micro-business entrepreneurs of Bangladesh and the founders of social organizations in Europe, to the high-tech entrepreneurs of Silicon Valley. Entrepreneurship and structural change are not just limited to the economic sphere but occur in all domains and at all levels of socioeconomic systems. For poverty reduction and social welfare, entrepreneurship in commercial profit-oriented businesses is important, and so are social entrepreneurs introducing novelties and social changes into a diverse range of areas of life, from the political to the environmental, cultural or social (e.g. Bornstein 2004; Yunus 2007). As such, we employ a broad concept of entrepreneurship and consider entrepreneurial action as the active engagement of people in changing the status quo of their lives, families and socioeconomic environment, aiming to achieve higher levels of social welfare, power and wealth for themselves and others.

3.3.3 Inequality, networks and economic variety

In socioeconomic systems, people and their capabilities and opportunities cannot be properly understood by considering only their individual, physical and mental characteristics and the resources and things which they are entitled to use; it is also important to understand that each actor is embedded in a network of social, economic and political interrelations (Granovetter 1985). The influential concepts and work of Amartya Sen (e.g. 1995, 1998a, 1999) and other authors on social choice, human development and inequality (e.g. UNDP 1990; Nussbaum and Sen 1993; Bourguignon *et al.* 2005; Milanovic 2007) arguably have tended to insufficiently consider the structural and evolutionary aspects of socioeconomic systems and their impact on the opportunities of actors to be active agents in development processes. For instance, the evolution of the variety of local economic activities and social network structures (e.g. power, access to non-redundant information and finance) are decisive determinants of whether or not people can be active agents and adapt to the evolutionary changes of the socioeconomic systems in which they live. Social network analysis (e.g. Granovetter 1973, 1985; Burt 1992; Castells 1996) has shown that every person is embedded in a network of social and economic relations which determine their job opportunities, their access to finance and information, their power and capacity to address economic and social problems. Castells (1996) indicated that the modern network society (enabled by ICT technologies) provides opportunities for better social inclusion yet also brings with it the threat of further exclusion of certain people, depending on their position and their access to social network structures. The position of individuals in local, national and global network structures is crucially important for their social and economic opportunities, their capacity for qualitative entrepreneurship, their opportunities to engage in learning processes and their ability to achieve a better standard of living (e.g. Castells 1996; Granovetter 1973, 1985; Woolcock and Narayan 2000; Hoang and Antoncic 2003; Casson and Della Giusta 2007). Several innovation and development economists have shown that economic diversification and the composition of economic systems are core drivers and outcomes of economic development. Economic diversity both promotes and is an outcome of creativity, recombination, entrepreneurship, innovation and growth (e.g. Jacobs 1969; Pasinetti 1981, 1983; Saviotti 1996; Hidalgo *et al.* 2007; Saviotti and Frenken 2008). It is important to note that social network structures and the composition of economic activities are not static, but follow evolutionary development paths, changing at different speeds over space, time, people and cultures. The type and speed of these structural changes depend on a series of endogenous and exogenous factors such as the entrance and exit of agents (e.g. through birth and death), the distribution of wealth and power, existing technologies, learning processes, the accumulation of knowledge, and innovation.

3.3.4 *Structure and dynamics of occupational choices*

The labour market and capabilities of choosing a different occupation are highly relevant practical examples of where strong feedbacks between capabilities, functionings, social choices and the structure and dynamics of socioeconomic systems exist. Occupational choices are essential for an individual's standard of living and well-being (Banerjee and Newman 1993; Miller *et al.* 2008). They determine individuals' income levels, lead to social recognition and are vital for individuals' own sense of satisfaction and motivation. Furthermore, they determine the freedom of individuals in choosing decent jobs or engaging in qualitative entrepreneurship.

Occupational choices and entrepreneurship and innovation can hardly be understood without taking into account the interactions between heterogeneous agents (Simon 1957). Social interaction and network access to information influences what people learn and what they consider as desirable and feasible (Liñán and Santos 2007). The literature on social capital has shown that social relations strongly impact the economic performance of individuals and countries (Burt 1992; Putnam 1993, 2000; Woolcock and Narayan 2000; Eagle *et al.* 2010). For example, people often receive information about job opportunities and are hired via social networks (Granovetter 1973). People also often (maybe even in most cases) evaluate occupational opportunities and choices via observing and asking their social networks. The evaluation of choices from their social peers, such as friends and family, in conjunction with their own capabilities and desires, leads to preferences of the individuals and groups which in turn feed back into the process of economic development via occupational demand evolution and learning processes. This, in consequence, affects the direction and scope of diversification processes. People aim to work in a specific occupation for various reasons, such as simply liking the activity (e.g. of writing, managing or constructing), because they expect to be socially rewarded or expect a good economic payoff.

It follows that in addition to socially constructed expectations and individual desires, occupational choices are formed in a matching process between the individual's capabilities, the social networks and the structures and dynamics of an economic system.

3.3.5 The freedom to innovate in complex systems

Another field where a 'Sen meets Schumpeter' approach is required and could provide important new insights are the capabilities of people to network and to learn and engage in entrepreneurial actions. Innovation economics has drawn attention to the role of interactive learning, networks and entrepreneurship as key drivers and determinants of innovation (e.g. Fagerberg *et al.* 2005; Hanusch and Pyka 2007a, 2007b). Recent literature on entrepreneurship shows that entrepreneurs essentially draw on and are embedded in social network structures (Aldrich and Zimmer 1986; Hoang and Antoncic 2003; Casson and Della Giusta 2007; Bornstein 2004). Furthermore, research into innovation systems in developing countries has revealed that it is a combination of capabilities and opportunities that paves the way for sustained learning processes and innovation (Johnson *et al.* 2003; Arocena and Sutz 2005; Hartmann *et al.* 2010). These theoretical and empirical insights generate the possibility of two new dimensions to people's freedom: namely their capabilities and opportunities for networking, learning and engaging in entrepreneurial action. These freedoms are formed and evolve in the interaction between individuals' capabilities and the structure of systems and their evolution. Furthermore, they go hand in hand with the ability of finding a good job. The unequal distribution of capabilities and opportunities for networking, learning and entrepreneurship essentially contributes to inequalities in terms of occupational choices and achieving certain living standards. Exclusion from social network structures and lack of opportunities for qualitative entrepreneurship and for applied learning limit the freedom of agents to be and to do what they wish and introduce qualitative change into their lives. As such, social network structures and the variety of technological and economic opportunities in a system have a decisive impact on the set of individuals' social choices to translate their capabilities into functionings and to expand their capabilities through learning processes. The personal traits of individual, as well as their network of social contacts, affect their motivation for learning and entrepreneurship and their preference for one type of occupation. For example, the decision of whether to choose a paid occupation or to be an entrepreneur depends on the opportunities and former experiences of different functionings. Furthermore, the capabilities to learn depend on such factors as opportunities and motivations; thus, the capabilities, opportunities, functionings and preferences for networking, learning, achieving a decent job and/or qualitative entrepreneurship are interrelated. Naturally, the importance and interdependence of these factors differ from one socioeconomic system to another. However, from a theoretical perspective it is fundamental to: (a) show that these elements and intersections exist; (b) link socioeconomic inequality directly with the capacity for innovation and structural change; and (c) take into account that social networks and economic variety (as structural elements of the system in which people live) have substantial impacts on the agency and capabilities of the people.

3.4 Chapter conclusion

This chapter has discussed how the Neo-Schumpeterian and the human development approach can be connected by taking key concepts from complexity thinking into account (i.e. heterogeneous agents, networks and diversity). This aims to contribute to an emerging research community, by analysing the relations between innovation and human development. It does, however, depart from the core emphasis of each specialised discipline on either innovation or human development towards deliberate study of the linkages between economic complexity and human development. Instead of creating lists of further crucial issues to consider, key emphasis is put on how networks and diversity thinking can contribute to an understanding of how the positive, negative and dynamic effects of structural economic change and the embeddedness of individuals within social networks affects human agency and welfare. The key goal is to contribute to the emergence of innovation and structural economic change policies that deliberately aim to improve human welfare instead of merely expanding production.

4 Economic diversification and human development

Economic diversification, defined as the change in the degree, type, composition and quality of the economic sectors in an economy, affects human development in multiple ways. Modern approaches in development economics show that diversification is a driver and outcome of production expansion and income (Saviotti 1996; Hidalgo *et al.* 2007). Economic diversification leads to changes in the available choices in an economy, determining the number, type and quality of occupational choices, consumption goods and also life styles and the agency of the people. It goes together with institutional and technological changes which make the diversification of the economy into different sectors possible. This point was made in the opening words of Simon Kuznets' Nobel Prize Lecture in Economics in 1971 (Kuznets 1971, p. 1):

> A country's economic growth may be defined as a long-term rise in capacity to supply increasingly diverse economic goods to its population, this growing capacity based on advancing technology and the institutional and ideological adjustments that it demands.

The technological and institutional change underpinning the economic diversification process has deep influences on the capabilities of the people in an economy, as it might require a changing set of capabilities and skills to become an active agent of development. Whereas physical skills may have been crucial in one epoch of mankind, Internet literacy is increasingly a crucial determinant for becoming a full member of modern society. And whereas minimum standards of education and health are required in any society, the precise skills and capabilities that are demanded from the citizens in different countries can significantly differ and change over time. One important factor influencing the agency and well-being of persons is the economic diversification of the country they are born and raised in. The life of a person raised in a rural place with few occupational choices, such as small-scale farming or mining, can be hugely different from the life of a person raised in a city with multiple occupational choices, such as retailer, software engineering companies, business consultancies or theatre. This factor can be considered in two different ways: on the one hand the sectoral setup illustrates the productive capabilities of a country (Hidalgo *et al.* 2007; Hausmann *et al.* 2011), while on the other hand, it has a deep influence on the learning processes, values and desires, occupational choices and life quality of the people.

The human development approach focuses on the welfare of individuals – their choices, capabilities and freedoms. Accordingly, it challenges the implicit assumption behind many economic approaches that macroeconomic growth automatically trickles down to individuals. This is an important shift, away from putting economic growth at the centre of development policies and towards making the individual the centre of attention. However, proposing a bottom-up view from the individual's perspective can led to an equally problematic 'trickle up' assumption: that the provision of basic capabilities for individuals automatically leads to the structural features, institutions, incentives and scale effects required for innovation and structural change. This perspective, by viewing the individuals as both means and ends of development, potentially neglects structural and dynamic economic features of development, such as the historical path dependency of the sectoral setup in a country, the set of economic sectors in which people can work in their home country or the necessity of reaching a critical mass allowing sectors to produce efficiently, provide well-paid and stable jobs and create tax revenues for the governments. For example, to produce at competitive prices taking into account scale economies and agglomeration effects, it is often necessary for a sector to have in its production areas a minimum number of companies (including supplier companies and retailers), as well as business and logistics infrastructure.

This book argues that both individual capabilities and economic diversification are crucial for human development. Policies should not rely on managing only one aspect and assuming the other will automatically follow. Instead, policies that address the relationships between both are necessary. For instance, economic diversification has several ambiguous, positive and negative effects on human development (such as the expansion of choices and positive recombination effects), while also having the potential to create decision paralysis through complexity. An economic development policy aiming to promote human agency and welfare should take these complex effects into account. Sustainable human development policies must go hand in hand with adequate structural economic policies. The fact that individual capabilities exist may by itself not provide the structural economic demand for such capabilities. Arguably without an economic policy based on endogenous economic development and qualitative diversification, human development and inequality reduction policies will fail to foster well-being and human capabilities in the long term. This is because of strong economic success-breeds-success mechanisms and barriers to entry to such self-reinforcing economic effects. Conversely, economic diversification without a free, healthy and creative workforce hardly seems possible to sustain in the long run.

This chapter attempts to contribute to development structural change policies for human development by showing the multiple effects of innovation-driven economic diversification on human development. It is structured as follows. First, the role of economic diversification in the history of economic thought is briefly discussed and different dimensions of economic diversity, such as related and unrelated variety, summarized. Subsequently, key reasons are discussed as to why economic diversification matters for human development. Then different positive, negative and ambiguous effects of economic diversification are reviewed and systematized. It becomes obvious that economic diversification has multiple positive, negative and changing effects on human development which can be explored in qualitative and empirical studies. In terms of the absolute and marginal effects of diversification on income and human development, the interplay of the multiple effects suggests that economic diversification tends to have a marginally increasing positive effect on income, whereas the effects of economic diversification on human development tend to show a positive, but marginally decreasing effect. A subsequent empirical study on the economic diversification, income and human development of 121 countries confirms this theoretical hypothesis. The study furthermore confirms that unrelated variety (i.e. having several very different sectors) seems to have a more pronounced effect on human development than related variety (i.e. being sophisticated in few sectors).

4.1 Economic diversification in the history of economic thought

From the classical authors to the present, a central theme of economic research has been the way economic systems grow and transform. This section briefly reviews the role of some main contributions on economic diversification in the history of economic thought. Several lines of research can be traced back to Adam Smith, Karl Marx and Joseph Schumpeter, giving different explanations for why economies grow and diversify their economic activities over time. While the term has not always been used, diversity has been an important concept in economics, at least since Adam Smith (1776), who identified the division of labour as a driving force of economic development. Specialization of activities at a lower level of aggregation (e.g. in a company or a region) often leads to the diversification of activities and outcomes at a higher level of aggregation (e.g. in the national economy). Increasing specialization and hence also diversification can be found at all levels of the economic production processes and activities on the regional, national and international levels. The division of labour led to an enormous number of new professions and skills, the saving of time, more output and technical progress.

In his theory of economic development, Joseph Schumpeter (1912) saw economic development as a structural transformation process in which innovation leads to the emergence of new sectors and the obsolescence of some old sectors. He coined the term 'creative destruction' to describe this process. Creative destruction processes lead to qualitative changes in the composition of sectors, job opportunities, skill requirements and demands, consumption possibilities and standards of life. In the long term, economic systems diversify, but in the short term many jobs and competences may become obsolete. Structural transformation processes and the direction of economic specialization and diversification deeply affect people's learning processes, their choices and functionings.

Based on ideas of Schumpeter, Marx and Keynes, several schools in development economics have traditionally put strong emphasis on structural change and economic diversification. Early approaches focused on: (a) how developing countries can transform their activities from agricultural production into higher value added industrialized activities (Rosenstein-Rodan 1943; Nurkse 1953; Lewis 1954; Hirschman 1958); and (b) how the embeddedness of developing countries in the global production system can produce structural dependency and underdevelopment due to specific types of productive specialization and diversification (Prebisch 1949, 1959; Furtado 1961). LASA viewed the periphery of the world economy as serving to meet the dynamic centres of development's demand for primary products. Whereas the centre continuously innovates and increases the diversity of its products and services, the periphery is deemed to specialize in the provision of basic primary goods which show a low income elasticity of demand. This means that when the income of people rises they do not equally consume more coffee or sugar produced in the periphery of the world economy, but rather spend their money on industrialized products (such as mobile phones or cars) made by the centre of the world economy. The result is a dependent development of the periphery whose products continuously lose their relative importance in the global consumption basket.

The policy implication of this phenomenon was that governments of the developing countries in Latin America and elsewhere closed their markets and tried to diversify their economies through industrialization policies driven by import substitution. In some cases, this has been successful and has provided the basis for current competitive sectors, for example some industrial sectors in Brazil, or the economic success story of several East-Asian Tiger states. But it led also to economic inefficiency, high debt rates, inflation and even economic collapse in several countries that did not have sufficiently large internal markets and did not combine the import substitution model with an export oriented strategy.

The field of urban studies and economic geography has also put emphasis on economic diversity. Examining growth in cities, Jane Jacobs (1969) identified the variety of activities, ideas and resources as a source of creativity, recombination, innovation and growth. Work from the field of economic geography also highlights the crucial role of proactive specialization and geographic agglomeration of related activities and companies (Becattini 1979; Pyke *et al.* 1990; Porter 1990, 1998; Glaeser *et al.* 1992). However, even the most famous industrial clusters such as Silicon Valley or Route 128 (Saxenian 1994) are certainly not perfectly homogenous; at lower levels of sectoral disaggregation there is enormous complexity and variety of related activities and processes. Furthermore, regional specialization does not necessarily make for a reduction of activities on the national or global level, but can even add to the number of activities and complex interactions between them.

Economic diversity and structural transformation is a recurrent key issue in economics, and especially in development economics. Many influential economists have highlighted economic diversity as a crucial factor and outcome of economic growth. For instance Kuznets (1971) defined economic growth as the long-term rise in capacity to supply increasingly diverse economic goods. Weitzman (1998) presented development as recombinant growth, where new ideas built upon the recombination of old ideas. The influential Dixit-Stiglitz (1977) model also puts emphasis on the demand of consumers for variety. Hausmann and Rodrik (2003) view economic development as a self-discovery process, in which companies discover which variety of products they can produce in a cost efficient and effective way.

Increased data availability and modern analysis techniques permit empirical analysis of the theories of the early development pioneers about the role and dynamics of polarization, structural transformation and economic diversification. Several works have shown that that economic diversification and position in the global productive space are crucial for the economic performance of countries (Hidalgo *et al.* 2007; Funke and Ruhwedel 2001; Saviotti and Frenken 2008) and regions (Frenken *et al.* 2007). With the exception of some oil-rich countries, most rich countries can draw upon highly diversified economic structures. Diversification also requires and draws upon a large variety of productive capabilities such as infrastructure, knowledge, institutions etc., within these countries (Hidalgo *et al.* 2007; Hidalgo and Hausmann 2009). Productive capabilities allow countries to produce high value added and complex products, recombine capabilities and further diversify and grow. By using employment and aggregated export data, Imbs and Wacziarg (2003) showed that countries diversify until they have very high levels of income. At around US\$7,000–11,000 per capita, depending on the measure and data applied, a tendency towards more specialization is observable. However, in the long term and at lower levels of disaggregation, the economic system has to constantly diversify, producing more and better products, processes and services, to maintain economic development (Pasinetti 1981, 1983; Saviotti 1996). This is not only true for the global economy, but also for countries and regions, to enable them to maintain flexibility and economic competitiveness (Tödtling and Trippl 2005).

To understand the effects of diversification on socioeconomic development, the abstract term 'diversification' needs to be defined and different types and dimensions of the terms 'diversity' and 'economic diversification' need to be distinguished. Over time, many different dimensions of diversity in general and economic diversification in particular have been discussed. Regarding the measurement of diversity in general, Andy Stirling (2007) argues that a comprehensive composite measure of diversity should include variety, disparity and balance as different core aspects of diversity. While variety measures the number of elements (here, sectors), balance measures the quantity of each element and disparity how different the elements are. Indeed, the evolution and measurement of each aspect may have distinct impacts on economic development. For our topic of interest, growth in the variety, balance and disparity of sectors may have different effects on the social choices and required capabilities of people. Economic diversification in terms of the growth of activity in a variety of similar sectors (e.g. in low-paid services) may not necessarily lead to a greater balance in the economic income distribution, significantly new social choices or more creative jobs. On the other hand, economic diversity measured in terms of a high level of balance between the sectors of an economy does not necessarily mean that the economy has a great variety of competitive sectors, providing well-paid and creative jobs.

To differentiate between the effects of different types of economic diversity on regional and national economic growth, Frenken *et al.* (2007) and Saviotti and Frenken (2008) made a distinction between related and unrelated economic variety, where related variety growth indicates diversification into related economic activities and unrelated variety growth covers the diversification of economic activities into essentially different activities and knowledge bases.

Hidalgo *et al.* (2007) draw attention to the complexity of the products a country is capable of producing (i.e. whether many other countries are able to produce and export the same types of products). In their analysis based on export data, they obtain highly significant results showing that the combination of the number and complexity of products matter for the past and future economic development of countries, because this indicates their existing and potential future productive capabilities.

In summary, however, in spite of the recent significant advances made in the analysis of economic diversification and its role in economic development, the effects of economic diversification on human development and well-being are still poorly understood.

4.2 The relevance of economic diversification for human development

Due to a focus on the well-being and human rights of people, economic topics such as technological innovation and economic diversification have not always been a major concern of the human development community. Of course, this lack of emphasis does not mean that knowledge, consumption and production are not considered as elements of the well-being of individuals. For example, income and education are two of the three constitutional pillars of the HDI (UNDP 1990, 2010). The differences and relationship between economic growth and human development is a passionate topic in the human development community. Amartya Sen (1999), for instance, emphasizes the interconnectedness of different dimensions of instrumental freedoms in the social, political and economic space. He argues that economic unfreedom can lead also to social and political unfreedom. Ranis *et al.* (2000) have analysed the causal chains linking human development to economic growth as well as economic growth to human development. However, topics such as production and economic structures are generally not core topics of interest in the human development debate. From a human development perspective, arguably, this is because a series of basic needs and capabilities such as education and health have to be ensured first (Streeten *et al.* 1981). With this said, it is important to also remember that economic dimensions, such as employment, consumption and income continue to be crucial elements of people's lives, their self-esteem and their happiness.

Some materialistic and economic issues such as money, income and a decent job continue to be core dimensions of daily life, desires, preoccupations social recognition and well-being, for the economically poor and deprived most of all. Amsden (2010) argued that grass-roots methods of poverty alleviation and human development policies will fail until jobs are created. Expanding people's capabilities through health expenditure and better education is not enough; long-term poverty reduction also requires determined investment in the creation of paid employment and self-employment above starvation wages. Development policy and anti-poverty programmes often neglect the crucial employment dimension, supposing, in a Say's law style assumption, that a supply of capabilities means there will also be a corresponding economic demand for these capabilities. However, this does not always hold true; supplying capabilities does not automatically contribute to long-term poverty reduction and development in countries. The people in the bottom quintiles of the income distribution may be forced into self-employment with low potential economic gains or into paid employment at starvation wages. And if people do not find proper occupational choices at home, they may try to emigrate. This can lead to a brain drain and contribute to further inequalities in the human capital and long-term economic development of countries. Countries need motivated and skilled people to promote endogenous economic, technological and institutional development. They need free and capable people to build up innovative and competitive companies able to transform and diversify the productive structure of their countries. However, without the initial set of economic opportunities and systemic interrelations between institutions, knowledge, production and demand, the virtuous circles of recombinant growth, evolutionary learning and innovation cannot start. This is what makes countries' productive structure and economic diversification so important. One cannot assume that expansion of capabilities alone (education, health, democracy and infrastructure) is enough to enable the emergence of prolific innovation systems, recombinant growth and development. Industrial and employment policies are needed to create the incentives, the institutional environment and economies of scale required to allow enterprises in developing countries to grow, to innovate and to be competitive on global markets (Rodrik 2004).

If it is true that economic development alone does not automatically translate into (well-distributed) human development, and within a globalized economy, it is hard to imagine sustaining regional human development without innovation and well-distributed economic development. This is where innovation and evolutionary economics come into play. The development of countries is dependent on their former technological and productive capabilities as well as on the historically and spatially evolved interrelations between all parts of the socioeconomic system affecting the creation, diffusion and application of knowledge and new technologies. The economic diversification of countries can be considered as an aggregate proxy indicator of these productive capabilities. Diversification, furthermore, determines the type, quality and variety of occupational choices that individuals have in their home region or country.

4.3 Disentangling positive, negative and dynamic effects

This section aims to reveal and systemize some of the multiple effects of economic diversification on human development. Some effects are positive, while others are negative and still others change over time or depend upon the level of economic diversity already achieved beforehand. It becomes obvious that economic diversification and human development are closely related to each other and that the study of the complex relations between them provides policy relevant insights.

4.3.1 Positive effects

Economic diversity, in the sense of variety of economic sectors and activities in an economy, deeply affects the social choices and capabilities of individuals. The difference to learning processes, choices and lifestyle of an individual who lives in a place which offers few occupational choices (such as subsistence agriculture or informal mining), compared to those of someone who lives in a place with multiple different occupations (such as in arts, software or tourism sectors) can be considerable. The most important effect of economic diversification is the expansion of social choices in terms of occupational choices, consumption choices and life style. This expansion of choices also favours a better potential adaptation to individual needs and demands of the people. It allows people to choose from a variety of different ideas and lifestyle possibilities and expands the possible functioning and capabilities space.

Other important effects of economic diversification are that it potentially favours a more equal or balanced power distribution within a society and has a tendency to go hand in hand with co-evolutionary institutional changes. It makes a difference to the power distribution between people, sectors and regions in an economy whether the country is dependent on one large sector (such as for example oil or minerals) or multiple different sectors (such as oil, software, car industry and arts). With just one dominant lead sector, a tendency for strong vertical hierarchies emerges, whereas an economy with multiple sectors and agents can promote a more horizontal and balanced power distribution among multiple different groups and people. It makes also a difference whether there is just a single or a limited number of lead companies within a dominant sector in a country (such as for instance gold mining or a manufacturing industry) producing one or few certain types of products, or multiple slightly different companies producing many slightly different products (e.g. different cars or using different technologies in the mining process). In the latter case, there is an increased chance of there being different development paths through the innovation process as well as a tendency to support the emergence of multiple interest groups and a better distribution of power. Furthermore, achieving economic diversity often requires well-developed and well-governed institutions, and qualitative diversification into new and more knowledge-intensive sectors tends to go hand in hand with co-evolutionary institutional advances. All major technological revolutions and waves of rapid productive diversification have been strongly connected with innovations in infrastructures (e.g. railways, automobile industry, telecommunication technologies) and the emergence of institutions such as appropriate new legal frameworks, new educational institutions and new types of social and productive organization that enable the new technologies to unfold their full potentials (Perez 2002, 2007). For instance, diversification often requires new skill-sets and educational institutions, increasing the amount of and choices within education (such as new online courses). Institutional change (e.g. in education or in proactive attitudes) and improvements in transportation allow people to be more mobile and access more information and choices. This tends to provide society with a more varied set of choices and capabilities. As such, institutional development, occurring along with the creation of qualitative diversification, tends to provide a further positive effect on human development.

Another positive effect is that diversification in the sense of more sectors and/ or a better balance between a variety of sectors makes an economy less vulnerable to external economic shocks (e.g. Tödtling and Trippl 2005). Economic development alone does not necessarily lead to human development in a country, but certainly economic crises do have a negative feedback on human development. Prolific economic diversification reduces the risk of such a crisis. A country whose economic production and welfare expansion is very dependent on few sectors (such as for instance the construction or tourism sectors), can end up in a serious economic and social crisis if these sectors have problems, prices sharply drop or they are not able to be competitive. Therefore it is important not to miss the opportunity during periods of economic growth to invest in the diversification of other sectors.

As an example, consider the housing market in Spain. The housing bubble explosion in Spain led to a severe structural economic crisis with very high rates of unemployment and a 'lost decade' for many Spaniards unable to find a job or obtain access to bank credits to open new businesses. They were forced to move back into the houses of their parents and/or try to find a job in another country. A similar thing happened on the regional level in the German Ruhr district, when its dominant steel industry was unable to compete internationally and subsequently entered into a deep crisis. However, in rich and diversified economies such as in Europe the effects are not as severe as those seen in many developing countries with much less developed social security systems.

Many developing countries focus on the exploitation of resources such as minerals and metals and then face a serious economic, social and political crisis if the global market prices of their main minerals and metals sharply decline. If the dominant sector collapses there are few other jobs available; unemployment and underemployment rise while at the same time the government receives less tax revenues. The result can be sharp cuts in social expenditure and subsequently social and political instability, leading to a vicious circle. Therefore, emphasis on economic diversification is crucial to alleviate the negative effects of external shocks and prevent socioeconomic crises.

A high level of economic diversity also has a positive impact on entrepreneurship as functioning (Gries and Naude 2010). If economies lack well-paid and diverse occupational choices, many people (especially in developing countries) are forced into necessity and subsistence-level entrepreneurship or have to work for very low incomes in poor conditions. In contrast, if there are many different job possibilities available, those who become entrepreneurs do this out of their own free will (see Chapter 6).

A further positive effect of economic diversification emerges when we consider what would happen if an economy's growth is merely based on efficiency improvements in existing sectors and not due to diversification and opening up new investment and employment opportunities in new sectors. Economic growth based on efficiency growth in the existing sectors alone creates a decreasing demand for labour over time (Pasinetti 1981, 1983), because for the same or more output fewer and fewer workers would be necessary. If no other sectors emerge, this can result in rising unemployment. Assuming that income, social recognition and well-being are correlated with the occupational status of persons (Miller *et al.* 2008) this would also mean unfreedom and a decline in the well-being of the people. It would furthermore mean a tendency for a more unequal income distribution, lack of demand (owing to the high rate of unemployment) and also imply the threat of social instability. This is why a capitalist economic system needs to constantly diversify and create new jobs to prevent a collapse due to constraints on the demand side and rising socioeconomic inequality (Pasinetti 1981, 1983; Saviotti 1996). Conversely, economic growth based on economic diversification can lead to virtuous diversity-breeds-diversity mechanisms, where the rise of new sectors (e.g. railways or ICT) leads to the rise of further new sectors (e.g. knowledge-intensive business sectors, supplier networks, new trade possibilities). Various theories support the existence of an economic Matthew effect, in which success-breeds-success mechanisms and economic diversity favour the emergence of further and/or qualitatively better sectors (e.g. Myrdal 1957; Jacobs 1969; Weitzman 1998). Economic diversity both indicates and triggers the level of productive capabilities deriving from institutional development, education, infrastructure etc. This in turns favours the improvement of human capabilities and social choices. In contrast, economic growth merely based on the growth of efficiency can lead to unemployment, social instability and more crucially, technological lock-in, lack of recombination and ultimately running out of creative steam. Jane Jacobs (1969) showed that growth in cities is triggered by the availability and recombination of diverse ideas. Development pioneers (such as Nurkse or Myrdal) have shown that in dynamic, growing centres of the world several sectors complement each other and trigger the emergence of other economic sectors. Saviotti summarizes and contributes to the literature by showing that economic diversity is a key driver and outcome of economic development (Saviotti 1996). Hidalgo *et al.* (2007) show that the type and variety of products a country produces conditions its development and that economic complexity is a good proxy indicator for the productive capabilities of a country. The capability of being able to produce high standard and complex products often depends on the capabilities of the multiple agents in a country to connect and produce a variety of further products, service and technological solutions. For instance, to diversify and build up competitiveness in the nanotechnology sector requires a number of other factors to be in place: measurement tools, models and competence structures, appropriate education institutions, skilled and creative workers, supplier companies (e.g. of resources and tailor-made instruments) and consumer companies (e.g an aerospace industry) demanding such products.

In sum, economic diversification tends to expand the extent of social choices and human capabilities in an economy, triggers co-evolutionary change and institutional development, promotes recombinant growth, reduces the risk of external shocks, and favours a more democratic growth process through a more equal distribution of economic, political and social power. However, while there are many economic reasons why diversification has positive effects on human development, we should not forget to take potential negative effects into account and consider how they evolve over time, according to the level of diversification an economy has already achieved.

4.3.2 Negative and ambiguous effects

The emphasis of research on economic diversification tends to be on the positive effects. But it is also important to systematically analyse the negative and ambiguous effects of diversification on human development. Some positive effects of diversification, such as expansion of choice, can end up creating too many choices, making life more difficult rather than promoting a true increase in agency and life quality. This, though, may trigger new solutions helping people to deal with complexity, for example current efforts in functional design and frugal innovation.

During the process of creative destruction and economic diversification, the set of required capabilities changes, with some capabilities becoming obsolete and some becoming increasingly important; entirely new capabilities may be necessary to become an active agent of society. Not all people (particularly those who are deprived) are necessarily able to quickly develop new capability sets. Increasing economic diversity can also make it more difficult for both the people and governments to understand and manage the diversity of choices. This section aims to contribute to a constructive critique of a one-sided positive perspective on economic diversity by presenting the following two negative effects: (a) creative destruction and inequality reproduction, and (b) more is not always better; and briefly discusses which types of diversification should be promoted.

Economic diversification is driven by creative destruction processes in which innovations can lead to the emergence of new sectors, but can also cause the decline or sometimes even obsolescence of some traditional sectors. Within these creative destruction processes, multiple new occupations and possibilities are created; nevertheless, many workplaces, skills and competences become obsolete. Over the last centuries, structural change and diversification have led to a massive expansion in the variety of activities, products, jobs and factors to consider in life planning. Still, in the short to medium term, difficult structural adaptation processes do have negative impacts on some sectors and on parts of the population, and can cause severe social problems and economic crisis. Older sectors decline and many people lose their jobs and are forced to reorient themselves or are excluded from their society's recognition system.

The process of creative destruction and structural transformation evolves in cyclical phases of emergence, expansion, maturity and decline of industries.

In expansionary phases, economic variety, job opportunities and social expenditure may increase simultaneously, having a positive impact on human development. By contrast, in phases of contraction or crisis, the social expenditures tend to shrink, companies go bankrupt and unemployment and uncertainty rises. However, crises can also be fertile ground for new ideas, radical changes and the demand for both economic and social innovation. For instance, in times of economic crisis and huge unemployment, the need for better social security and education systems, or legal frameworks that fight against crime and corruption, can become obvious and an urgent development task. For these reasons, crises can have a negative direct impact on human development in the short to medium term, but also have positive effects in the long run.

In addition, not all regions and agents may be equally affected by creative destruction processes. This can lead to increasing levels of inequality and relative deprivation. As the development pioneers (e.g. Myrdal 1957) and LASA have shown, the diversification of one region can lead to the structural dependence and underdevelopment of other regions. Young and highly qualified workers may leave their less developed region and emigrate to the dynamic and diversified centres of development, adding further to the innovation and productive capabilities of the centre and the economic problems in the periphery. Further, the relative importance of the products produced in the periphery may decline in comparison to the increasing number of products and services made in the dynamic centres. The economic opportunities and growth in the centre and the periphery diverge.

There is a critical question to be asked (Schwartz 2004): do more choices, products and services always contribute to human well-being and agency? There is little doubt from a human development perspective that the existence of a varied set of choices (e.g. occupations, life styles, access to education and health services) is better for the human freedom of people than the availability of just few compulsory choices (e.g. subsistence farming, being a street vendor). The poor often lack social choices such as access to good education, health services and occupations. The expansion of potential choices through the improvement of human capabilities and new choices (e.g. new occupations, cheaper access to microcredits or better education services) tends to raise human agency. However, the same generalization cannot be made at very high levels of economic development and diversification, where further choices can have negative effects on the well-being and (at least temporarily) even reduce the agency of people.

Barry Schwartz (2004) argues that the paradigm of individual freedom suggests that the more choices there are, the better, because individuals can make their own optimal choices. He shows, however, that this is not necessarily true and that more is not necessarily always better, because the abundance of choices can lead to excessive expectations and decision paralysis. In the wealthier parts of the world, we see a massive expansion in the numbers of choices and decisions that individuals have to make. Think, for example, about a choice between multiple different cereals, jams, internet providers, mobile phones, university courses, occupations, leisure activities or life styles. Increasing information availability and numbers of choices has made the decision processes in all areas of human life very complex and time-consuming. Schwartz (2004) argues that the rising complexity of decision processes together with rising expectations (to get the optimal choice) and the rising opportunity costs (of not having made other choices) can lead to pre-regret and stress. Instead of making an optimal or at least satisfactory choice, many people postpone their decision or do not decide at all. For this reason, at a very high level of diversification the effects of further choices can in some cases become negatively correlated with human agency and well-being.

An important question for policy makers is which types of economic diversification they should promote. To assess the contribution of economic diversification to human agency and welfare, an important distinction can be made between different types of diversification, for example related and unrelated variety growth (in other words, the diversification into very similar sectors or completely new sectors). Saviotti and Frenken (2008) have shown that whereas related variety growth is crucial for economic development in the short to medium term, unrelated variety growth is essential for the long-term growth of countries. The empirical study in Section 4.5 also suggests that unrelated variety growth may be more positively influential on human development than mere economic growth. The main reason for this seems to be that unrelated variety growth provides completely new choices and tends to distribute the economic, social and political power more evenly. The introduction of railroads, electricity or the Internet has certainly massively improved the capabilities and availability of social choices of people around the world. The realization of the positive effects of related and unrelated variety growth, however, depends on co-evolutionary institutional processes. In theory, a more diversified economy with multiple sectors can favour the establishment of a pluralistic society with multiple different occupations and life styles, with a better distribution of economic and political power. But this will only occur if people have appropriate access to information and the capabilities to understand systemic relations and actively contribute to the development processes. Otherwise they might become trapped within blinkered specializations and, instead of being active agents of development, become increasingly ignorant or exploited within a steadily diversifying and demanding system. Charles Chaplin's *Modern Times* from 1936 is a great illustration of this. He shows factory workers in an assembly production chain, each worker specializing in one single activity.

Increasing economic diversity tends to require growing and changing capabilities from the people if they are to be active agents of development. This makes it crucial to develop appropriate institutions which prevent increasing inequalities in people's skills and capabilities. Even people living in a highly diversified economy such as the USA or Germany do not necessarily have the capabilities to choose among diverse attractive occupations, if the educational standards and institutional support of different social groups differ. This is where the human development approach can make a significant contribution to human agency and well-being, even in advanced countries where people sometimes suffer from there being too many rather than too few choices. In these countries, the level of human agency and well-being certainly also depend upon the capabilities of the people to deal with increasingly complex decision processes. It must be noted, though, that short to medium-term negative effects of the increasing capabilities demand can also trigger further learning processes and the evolution of capabilities and choices in the medium to long run. Therefore, appropriate institutions and/or new technologies must be created to help people to deal with complexity.

4.3.3 *Interplay between the effects*

Different positive, negative and ambiguous effects of diversification on human development have been explored above. It has become obvious that diversification affects human development and well-being in multiple essential ways. The positive, negative and ambiguous effects of economic diversification seem to be strongly connected to each other, depending on the type of diversification, and are influenced by co-evolutionary institutional processes. Economic diversification expands the amount of potential social choice, but can also trigger further inequality reproduction and relative deprivation. The direction of the effects (positive, negative or ambiguous) can change over time. There is a tendency for economic diversification to put increasing and changing requirements on people to become full members of the society. Nevertheless, some technologies deliberately aim to reduce complexity and make usage easier; examples are functional design of hardware and software devices or frugal innovation (e.g. in medical equipment) to reduce nonessential elements of goods. Furthermore, multiple learning, adaptation and selection processes help to reduce the complexity of decision processes and enable people to enlarge their functionings. All of these dynamic and interrelated factors make the analysis of the effects of diversification on human development very difficult and complex, but also offer multiple insights and opportunities for in-depth theoretical and empirical research. Policy makers, researchers and society in general should take these effects into account when designing economic and social policies and discuss what the expected effects of different types of diversification might be over time. Naturally, it is not possible to perfectly predict the net outcome of such complex and dynamic relations. Nevertheless, some patterns emerge when we make an overview of all the mentioned effects. Table 4.1 summarizes the effects and distinguishes between the expected type and direction (positive, neutral or negative) of the effects of economic diversification on a low and high level of economic complexity.

Table 4.1 shows that the positive impacts of qualitative economic diversification on human development are expected to be stronger in cases of low complexity; in other words economic diversification in weakly diversified and networked economies has a more profound positive effect than in already highly diversified economies. The difficulty, however, is in successfully triggering a virtuous cycle of qualitative diversification, which is much easier to achieve in countries which already have a considerable set of productive and human capabilities than it is in countries with a low endowment of capabilities. This is closely related to the ideas of the early development pioneers (such as Nurkse, Hirschman or Myrdal) that first a certain level of systemic effects between demand, supply and productive capabilities has to be achieved before the system starts running. Conversely,

Table 4.1 Theoretical effects of economic diversification on human development

Type of effect	Effects of further diversification on human development[a]		Expected absolute and marginal effects of diversification[a]	
	at a low level of previous economic diversity	at a high level of previous economic diversity	absolute effects (positive or negative)	marginal effects (increasing or decreasing returns)
Expansion of choices				
Unrelated variety	+	+	+	?
Related variety	+	–	+	–
More equal/balanced distribution of the economic and political power				
Unrelated variety	+	+	+	–
Related variety	?	?	?	–
Demand for individual capabilities (e.g. education and health)				
Unrelated variety	+	+	+	+
Related variety	o	o	o	+
Addressing vulnerability of external shocks and economic crises				
Unrelated variety	+	+	+	?
Related variety	–	–	–	?
Job creation and destruction				
Unrelated variety	+/–	+	+	+
Related variety	+	+	+	–

Note

a The signs '+ – o' are used to indicate the expected effects resulting from the theoretical analysis, with '+' indicating a positive effect, '–' a negative effect, '+/–' a effect in both directions, '?' an unclear effect and 'o' a neutral effect of diversification on human development.

the negative effects on human development and especially on well-being seem to increase at higher levels of diversification, where people are confronted with difficulties in deciding between the enormous quantity of choices in all dimensions of their lives (e.g. consumption, life planning), with the consequence that expectation levels and opportunity costs become higher and higher. The capabilities of human beings to deal with complexity are limited; biological constraints (e.g. for information processing) have to be taken into account (Simon 1957). This can lead to an increasing mismatch between theoretical capabilities and people's true functioning space, and hence to increasing relative deprivation. In sum, a certain tendency in the effects of economic diversification seems to emerge. Of course, the complexity of interrelations does not allow for completely reliable predictions, however, there seem to be underlying trends in the direction and impact of diversification on human development over time which are strongly confirmed by theoretical and empirical analysis (Myrdal 1957; Hirschman 1958; Hidalgo 2007, 2010; Schwartz 2004).

1   At low levels of economic diversity, new varieties produce increasing returns and have cumulative effects on human development (due to systemic inter-action effects: Nurkse 1953; Myrdal 1957; Jacobs 1969). Increased variety strongly correlates with an improved basis for sound decision-making allow-ing for further development.
2   At higher levels of diversification, the positive effects of diversification on human development can be expected to decrease. When the limits of vari-ety processing capabilities are reached, the well-being of economic agents becomes constrained by the increasing scope of choices to be made.

These trends can be graphically illustrated. Figure 4.1 illustrates increasing returns of diversification for human development at low levels of diversification and then decreasing returns of diversification for human development at higher levels of diversification and complexity.

Figure 4.2 illustrates divergent evolutions of economic variety and human development and well-being over time.

As a result of innovation and recombinant growth, the diversity of economic activities tends to increase over time, sometimes at a slow pace or even tem-porarily declining due to selection processes, but sometimes rapidly due to the diffusion of radical innovations and the related opportunities for incremental innovations. This leads to the cyclical shape of the economic variety curve in Figure 4.2. With respect to the evolution of human development and well-being over time, an over-proportionate growth can be achieved together with economic diversification at low levels of development. However, once the natural limits of learning and processing information of a person have been reached, the posi-tive effect of diversification of agency and well-being can marginally decrease or even become negative. As highlighted in the section on negative effects of

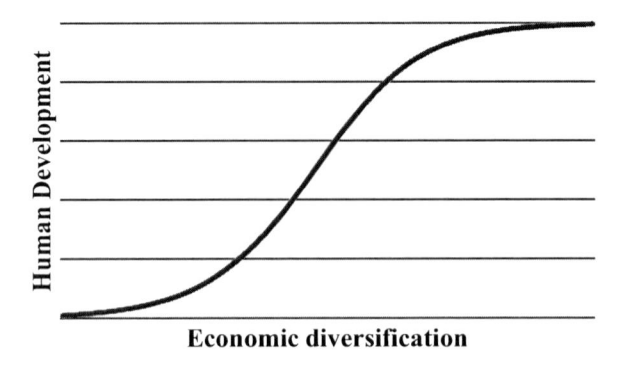

Economic diversification

Figure 4.1 Relation between economic diversification and
human development

Development

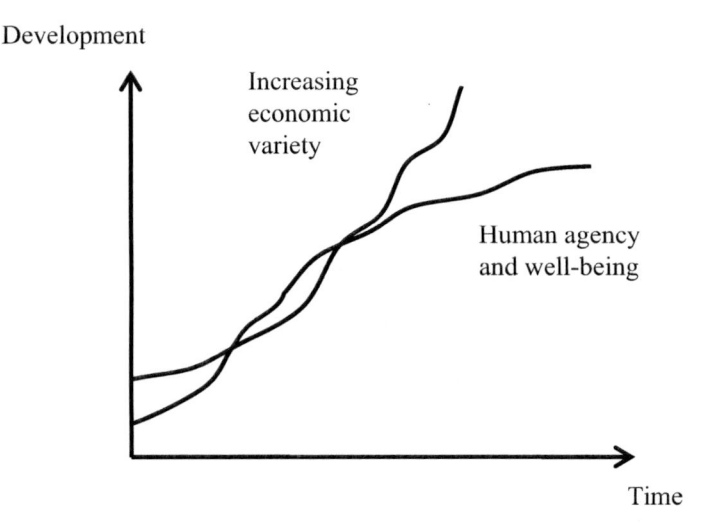

Figure 4.2 Evolution of economic variety and human development over time

diversification, some psychological studies even argue that the massive explosion of choices in the most highly industrialized countries negatively affects people's well-being. Without a doubt, the exact shape of the curves depends on the interplay and the varying relative influence of the varied effects of diversification over time and the level of underlying complexity. Table 4.1 and Figures 4.1 and 4.2 can serve as a point of orientation for new empirical research on economic development and human well-being, as well as guidance for policy makers seeking to advance the socioeconomic development of their countries, by promoting the positive and preventing the negative effects of diversification.

4.4 Addressing constructive critiques

During the elaboration of this book, leading scholars from economic geography and international development asked some constructive questions and voiced some doubts as to whether economic diversification of a region is really so important in a globalized and mobile world. Or is specialization and accessing diversity through international networks more important? The following three critical comments are addressed in this chapter.

1   People are not restricted to regional borders but can migrate on the international and national level; therefore the real variety of choices might not be limited by narrow spatial boundaries (and the corresponding regional or national data).
2   Economic diversification might not be more important for economic development than clustering and specialization, (especially in poor regions).
3   Spatial units, e.g. regions or countries, may be specialized, but can access economic diversity via networks, for instance through imports.

These critiques also lead to doubts about the feasibility of measuring and analysing diversification within regional and nationally defined spatial boundaries. However, these critical points might underestimate the role of long-term economic diversification on the one hand and many people's individual preferences to stay and work in their home region on the other.

As several statistics and reports of the International Labour Organization (e.g. ILO 2008, 2009) show, the set of occupational choices is very unevenly distributed across regions and countries (ILO 2008, 2009), affecting the capabilities and agency of people in a profound way. But due to a varied set of political, social and economic causes, even in the globalized and connected world of the twenty-first century, people cannot freely move and nor do all citizens want to move across national and regional borders to get a better job in other places. A free global labour market does not yet exist (UNDP 2009; ILO 2010; De Haas and Rodriguez 2010). Apart from political borders, the social choice made by a large proportion of the population against mobility suggests that closeness to the home region and strong social bonds continues to be an important factor for occupational choices. Most people want to stay close to their home, their families and friends, traditions, norms and routines. Empirical research shows that even high-skilled entrepreneurs prefer to stay and build up their companies in their home regions (Dahl and Sorensen 2009, 2010). This is a rational and natural decision in the sense that being close to friends and family provides psychological well-being (e.g. Bauer 2007) and helps people to find jobs or engage in entrepreneurial action by making use of the social capital they have built up in their region through frequent interactions (Aldrich and Zimmer 1986; Aldrich *et al.* 1987; Coleman 1988; Dahl and Sorenson 2009, 2010). Even in an increasingly globalized world, the set of choices and the required and desired capabilities of people often depend on their home region, local strong ties and the regional environment where they grew up. Of course, some distances can be bridged through information and trade networks, but to benefit from these channels requires a set of capabilities that many poor people may not have, such as literacy, access to ICT, income and the absorptive capacity to use information. Moving within a country or to another country may improve economic opportunities for some migrants, but may not always be the result of a free choice, but may rather indicate the comparative level of deprivation and unfreedom at home. For this reason, it seems reasonable to argue that the set of occupational choices at the local level has a relevant impact on the capabilities and agency of the people.

Some scholars emphasize the importance of clusters, the spatial agglomeration of specialized economic activities (e.g. Porter 1990, 1998), as well as the Ricardian comparative advantages, as empirical and theoretical counter-arguments to the perspective of development as a process of constant diversification and complexity growth. Economic concentration and specialization certainly matter for value creation and competitiveness (Pyke *et al.* 1990; Maskell *et al.* 1998; Brenner 2004), at least in the short term and on the local and regional level. However, there is a strong debate within the field of economic geography on to what extent the sectoral concentration or diversification, cooperation or competition, temporary monopolies, oligopolies or competition drive regional innovation and development (e.g. Glaeser *et al.* 1992; Boix Domenech 2004; Boschma and Martin 2010). Probably all of these effects matter at different stages of the life cycles of clusters and industries (Klepper 1997; Brenner 2004; Tödtling and Trippl 2005; Neffke *et al.* 2008). In a long-term perspective, however, successful regions require the flexibility and hence a diversified set of capabilities to achieve sustained economic development, overcome rigidities, adapt to new challenges and diversify into and produce new products and services (Tödtling and Trippl 2005). For this reason, regions which are successful in the long run may also be characterized by higher degrees of complexity and fairly diversified structures (Jacobs 1969; Frenken and Boschma 2007; Boschma and Martin 2010). Furthermore, as Adam Smith (1776) showed, the very same process of specialization and division of labour leads to a greater variety of activities and the increasing wealth of nations. The most successful clusters such as the Silicon Valley (e.g. Saxenian 1994) show high levels of concentration of certain sectors within one region; however, they are also often highly sophisticated and vertically diversified. The categorization into specialized or diversified depends on the level of analysis as well as the type of diversity under consideration. We may observe, for instance, a high spatial concentration of automobile or mobile industry at country level. But at a more micro-level of observation within these clusters, we may see enormous sophistication, diversity and complexity of activities. For example, within a cluster of software services and related activities we may find myriads of interrelated tiers of suppliers, research institutions, consultants and plenty of different activities and jobs, and thus a great level of vertical and related diversification.

4.5 Empirical exploration of the effects of economic diversification on human development

This section introduces the promising new field of empirical research on the interrelations between human development and economic diversification. There are many different taxonomies and methodologies available with which to measure the well-being and economic diversification of countries. The subsequent cross-sectional analysis compares the impact of different export diversification measures on human development and economic growth. Interestingly even this rather simple approach leads to quite robust results. Of course, much further empirical work can and needs to be done, using for instance panel data, applying network analysis techniques and controlling for several factors influencing the results. But one essential contribution of the analysis described below has been to open up an enormous range of interesting areas for analysis and in-depth insights into the relations between structural change and human welfare. This promises to provide us with a better understanding of the complex relations between economic and human development.

4.5.1 Measurement

This section discusses the variables and the methodologies that were applied. From around the start of the twenty-first century, there has been an increased focus on different taxonomies with which to measure human capabilities, well-being and social progress. The composed indicators range from objective measures of well-being and deprivation, such as the HDI (UNDP 1990) or the MPI (Alkire and Foster 2007; UNDP 2010), to more subjective measures of well-being, such as surveys of happiness and life satisfaction. New taxonomies tend to be multidimensional and combine several elements of both objective indicators such as life expectancy and health, and relatively subjective indicators such as community and family life or work-time balance, which might vary across cultures (e.g. Economist Intelligence Unit 2005; Stiglitz *et al.* 2009; Hall *et al.* 2010). For the sake of simplicity, we choose in this study the HDI as dependent variable because it the most commonly discussed and most broadly accepted and available indicator for human capabilities and well-being. It is certainly not a comprehensive indicator for all the different elements constituting human well-being and freedom, but at least it considers three basic elements which most people around the world would agree to be vital, namely income, health and education (UNDP 1990).

Regarding the measurement of economic diversification, great advances have been made using export and employment data (e.g. Funke and Ruhwedel 2001; Hidalgo *et al.* 2007; Frenken *et al.* 2007; Saviotti and Frenken 2008; Hausmann and Hidalgo 2010). To calculate different dimensions of economic diversification (related and unrelated variety), we use export data for the year 2000 from a NBER dataset created by Feenstra *et al.* (2005). The dataset contains the exports of virtually all countries in the world to all other countries, distinguishing between 772 product categories at the 4-digit level of the Standard International Trade Classification (SITC-4). Export data is used because of its broad availability and relatively good comparability. Naturally, there might be some bias, in that larger countries tend to be more diversified (e.g. India in contrast to Lebanon); however, the study also applies the methodology suggested by Hidalgo *et al.* (2007) and Hausmann and Hidalgo (2010) to handle this problem by considering revealed comparative advantages above certain thresholds. The results also show that larger countries in terms of population, such as China and India, do not necessarily show a higher level of diversification than smaller countries, such as Belgium or Switzerland.

Based on the export data we calculate different proxy indicators for the economic diversity of countries; namely entropy, HHI, the number of revealed comparative advantages and the product ubiquity. Each of these measures considers different dimensions of diversity, such as the variety, balance and quality of the economic sectors in which the economies are able to reach a level of competitiveness and comparative advantage allowing them to export these goods.

- *Entropy* places a higher value on smaller sectors, measures both variety and balance, and allows for the differentiation between unrelated, semi-related and related variety (Frenken *et al.* 2007; Saviotti and Frenken 2008). The entropy H can be calculated as follows:

$$H = \sum_{i=1}^{n} p_i \log_2\left(\frac{1}{p_i}\right),$$

where p_i stands for the share of a given sector i in the total exports of a country. The value of entropy grows along with an increase in the number of sectors and with the evenness of the distribution of the share of the total exports (Saviotti and Frenken 2008). An essential advantage of the entropy measure is that a hierarchical decomposition of the contribution of each sectoral level (e.g. 1- to 6-digit level in the SITC system) on the overall diversity can be made (Frenken 2007). Entropy values at different digit levels can be introduced into a regression analysis without necessarily leading to collinearity problems (Jacquemin and Berry 1979). This allows unrelated, semi-related and related variety to be distinguished by measuring the level of variety on different levels of sectoral aggregations (Frenken *et al.* 2007). In our empirical application, the different types of variety are proxied by the entropies on the 1-digit, 2-digit and 4-digit level, respectively.

- The *Hirschman-Herfindahl Index* (HHI) places a higher weighting on larger sectors and basically measures concentration and balance of the sectors.

$$HHI = \sum_{i}\left(\frac{X_i}{\sum_{j}^{N} X_j}\right)^2$$

The value of the HHI ranges between 0 and 1, where 1 supposes an absolute concentration of the exports x in one product sector i. Hence, the lower the value, the more balanced and less concentrated the sectors are.

- The *number of revealed comparative advantages* and the *ubiquity* of the exports (Hidalgo *et al.* 2007; Hidalgo and Hausmann 2009; Hausmann and Hidalgo 2010; Balassa 1965) are indicators which measure the amount and ubiquity/quality of export diversification. The revealed comparative advantage (RCA) measures whether a country c exports more of product i, as a share of its total exports, than other countries. It is calculated as follows:

$$RCA = \frac{x(c, i)/\sum_{i} x(c, i)}{\sum_{c} x(c, i)/\sum_{c, i} x(c, i)}$$

If the RCA is higher than 1, country c has a comparative advantage in the export of the product i. If it is lower than 1, then the country has a comparative disadvantage. Furthermore, the empirical analysis calculates the average ubiquity of the products i exported by country c by using the method introduced by Hidalgo and Hausmann (2009).

$$k_{c, N} = \frac{1}{k_{c, 0}} \sum_{i} M_{ci} k_{i, N-1}$$

where k_c stands for the observed level of diversification of the exports of a country and k_i for the ubiquity of a product, or in other words, the number of countries who export product i. M_{ci} represents an adjacency matrix which measures the *RCAs* for each country (rows) in the 772 product categories (columns). Further information is available in Hidalgo and Hausmann (2009).

4.5.2 Results

A set of simple linear regression models are used to analyse the impact of the different types of diversification on human development and on gross domestic product at purchasing power parity per capital (GDP PPP per capita), respectively. The available data on exports, human development and GDP PPP per capita for the year 2000 allows for the analysis of a comprehensive set of 121 countries, ranging from countries with very low to very high human development and from highly concentrated to very diversified export portfolios. The dependent variables of the cross-sectional analysis are the HDI and GDP PPP per capita for the year 2000; and the explanatory variables are the entropies on the 4-, 2- and 1-digit level, the HHI, the number of RCAs and the average product ubiquity. This allows us to compare and plot 16 different simple linear regressions. The method is simple but provides robust results. First, economic diversification has a highly significant positive effect on both GDP and human development, independent of the diversification indicator applied (see Table 4.2). The effect is so strong that, regardless of whether the measurement focuses on variety, balance, disparity or quality at the 1-, 2- or 4-digit levels, export diversification always plays a significant role in the explanation of the GDP and the human development of a country.

Second, it is striking that economic diversification explains more of the variance in the HDI than in mere economic income (see Table 4.3). The determination

Table 4.2 Empirical effects of economic diversification on human development and GDP

Effects of different types of diversity on HDI and GDP[a]		Human development in 2000			GDP PPP per capita in 2000		
Simple linear regressions N = 121 countries		Stand. Coeff. Beta	T	Sig	Stand. Coeff. Beta	T	Sig
Entropy at the	4-digit SITC level	0.692	10.459	0.000	0.484	6.042	0.000
	2-digit SITC level	0.648	9.285	0.000	0.453	5.545	0.000
	1-digit SITC level	0.531	6.830	0.000	0.302	3.456	0.001
HHI at the	4-digit SITC level	0.538	6.954	0.000	0.279	3.166	0.002
	2-digit SITC level	0.543	7.048	0.000	0.315	3.624	0.000
	1-digit SITC level	0.455	5.571	0.000	0.230	2.579	0.011
RCAs	No. RCA > 1 at the 4-digit level	0.637	9.004	0.000	0.524	6.712	0.000
	Average ubiquity	0.584	7.839	0.000	0.388	4.598	0.000

Source: Human development data and charts (2013), Feenstra *et al.* (2005).

Note
a Diversity measures based on Feenstra *et al.* (2005) export data from 2000, at the 1-, 2- and 4-digit level of the Standard Industrial Trade Classification (SITC).

Table 4.3 Explanatory power of economic diversificationa for human development[a]

Coefficients of determination (R²) N = 121 countries		Human development in 2000 R²	GDP in 2000 R²
Entropy at the	4-digit SITC level	0.479	0.235
	2-digit SITC level	0.420	0.205
	1-digit SITC level	0.282	0.091
1- HHI at the	4-digit SITC level	0.289	0.078
	2-digit SITC level	0.294	0.099
	1-digit SITC level	0.207	0.053
RCAs	No. RCA > 1 at the 4-digit level	0.405	0.275
	Average ubiquity	0.341	0.151

Source: Human development data and charts (2013), Feenstra *et al.* (2005).

Note
a Diversity measures based on Feenstra *et al.* (2005) export data from 2000, at the 1-, 2- and 4-digit level of the Standard Industrial Trade Classification (SITC).

coefficient (R^2) is significantly higher for all the simple linear models explaining human development.

The high variance in the relation between economic diversification and economic growth can also be observed in Figure 4.3, Figure 4.4 and Figure 4.5. It is important to note that these results imply that the significant positive effect of diversification on human development does not just result from the fact that the HDI includes income. Economic diversification is a better predictor of human development than income taken alone. As such, economic diversification must also be positively related with other components of human development, such as education and life expectancy (which constitute the other two components of the HDI). Several reasons have been highlighted in the theoretical section of this chapter, including: (a) it results in a better distribution of power within an economy; (b) the requirement of productive capabilities positively affects human development such as infrastructure, institutions, health and education; and (c) it gives more occupational choices.

The implications for human development policy are straightforward: qualitative economic diversification is not only crucial for sustained economic growth, but appears to be even more important for human development. Accordingly, proper economic policy can substantially contribute to human development. Now the question arises: what are the impacts of different types of diversification and thus, which type(s) of diversification policy should be promoted? In an attempt to address these questions, this study contrasts the effects of unrelated, semi-related and related variety on economic and human development. Figure 4.3, Figure 4.4. and Figure 4.5 plot (a) the related variety of countries at the 4-digit level (measured by Shannon entropy, Shannon 1948) (Figure 4.3), (b) the semi-related variety at the 2-digit level (Figure 4.4) and (c) unrelated variety at the 1-digit level (Figure 4.5) against the HDI and GDP per capita. Trendlines are added to the figures to show general tendencies in the described relations. A set of interesting observations can be made for further qualitative and empirical exploration. Whereas unrelated variety seems to have a marginally increasing positive effect on human development, related variety has – as predicted in theory section – a marginally decreasing positive effect on human development. In contrast,

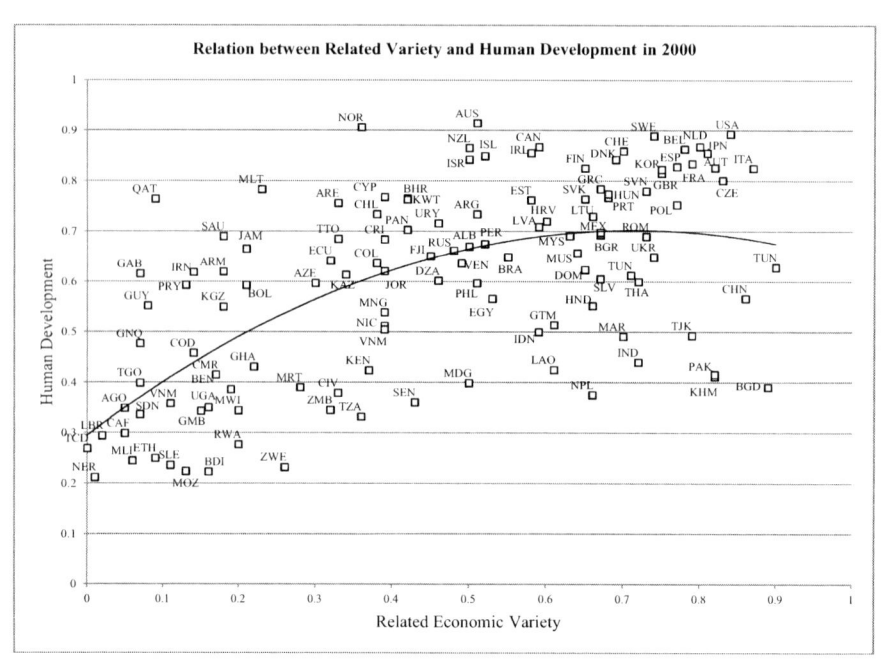

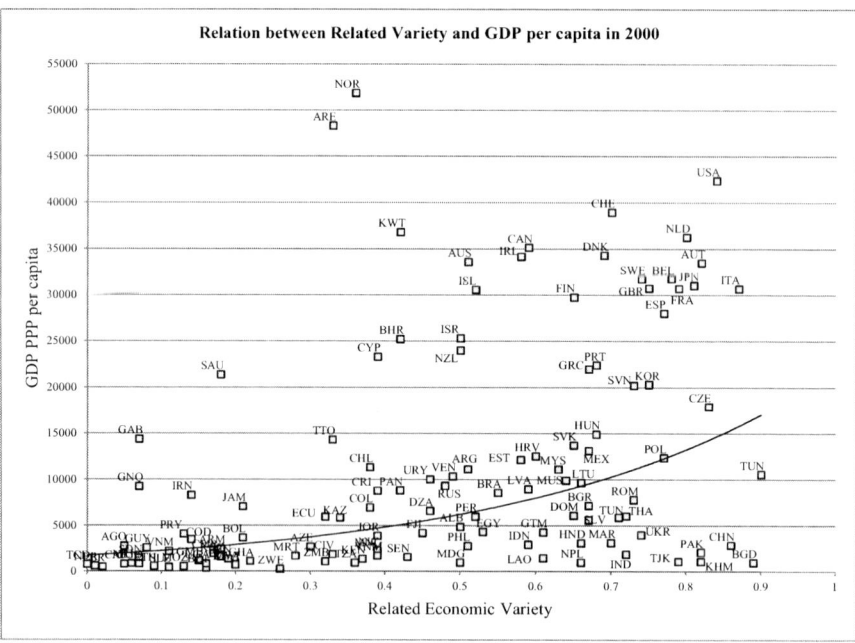

Figure 4.3 The effects of related variety on human development and GDP[a]

Source: Human Development Index in 2000 (UNDP 2010). SITC export data in 2000 (Feenstra *et al.* 2005).

Note
a The country codes are based on ISO 3166. Related variety is measured by the Shannon entropy on the 4-digit SITC level subtracted by the Shannon entropy on the 2-digit SITC level. The trendlines show a general tendency of the described relations.

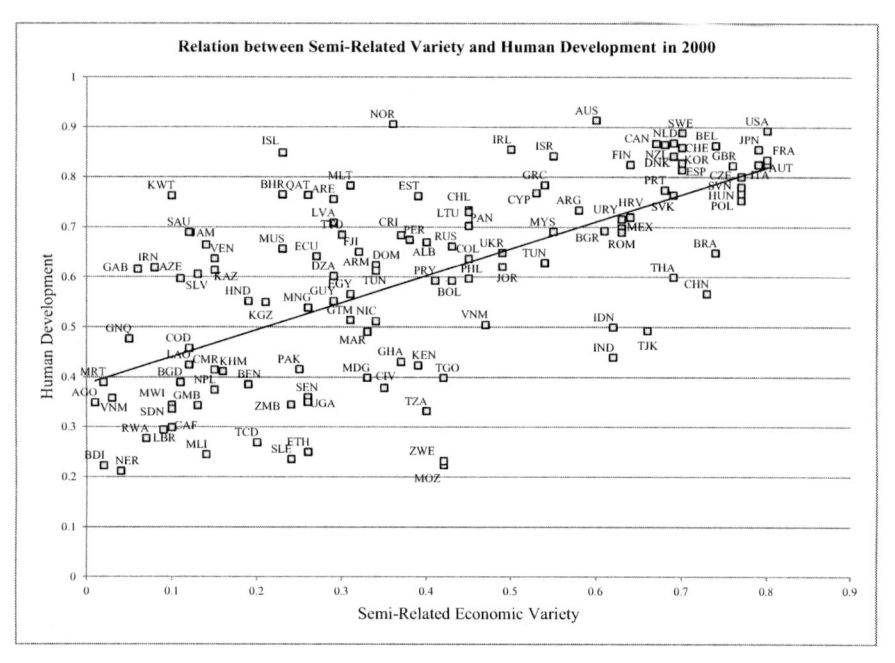

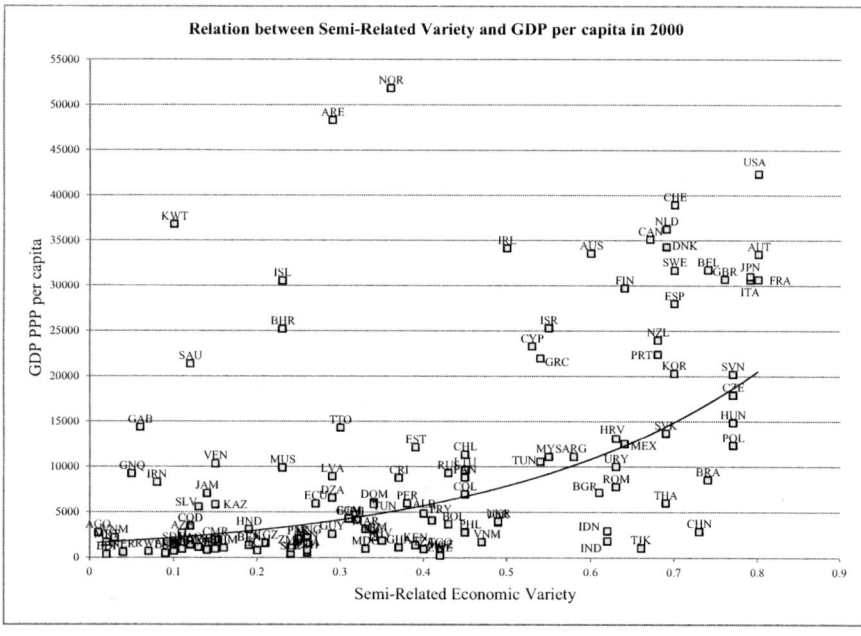

Figure 4.4 The effects of semi-related variety on human development and GDP[a]

Source: Human Development Index in 2000 (UNDP 2010). SITC export data in 2000 (Feenstra *et al.* 2005).

Note

a The country codes are based on ISO 3166. Semi-related variety is measured by the Shannon entropy on the 2-digit SITC level subtracted by the Shannon entropy on the 1-digit SITC level. The trendlines show a general tendency of the described relations.

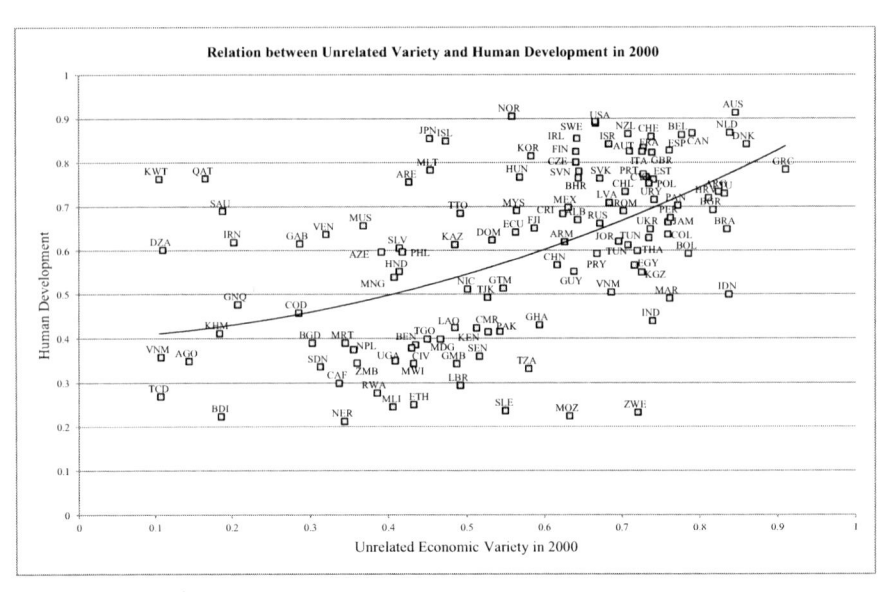

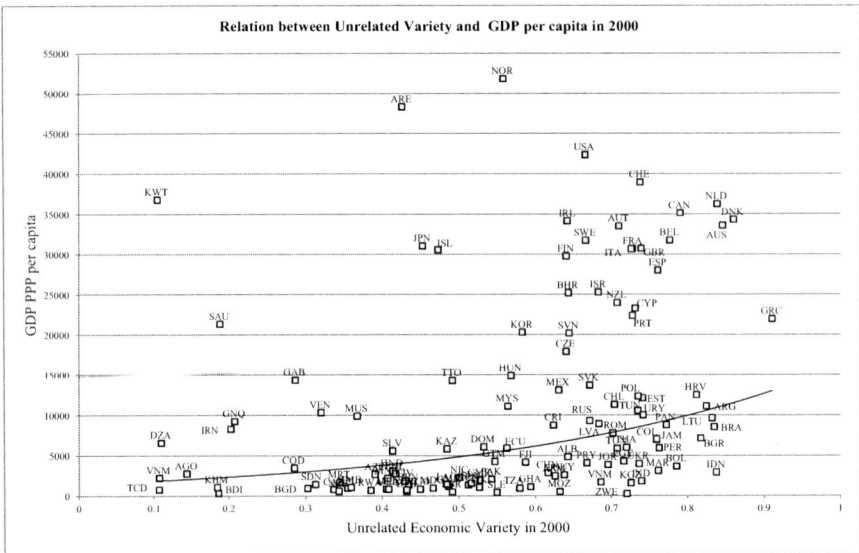

Figure 4.5 The effects of unrelated variety on human development and GDP[a]

Source: Human Development Index in 2000 (UNDP 2010). SITC export data in 2000 (Feenstra *et al.* 2005).

Note

a The country codes are based on ISO 3166. Unrelated variety is measured by the Shannon entropy on the 1-digit SITC level. The trendlines show a general tendency of the described relations.

marginally increasing positive returns of diversification for GDP can be observed in all three types of measured diversity.

As predicted in the theoretical section, economic diversity indeed seems to have a marginally increasing positive effect on GDP ($f'>0$, $f''>0$). However, quite a high level of variance is evident. Some resource and oil-rich countries (such as Kuwait, Argentina and Norway) achieve very high levels of income despite comparatively low economic diversity values; in contrast, some large developing countries (such as India and Pakistan) have low levels of average income but relatively high levels of economic variety. Nevertheless, a general tendency of marginally increasing returns of economic diversification on GDP can be observed, in line with theoretical approaches highlighting cumulative effects, increasing returns and recombinant growth (Myrdal 1957; Jacobs 1969; Romer 1986; Weitzman 1998).

Recombinant growth, however, seems to be realizable and gain full power only at high levels of economic diversity. One key reason for this seems to be the need to fill the gaps in the productive capabilities between different sectors before advanced recombinant growth can fully set in (Hidalgo *et al.* 2007). Gaps in the product space and structural heterogeneity can prevent learning and interactive innovation between the sectors and can also imply very strong differences in productivity and income generation (e.g. Furtado 1961; Katz 2007; ECLAC 2008). This also partially explains the tendency of increasing positive returns of unrelated economic variety on human development. However, while virtually all countries with a high level of unrelated variety also have a medium to high level of human development, it is not the same picture when GDP is considered. In addition, as predicted theoretically, marginally decreasing positive effects of related economic variety on human development can be observed, whereas the effect on GDP continues to have a marginally increasing tendency. The empirical results sustain the theoretical analysis and show the need to further explore the different effects of economic diversification on GDP and on human development. The core research hypothesis for further empirical proof and refinement in more advanced econometric studies as well as qualitative case studies can be summarized as follows.

1   Economic diversification has a positive effect on both human and economic development.
2   Whereas unrelated variety has a marginally increasing positive effect on human development ($f'>0$, $f''>0$), related variety has a marginally decreasing positive effect on human development ($f'>0$, $f''<0$).
3   Both unrelated and related economic diversification have a marginally increasing positive effect on economic growth ($f'>0$, $f''>0$).
4   Economic diversification is even more essential for human development than for income per capita, because it demands human capabilities and tends to distribute the economic and political power.

This study has been a modest preliminary attempt to explore the empirical relations between economic diversification and human development. Naturally, these hypotheses must be confirmed and further studied within systematic empirical work, using also panel data, introducing control variables and distinguishing between different dimensions of human development and types of economic diversification. In addition, the positive effects between economic diversification and human development certainly go in both directions. While diversification provides more choices and increases the demand for higher levels of human capabilities, human development is essential for the productive capabilities of a country to innovate and diversify. The strengths and directions of the effects, dependent on different types of economic diversification and dimensions of human development, must be further explored. Nevertheless, the main purpose to show possibilities for new studies and insights of the complex relations between structural change and human development has been achieved.

4.6 Chapter conclusion

This chapter has shown that economic diversification has multiple positive, negative, complex and changing effects on human development which deeply affect human development across space and over time. The data now available to researchers, along with interdisciplinary research approaches, however, enables more comprehensive examination of these complex effects. This in turn provides new insights allowing for a democratic debate and policy measures to make structural change and economic diversity work for human development.

The diverse theoretical effects outlined above can be studied at national, regional or individual level, using a varied set of diversity measures. This provides societies with many potential benefits, as it can contribute to a new understanding of socioeconomic development and help policy makers to foster economic and human development simultaneously. Studying the effects of economic diversification on the choices and capabilities of people opens up a large number of further promising possibilities for more comprehensively considering the relations between human and economic development. These include panel analysis, or triangulating with other data sources (e.g. employment data, different indicators of well-being and life standards, polynomial functions). A variety of new possibilities for theoretical and applied research in welfare economics and complexity research can be opened up. However, the main aim and value of the theoretical and empirical research on the effects of economic diversification on human development can provide the civil society, companies and policy-makers with new insights on how to simultaneously foster economic and human development in their regions and countries.

We have seen that a future-oriented policy to fostering individuals' capabilities and choices goes hand in hand with an industrial policy promoting adequate economic diversification. Governments should foster different types of diversification – for instance, related or unrelated variety growth – according to their productive structure at a given point in time. To design proper innovation and development policies, a fruitful mix of selection and variation processes has to be found. At lower complexity levels, countries need to foster endogenous capability upgrading and diversification evolution, which allow for systemic feedbacks. This is similar to the idea of development push strategies (e.g. Rosenstein-Rodan 1943; Nurkse 1953; Hirschman 1958). At higher levels of complexity, the emphasis of policy design should increasingly shift towards proper selection mechanisms within complexity, focusing less on fostering the quantity of further consumption and employment choices, and more on the quality of choices and their impact on the well-being of people.

Increasing the number of choices exponentially does not necessarily lead to more freedom and well-being, and can even have negative effects due to rising costs in decision processes. In countries with both higher and lower complexity and productive capabilities, the focus on short and medium-term related variety growth should be evaluated against the long-term welfare effects of unrelated variety growth. It seems that long-term unrelated variety growth deserves major attention, because it distributes the economic and political power within countries and leads to more democratic regimes with more choices for people. However, this does not mean randomly diversifying into all possible product areas. Instead, the endogenous exploration of local, regional and national productive capabilities has to be emphasized to promote competitive diversification which in turn promotes both economic growth and social welfare simultaneously. A final factor is that to promote qualitative diversification, prolific knowledge exchange, cooperation and competition between the multiple agents involved in the economy is necessary. The subsequent chapters 5, 6 and 7 will explore this in more detail.

5 Social networks, innovation and human development

Economists and the public media often highlight individual skills as key factors for success, but in fact individuals do not depend only on their own skills for their achievements and well-being, but also on their social contacts and associations. For instance, it is often not a matter of what individuals know, but rather who they know which gives rise to employment options (Woolcock and Narayan 2000). While it is necessary to promote human agency, especially for the poor, through the attendance of basic needs and expenditure in basic shelter, education and health services, on their own these measures are insufficient if people cannot access social networks that empower them, or if the structure of the socio-economic systems reproduces inequalities as a result of very unequal access to information and power over the information flow. Consequently it is unrealistic for economic approaches to assume that people are rational individuals merely interacting with each other for the sake of profit maximization and not consider the social embeddedness of economic actions (Granovetter 1985). The network of social contacts affects the capabilities and choices of people, as it also affects the learning and innovation patterns and directions of structural economic change.

The 'Sen meets Schumpeter' approach aims to contribute dynamic and structural insights on the complex relations between economic growth and human development. Social capital and network theory can help to link together the human development and structural change approaches, as networks are crucial for the enhancement of capabilities of people and the evolutionary dynamics and directions of structural change. The positive, negative and changing effects of social networks need to be taken into account to design proper network and structural change policies. Most works on social capital, as well as those on collective or group capabilities, highlight the positive effects of social networks or the negative consequences stemming from the lack of social networks and trust (e.g. Putnam 2000; Steward 2005). However, networks can also have direct and indirect negative effects on human development.

Social networks can be a key structural device for inclusion (e.g. community networks), empowerment and learning processes (entrepreneurship, information access or distance learning via the Internet). But network dynamics and differences in network positions, structures and power often relate to inequalities, central and peripheral structures, rich-get-richer mechanisms, social exclusion and ultimately harm. There are a few works that draw connections between economic development, social networks and human development (e.g. Evans 2002; Ibrahim 2006; Foster and Handy 2008) but, to our best knowledge, there is no work that analyses systematically the positive and negative effects of social networks on human development.

This chapter discusses this subject as follows. First, it is shown how basic concepts from social capital and network theory can be useful for the human development approach (Section 5.1). The role network concepts play in Neo-Schumpeterian Economics is then analysed in Section 5.2. Section 5.3 briefly summarizes the positive and negative effects of social networks. Section 5.4 discusses how network measures (such as network centrality, the composition of ego-networks, network cohesion or preferential attachment) can help to understand the complex relations between social networks, structural economic change and human agency. Then some of these methods of exploratory social network analysis (SNA) are applied in an empirical case study in Section 5.5 on the relations between social capital and the innovative behaviour of smallholder farmers in Peru. This shows how social networks are crucial in virtually all realms of socioeconomic life, from family and community life to work and leisure, and enables an analysis of multiple positive and negative effects in diverse fields. Emphasis is placed on the following core aspects that seem to connect human and economic development.

1 The relational/external and group capabilities of the human development approach.
2 Institutional aspects such as trust and cooperation.
3 A network-based perspective on social capital.
4 Social capital and entrepreneurship.
5 Innovation networks and knowledge transfer in less developed regions.

These aspects open up many possible ways in which social network thinking can be used to help bridge Neo-Schumpeterian economics and the human development approach.

5.1 Social capital theory

Social capital theory highlights the importance of social relations for economic performance (Lin 1999, 2003; Woolcock and Narayan 2000). It moves beyond common perspectives in economics that assume individual rational decision-making processes based on full information. Furthermore, social capital theory identifies the role of different types of relations, such as strong and weak ties, as well triggering a debate on structural aspects of inequality and inequality reproduction.

5.1.1 Social networks matter

People are embedded in networks of social relations that have deep influences on their capabilities (Granovetter 1985; Castells 1996; Lin 2003). Their network position and the composition of their social contacts, such as friends, family and colleagues, decisively condition their choices and opportunities (Bourdieu 1983; Castells 1996; Lin 2003; Benkler 2006; Eagle *et al.* 2010). In economics, people are often regarded as individuals who make rational decisions based on full information about scarcities and prices in an economy. In reality, however, access to information and the preferences and capabilities of individuals are deeply influenced by the information and preferences of the social networks in which those individuals are embedded, such as their families, friends or colleagues. A common assumption in mainstream economics is that agents are rational beings who behave and interact rationally with other persons (purely) for the sake of trade and profit maximization. But the presumption of the existence of this representative rational agent does not take into account the full complexity of human behaviour and the enormous amount of information within complex socioeconomic system with millions, or even billions, of different agents, together with their actions and interactions. Human beings can virtually never make completely rational choices based on a full knowledge of all the possible choices and their effects. People can only be rational within the boundaries of their knowledge (Simon 1957), and can only evaluate their actions and decisions based upon the choices they know. There are no two people with precisely the same knowledge, network of social contacts, skills and capabilities. The normative principles and capabilities of individuals depend not just on their skills, but also on the experiences, preferences, knowledge and power of their social contacts, family, friends, and colleagues, as well as the socioeconomic environment and routines they are living in.

Social networks play an essential role in virtually all dimensions of human life (such as family, friends, work, religion, sports and leisure). It is through social networks that people access a range of information and opportunities and help each other. It is through social networks that economies and societies are structured and develop. Indeed, it is via social networks that people become aware of and evaluate opportunities and choices. Social interactions and network access to information influence what people learn, what they see as desirable as well as feasible (Liñán and Santos 2007). It is in this way that networks strongly affect people's capabilities, choices, desires and convictions. Sociologists have emphasized the social embeddedness of individual economic behaviour (e.g. Weber 1922; Parsons and Smelser 1956; Granovetter 1973). Economists such as Schumpeter (1954) and Veblen (1898, 1899) have also highlighted the need for economic sociology. The literature on social capital shows that social relations have a strong impact on the economic performance of individuals, social groups and countries (Coleman 1988, 1990; Burt 1992; Portes and Sensenbrenner 1993; Putnam 1993, 2000; Woolcock and Narayan 2000; Eagle *et al.* 2010). For instance, social networks are crucial for providing an individual with access to information on job opportunities (Granovetter 1973). Empirical work using large datasets has shown that network diversity is closely related to individuals' income and human development (Eagle *et al.* 2010).

Owing to its focus on the rights of the individuals and ethical foundations of justice, the human development approach has naturally not concentrated on how social relations directly affect individuals' choices and capabilities. It must be noted, though, that while grounded in ethical individualism, the human development approach does not follow methodological individualism (Robeyns 2008 cited in Alkire 2010). The human development approach emphasizes the multiple ways in which process freedoms and societal and institutional aspects have positive or negative effects on the capabilities of the individuals. Nevertheless, this emphasis on individuals has the potential to underemphasize the fact that human beings are 'social animals' (Aristotle 1253a2 cited in Barker 1958) who find physical well-being and motivation through networks (Bauer 2007). The capabilities of people often heavily depend on their social networks: social networks affect the formation of preferences, learning processes and human behaviour.

Several human development researchers stress that individuals can access capabilities by taking part in group and collective actions, such as self-help groups, credit and savings groups, producer associations or political parties (Steward 2005; Ibrahim 2006). Collective action is necessary to create capabilities, social security and well-being; especially for the poor and less privileged (Evans 2002 cited in Foster and Handy 2008). As such, it is not only the sum of the individual capabilities that generates collective capabilities: the group itself creates completely new capabilities (Steward 2005; Ibrahim 2006). Groups can provide access to resources, scale effects and/or a political voice, but also mobilize other social intangibles, such as self-respect and feelings of inclusion (Steward 2005). In addition, Deneulin and Steward (2002) argue that the structures of living together do not just influence the formation of individual capabilities and the choice of functionings, but they also have an intrinsic value, such as for example the values of families and friendships (Foster and Handy 2008). These approaches also take into account that groups and collectivities decisively affect the formation of individuals' preferences and their behaviour (Evans 2002; Steward 2005). Whereas group capabilities refer to capabilities provided by collective action and group assistance, Foster and Handy's (2008) external capabilities approach focuses on capabilities that can be directly provided by social contacts, such as the capabilities of an illiterate person to understand a written document with the help of a literate friend. For this purpose, a well-defined group which needs to be organized strategically to build up new group capabilities, such as an association of farmers, is not required. The external capabilities can be accessed through direct social interactions with other people. Foster and Handy (2008) provide several examples. Using a mobile phone, a farmer may check the current market prices, where to get the cheapest crops and where the clients currently pay the highest prices. He might give this information to a friend who is a farmer as well. This raises the capabilities of the second farmer. As it is dependent on the friendship of the first farmer, it can hardly be described as an individual capability of the second farmer. Instead, both farmers are involved in the creation of a new capability; a capability that has arisen out of social interaction. Note that the first farmer has the capability independently of the second farmer and can decide whether he wants to share it with the second farmer or not. Furthermore, the second farmer can use the information differently than the first farmer. But in comparison to a group capability (e.g. through a farmers association), the farmers in the example are not bound to a group action to obtain the same new capability. The additional capabilities are external to the individual and hence cannot merely be defined as internal individual capabilities. They add to the individual's capabilities, but they are neither completely dependent on the individuals' capabilities, nor are they social services provided by a government or any other organization. Hence, through direct network contacts, individuals can improve their own capabilities.

But human development research also points to potential negative effects. As Kaushik Basu remarked at the HDCA conference in Lima 2009 (Basu 2009), group identities, altruism and compassion can have both positive and negative effects on human well-being and agency. Altruistic behaviour and compassion can certainly be good, but it can also hamper the agency of the individual. For example, a literate person can help an illiterate person by reading texts for him/her, but it would be more effective in human development terms to teach the illiterate individual to read and write. Reliance on external sources can prevent an individual's capability enhancement and make the person vulnerable and dependent. The human development approach aims to empower people; as such, reliance on the social security network of the community network could also be interpreted as an indicator of deprivation. It is worth noting that the human development approach can benefit from social capital research, to analyse and understand how network structures can lead to inequality in different dimensions of human life, or how different types of social relations, such as strong and weak ties, affect the agency, capabilities, choices and functionings of the people.

5.1.2 Basic concepts of social capital theory

The emphasis of social capital theory has generally been on the positive contributions of social relations, such as the valuable access to information and synergies that social networks can provide (Granovetter 1973; Coleman 1988, 1990; Burt 1992; Putnam 1993). This is partly due to the choice of terminology. Similar to economic capital (i.e. money and machines) and human capital (e.g. skills), social capital seems to be a (scarce) input, and hence the more social contacts, the better the social capital. The negative effects are generally considered to be the lack of one or other dimensions of social capital. There has been less research emphasis on the intrinsically negative effects that social capital can have.

Three main concepts can be highlighted within the network-based social capital theory: (a) the strengths of weak ties (Granovetter 1973); (b) network closure as social capital (Coleman 1988); and (c) structural holes (Burt 1992). Coleman (1988) argues that strong (and even redundant) ties between people, based on frequent social interaction, are crucial to reducing opportunistic behaviour, enabling shared norms and providing the fertile climate of trust necessary for fine-grained information transfers and coping with information ambiguity. However, Granovetter's analysis (e.g. 1973, 1985) revealed that people access valuable new information (e.g. on job opportunities) through so-called weak ties. A weak tie is a connection from one person to another, who together do not form part of a group of people or clique, and who do not frequently interact and interchange information. The information flowing within a clique may be redundant, whereas connections with members outside the clique (weak ties) can provide new ideas and information (e.g. job opportunities). As Mark Granovetter explained in an interview with Richard Swedberg in May 1988 (Swedberg 1990, p. 99):

> Another thing I looked at was if it mattered what part of an information network a person was in for a specific bit of information to flow to him. One of the interesting findings in this context was that many people found their jobs through people they really did not know very well, something which I later described in an article called 'The Strength of Weak Ties'. My argument was that this was no accident, but rather that the people you don't know very well are probably moving in circles that are different from your own and therefore less likely to have the same information as you do. The people you know very well, on the other hand, know the same people as you do and therefore have the same information. ... I also found that the employers preferred to hire people through personal contacts, just as the workers themselves preferred to find jobs that way.

In a similar vein, Burt (1992) draws attention to the role strategic network positions play in the career ladder (for example, when individuals achieve better positions and gain better rewards within organizations). In Burt's view, a strategic position (brokerage) between otherwise unconnected groups provides an individual with power and access to distinct, rather than redundant, information. People who are closer to so-called structural holes are expected to attain greater economic rewards and will have a higher probability of advancement. Furthermore, Burt's (1992) strategic position of individuals must not merely be viewed from the perspective of the individual's advantages, but should also be used to reveal opportunities for social and economic integration by boundary spanners promoting knowledge transfers between otherwise disconnected groups.

In sum, it may be the adequate combination of strong and weak ties and a central network position that provides individuals with different capabilities and opportunities to access and control the material and immaterial network flows. An individual might require both a network of strong ties on which he or she can rely, as well as access to weak ties able to provide him or her with new information and opportunities. In addition, larger societies are formed by various different groups. It is not just the immediate bonding and bridging social ties between the groups that matter, but also the generalized level of trust and commonly shared norms that can find their expression in legal frameworks, participatory policy processes and countries' institutional setups (North 1990). High levels of civic engagement, trust and social interaction can lead to social stability, interactive learning and foster economic development (Putnam 1993).

A mixture of network and institutional arguments is presented in the so-called synergy view (Woolcock and Narayan 2000). This approach focuses on the role of the complementarities and embeddedness of different agents in a socioeconomic system (Evans 1995, 1996) and promotes participatory development. The state, society and private enterprises need to learn from each other and interact to promote mutual understanding, to solve both market and government failures and facilitate structural changes (see also Chapter 8 on policies for structural change and human development). Institutional macro aspects (such as democratic institutions, human rights and equality before the law) are important and affect the bridges between structural change and human development. Some essential points are outlined by Evans (1995), Putnam (2000) and Benkler (2006), but an in-depth review on the complex institutional effects on the creation of trust, democratic structures and proactive behaviour is beyond the scope and purpose of this book. It surely has its own future research agenda. Analysing and connecting the 'Sen meets Schumpeter' paradigm with the insights of Veblen (1898, 1899), North (1990), Coleman (1990), Evans (1995) and Benkler (2006) seems to be a promising path for future research.

5.1.3 Social capital in immigrant and minority groups

An example of where networks have important positive and negative effects on human development and agency are the social networks within minority groups. Social capital within minority or immigrant groups provides the means with which to open up small ventures, draw upon credits, help, labour and demand from the community, and/or access employment, education or initial housing. Portes and Sensenbrenner (1993, p. 1326) distinguish between four sources of social capital:

- value introjections and socialization into consensually established beliefs (Durkheim 1893; Parsons and Smelser 1956);
- the norm of reciprocity in face-to-face interactions (Simmel 1908; Blau 1964);
- bounded solidarity and situational reactive sentiments (Marx and Engels 1848); and
- enforceable trust through particularistic rewards and sanctions linked to group membership (Weber 1922; Aldrich and Zimmer 1986).

Both value introjections and reciprocity transactions are vital for generalized trust between individuals. Value introjections refer to values that are given to us by our parents and society. They often unconsciously affect how we feel and act and imply that our behaviour will be based on things other than sheer greed and selfishness. The norm of reciprocity allows for the exchange of both material goods and social intangibles, without a higher group morality, but based on the mutual expectations that valued items such as favours and information are given and received (Portes and Sensenbrenner 1993).

Bounded solidarity and enforceable trust can be a distinctive feature within minority and immigrant groups. Groups that confront common problems, discrimination or exploitation can develop bounded solidarity. They show solidarity towards the group members, but not necessarily to people outside the group. For example, discrimination based on phenotypical or cultural differences can lead to community members supporting each other altruistically, having shared goals as well as showing preferences for co-ethnics in economic transactions (Portes and Sensenbrenner 1993, p. 1345). The functioning of group solidarity and support, furthermore, depends on the degree to which trust is enforceable – how the violation of commonly shared expectations or norms is sanctioned by the community. Members of minority groups are often afraid of losing their good standing in their particular community and the threat of exclusion. Enforceable trust is based upon a community's monitoring and sanctioning capacity, but also upon the availability of in-group economic resources and the lack of outside social and economic opportunities.

Enforceable trust within groups can lead to privileged access to economic resources and reliable expectations concerning effects of malfeasance and flexibility in economic transactions through the reduction of formal contracts (Portes and Sensenbrenner 1993, p. 1345). A typical example is the provision of loans without guarantees but based instead upon the reputation of the family of the debtors. But social networks and groups can also suffer from lock-in effects, where groups isolate themselves. Portes and Sensenbrenner (1993) outline the negative effects that can result from bounded solidarity and enforceable trust within minority and immigrant groups. The positive effects of social capital within groups can be also negative if they (a) lead to freeriders abusing community bonds and norms, (b) create levelling pressures to maintain the group characteristics and/or (c) impose restrictions on individual freedom and outside contacts. These three effects can lead to a situation where groups downgrade, rather than enable the capabilities of the people. A typical example of this phenomenon is the situation when a member of a gang deems earning excellent marks at school as being 'uncool'. It is worth noting that in the case of bounded solidarity, the feeling of togetherness and mutual help results specifically from a commonly shared adverse situation. This can lead to levelling pressures that prevents the advancement of the group and its members. Someone trying to overcome a common adverse condition that bounds a group together, for example no access to higher education or lack of income, can be marked as a careerist or renegade and be excluded (Portes and Sensenbrenner 1993). It is as a result of levelling pressures that the combination of bounded solidarity and enforceable trust can constrain learning processes, entrepreneurial action, and the introduction of novelties and qualitative changes into the group. Lock-in from outside refers to factors which force people into narrow categories and judges them based upon the groups they belong to. Sen (2006) emphasizes the limits of choices and prejudices that can result from participation in specific groups (e.g. certain religious beliefs, music tastes, political parties and/

or research interests). Sen (2006) shows that the identity of individuals is shaped by their participation in multiple different groups; however, violence is often generated through prejudices and generalizations towards group members and their behaviour. It is worth noting that this also happens between academic paradigms and/or social interest groups and hinders mutual understanding and interactive learning.

5.1.4 Social networks and inequality

Social capital has the ability to enhance as well as constrain the capabilities of the individuals and/or the group. Serageldin (1996, p. 196) describes social capital as 'the glue that holds societies together'. If there is little civic engagement, commonly shared norms, trust or reciprocity then society can disintegrate; violence increases and structural change and economic development is hampered (Putnam 2000). However, participation or inclusion in networks may not always be good for the freedom and human development of the individuals within and/ or outside of the network, for instance in the case of a drug trade network. By their very definition, social networks also tend to introduce inequalities between people and groups, because different network contacts leads to different levels of power and social capital. Sociological research shows that networks differentiate between groups and lead to different sets of preferences, choices and capabilities (e.g. Bourdieu 1983). Research on social networks illustrates that a different number of contacts and positions within a network structure have a strong influence on the role, prestige and power of the corresponding agents, be they individuals, groups, regions or countries. Indeed, networks usually have hierarchies and there may be an unequal number of connections of nodes in a network.

One well-known example of structural dependence and inequality reproduction is that of centre-periphery structures in the world economy (Singer 1949; Prebisch 1949; Wallerstein 1974). Centre-periphery structures can lead to deteriorating terms of trade for the countries that merely export primary resources to the dynamic and economically diversified centre of the global economy. Their dependence on the demand from the centre limits their bargaining power in price negotiations; thus their position within a network can lead to dependence and inequality. It is important to note, however, that any social system (be it large countries and the global economy or a small families and friends circle), require some type of social organization, which almost by definition leads to different social roles and the existence of hierarchies at least within different activities. In the words of Georg Simmel (1908, cited in Blau 1964, p. 168):

> Any social order requires a hierarchy of superordinations and subordinations, even if only for technical reasons. Therefore, equality in the sense of justice can only be the exact correspondence of personal qualification with position in this hierarchy. Yet, this harmonious correspondence is in principle impossible for the very simple reason that there always are more persons qualified for superior positions than there are superior positions.

In other words, complete equality in societies is virtually impossible, or at least impracticable, because the bigger a society becomes, the more inequality in the network position and power emerges. Four friends may have virtually equal rights and power within their small circle. A hundred and fifty persons may form a fairly equalitarian society, but the larger the society gets the more organizations are necessary and the more hierarchies emerge, in which different people have different positions and power over the network. These hierarchies and power inequalities introduce competition, as typically more people may be willing and/or are capable of fulfilling powerful roles in the network management. In addition, the heterogeneity of capabilities, traits, luck, roles and the inheritance of individuals lead to inequality in the embeddedness of individuals in social networks. Conversely, the embeddedness in social networks affects the opportunities, choices and capability formation of the individuals. Complete network equality seems to be virtually impossible in large networks. Essentially it would mean that every single person would need to know everybody else or have exactly the same access to information and power over their social network. This is a rather unrealistic scenario, considering the millions of people with different interests, desires, skills and social contacts.

This tendency towards an unequal distribution of power in large networks requires an ethical debate about distributional justice and the equality of initial opportunities resulting in political and societal actions that enable the agency of all citizens and prevents socially unacceptable injustice. While this is beyond the scope of this book, the structural tendency for inequality and the hierarchies within large networks should be taken into account. Research on large natural, social and physical networks (such as the World Wide Web, power grids citation networks and innovation networks) show a power law distribution in the number of contacts of the elements (nodes) in the network (Albert and Barabasi 2002). This means that most nodes (e.g. researcher, web pages, Facebook members) have relatively few links (e.g. social contacts, citations) whereas some nodes (called hubs) have many contacts. This of course leads to inequality in access to information and power over information flow and prestige. Empirical research shows that many large networks are scale free (Barabasi and Albert 1999; Albert and Barabasi 2002), meaning that there is no typical number of linkages and that some hubs connect the network and make a fast transmission within the network possible. Scale-free networks go on to show a low probability of systemic failure and a faster information flow than random networks. If failures occur at random, the likelihood that the network disaggregates is very low. Even if a small number of hubs fail, the system remains connected. The simultanous failure of all hubs in a large scale free network as a result of random causes, errors, or disasters is very low. However, targeted simultaneous attacks on all key hubs could easily disrupt the entire network breaks it into pieces. The robustness against random failure and fast information diffusion seem to be a main reason why many physical network structures in the real world (including both physical and social networks) show a scale-free attribute (Albert and Barabasi 2002).

Researchers from physics have explained the emergence of such scale free characteristics and power law distributions in large networks by preferential attachment and 'success-breeds-success' mechanisms (de Solla Price 1965; Merton 1968; Barabasi and Albert 1999). Nodes with many links have a higher probability of getting more links. Or conversely, the probability of new nodes connecting with nodes that are already highly connected is higher than that of connecting with nodes that have few links. This is also happening in societies, where network effects tend to create stars, be it in science, life style, politics or any other field of human life. In most cases the effect is partly associated with the intrinsic quality of the nodes (e.g. skills, sociability etc.); however, to a significant extent it is a network effect. For example, film stars, internet companies, local leaders or scientists not only become successful due to the quality of their work, but also because of the fact that people know them. Then the diversity of network contacts enables these popular nodes to access more resources, learn and upgrade their capabilities. This leads to 'the rich-get-richer' mechanisms and endogenous inequality reproduction.

Thus network structures and dynamics, such as preferential attachment, have a strong influence on the evolution and distribution of choices, opportunities and capability upgrading within a system and between individuals. The intrinsic reproduction of inequality through network dynamics has both positive and negative implications. The same negative implications of varying power and capabilities may be partly positive in that they create a fast information flow as well as introducing competition and fighting for position/social struggle, which leads to innovation and socioeconomic change, a crucial driver of capability expansion. In social market economies the constant competitive struggles (e.g. between unions and employees, capitalists and philanthropists), as well as the natural force of people cooperating, is an essential driver of social innovation and economic, technological and societal progress. This constant interplay between competition and cooperation leads to higher economic specialization as well as variety of choices and opportunities, higher average incomes and better education and health. The problem is how these outcomes of progress are distributed between different people and groups. The initial position of individuals in a network determines their capabilities to contribute, adapt and gain from the outcome of the creative destruction processes of the socioeconomic environment they are living in. From a human, ethical and also economic perspective, however, a high level of inequality can have negative effects on long-run economic and human development, leading to risk-aversion, a lack of aggregated demand and demand multipliers, corruption and nepotism, under- and over-representation of the interests of particular groups, a lack of trust, social instability and crime. For reasons of both justice and human development, but also for better system functioning and knowledge flow, policy makers need to make great efforts to connect people to the networks of information and power. Access to ICT and the establishment of democratic structures, among other things, are essential policy measures that can impede social exclusion, reduce harmful levels of inequality and foster societal progress and human development.

5.2 Social networks and innovation

Schumpeter (1954) claimed that economic sociology, along with economic history, economic statistics and economic theory, is a fundamental field of economics. He argued against viewing individuals as 'mere clotheslines on which to hang propositions of economic logic' (Schumpeter 1954, p. 854). Consequently, taking the heterogeneous and bounded rational character of agents into account and understanding the crucial role of their interactions for innovation is at the core of Neo-Schumpeterian research approaches (Hanusch and Pyka 2007b). Innovation is considered to be an interactive and cumulative learning process (Lundvall 1992; Pyka 1999) in which multiple agents from public and private institutions (e.g. companies, employees, clients, researchers, state workers) exchange information and learn from each other. Despite the general perception of entrepreneurs being individual heroes, they are deeply embedded and need to create social networks (e.g. Grebel *et al.* 2003; Dahl and Sorenson 2009). Furthermore, innovation and creative destruction processes change the economic system and the modes of interactions and the roles of the different agents. Three key network-related issues in Neo-Schumpeterian research are social capital and entrepreneurship, innovation networks and commuting entrepreneurs.

5.2.1 Social capital and entrepreneurship

Social capital is a key resource in people's agency and their capacity to engage in entrepreneurial action. Entrepreneurs need to form and draw upon social networks to have access to critical factors such as information, finance, initial demand and social backing (Aldrich and Zimmer 1986; Johannison 1988; Hoang and Antoncic 2003; Casson and Della Giusta 2007). Strong ties (Coleman 1988, 1990) such as kinship and networks of close friends are essential for an individual's success in underdeveloped settings and for any venture undertaken. In developing countries, access to finance and the initial step of distribution are both often achieved through close family members and friends. It is only in the later stages, once the entrepreneurs are successful, that the importance of market interaction with unfamiliar customers becomes apparent.

Social networks affect the perceived desirability and feasibility of entrepreneurial action. The desire and ability of individuals to introduce novelties into the local production system depend on their own skills and intrinsic motivation, as well as on their social network (Liñán and Santos 2007). The desires and occupational activities of family members, friends and other social contacts influence the preferences and activities of the individuals, for example their desire for agency. If people have more entrepreneurial friends, they also tend to be more active, owing to a higher perceived desirability and feasibility of entrepreneurial action (e.g. Liñán and Santos 2007). The embeddedness of entrepreneurs does not just appear in economic space, but also in public and social space. For example, the capacity for building up networks of support and action is essential for the success of social entrepreneurs (Bornstein 2004). Social entrepreneurs introduce new structures, coordination and networks which empower other people and lead to new capabilities and choices for individuals (e.g. for healthcare, education or production).

5.2.2 Innovation networks

Social capital is also one of the main ingredients of innovation networks, and hence of interactive learning, innovation and structural change. This applies to R&D collaboration in global frontier research, as well as to local teams and inter-actions between, for instance, micro-entrepreneurs, microfinance institutions and consultants trying to introduce changes into the local environment. Innovation networks affect human development in multiple ways, such as through the creation of knowledge, new products, services and occupations and by causing changes in the economic structure and organization.

Modern innovation research identifies innovation as a collective and cumulative process (Freeman 1987; Lundvall 1988; Pyka 1999; Pyka *et al.* 2007; Pyka and Scharnhorst 2009). An agent's network of contacts determines the information that agent (e.g. an individual, a company or a community) can access, use, diffuse and recombine. For this reason, networks are crucial for learning, entrepreneurship and innovation (Grebel *et al.* 2003). It is worth noting that Schumpeter (1912) did not use the word 'innovation' in his theory of economic development but referred to new combinations leading to new products, processes, markets, organizations and inputs. This definition and wording goes hand in hand with other influential work in classical political economy as well as work in evolutionary economics that highlight that innovation and development are typically built upon previous experiences and knowledge of the agents (List 1841; Nelson and Winter 1982). Neo-Schumpeterian economics and complexity research highlights the fact that technological and economic development follows evolutionary paths within complex systems in which multiple agents interact, learn from each other, cooperate and compete (Nelson and Winter 1982; David 1985; Dosi *et al.* 1988; Arthur 1994, 1999). In an increasingly complex world, no single individual or firm is able to keep track of all the different types of technological advances, existing problems and solutions, but must draw upon networks of specialised partners (Pyka 2002). This is the case for global companies, but it is also important for people at the local level. The underlying argument is that interaction and mutual learning allow actors to discover new combinations of existing knowledge, find new solutions to known problems and identify new areas and markets for technological advance (Schumpeter 1912).

Regarding innovation in less developed regions, the focus has been on the importance of endogenous technological capability upgrading and the proper absorption of external knowledge (e.g. Rabellotti and Schmitz 1999; Juma *et al.* 2001; Vázquez-Barquero 2002). Both external and internal linkages matter and need to be fostered to promote sustainable endogenous development and fruitful embeddedness in national and global systems. Technology transfer from industrialized to developing countries can be a useful factor for economic development, but is not enough alone and can even lead to structural dependence and underdevelopment if no proper endogenous technological upgrading takes place (Myrdal 1957; Patel 1974). The awareness of missing knowledge and the local absorptive capacity must be advanced through applied learning-by-doing, using and solving activities (Arocena and Sutz 2005; Evers *et al.* 2006). Often it is precisely the awareness of missing knowledge and critical problems that allows us to advance. If technological products are just considered black boxes (e.g. donated computers for poor communities, a hydraulic water pump installed by external agents) without the local population having any knowledge about the processes, usage and possible problems with the product – any type of difficulty – will cause further demand for external help or the obsolescence of the imported artefacts. However, when the people have knowledge of the constitution and the functioning of the product and processes, they may be able to innovate and adapt the products and services to local needs themselves (Arocena and Sutz 2005). Therefore access of individuals to knowledge and how they are embedded in social networks are critical. Most case studies on endogenous development, local clusters and inno-vation systems in less advanced countries mention the crucial role of interactive learning, but tend to concentrate on agglomeration effects and the local top-down institutional setups (e.g. Cassiolato *et al.* 2003). Studies on agricultural innovation in less advanced regions have focused mostly on the qualitative aspects of spe-cific cases and technologies, or on the institutional aspects at the national/sectoral level (Omamo and Lynam 2003; Hall *et al.* 2006; World Bank 2006, 2008). Only recently have local structural features and the embeddedness of heterogeneous agents within networks of techno-economic relations received more attention (Giuliani and Bell 2005; Monge *et al.* 2008; Arora 2009; Spielman *et al.* 2011). Within clusters there is typically no 'free floating knowledge in the air' available to everyone (e.g. Breschi and Lissoni 2001), but the agents have significantly diverse and unequally distributed access to knowledge and absorptive capacities (Giuliani and Bell 2005). Especially in developing countries there is often a large gap between the technological capabilities and network contacts of medium and large enterprises on the one hand and small entrepreneurs and smallholder farmers on the other. Owing to the very limited resources and absorptive capacities of the agents in underdeveloped settings, linkages and information exchanges between advanced and less advanced agents are rather scarce; therefore one key issue in any attempt to foster development in such settings is the promotion of educa-tion and infrastructure for those agents with fewer network contacts and lower absorptive capacities. However, a better understanding of the innovative behav-iour and social embeddedness of micro-entrepreneurs is also necessary, as is an understanding of how novelties are introduced in less advanced regions and how innovation can contribute to and is driven by human agency.

5.2.3 *Knowledge circulation through commuting entrepreneurs*

An inspiring approach towards promoting economic win-win situations and inter-active learning between individuals from industrialized and developing countries is visible in the so-called commuting entrepreneurs. The international networks of migrants, often called diaspora networks, referring to, for example, the network of Chinese migrants around the world, can provide critical resources such as information, finance, housing, social backing support and remittances (The Economist 2011). They can also be a major source of knowledge flow and contribute to intercultural integration. They can furthermore lead to positive effects not just for the rich industrialized centres of the global economy (like Europe or North America), but can also be beneficial for developing countries (like China and India).

Saxenian (2006) discusses the old core/periphery model of economic development with an approach which is new in regards to the role of individuals who transfer competences from the core to the periphery regions, whom she labelled 'commuting entrepreneurs'. Knowledge transfers take place in innovation networks spawned between the core and the periphery by these individuals and their economic engagement in both regions. Commuting entrepreneurs immigrate to core regions to be academically trained and to create their first business and social networks in core regions. Later in their career they either stay in the core regions or return to their home regions in the periphery. In both cases they trigger the development of prolific network structures for knowledge and socioeconomic transactions and thereby significantly push development in the home regions. They can contribute to transfer of technological knowledge into their regions, contribute to structural change and economic competitiveness, create jobs and promote social innovations. Most importantly, commuting entrepreneurs and diaspora networks can contribute to the reduction of economic and technological inequality between different countries in the global economy.

In the traditional core/periphery model, new technologies emerge in highly industrialized core countries that combine their highly skilled workforces and high per capita incomes to develop new markets for innovations. The success in periphery countries strongly depends on these achievements, in a trickling-down fashion. These regions are destined to remain followers because cutting-edge skills remain in the companies and universities in the core. In contrast to the established core/periphery model of economic development, Saxenian's approach has to be considered as being much more appropriate to the contemporary situation, reflecting the changed conditions characteristic of knowledge-based economies, namely cheap transportation costs and easy coordination over long distances by means of modern information and communication technologies. The network organization of knowledge-based economies strongly contributes to the mutual transfer of knowledge and competences, thereby positively contributing to a knowledge-driven catching-up by the periphery regions. There has been considerable discussion on the role of foreign direct investment and how to attract MNEs (e.g. Dachs and Pyka 2009) to periphery regions so that they can benefit from knowledge spillovers and thereby trigger economic development in these regions. Saxenian (2006) shows that commuting entrepreneurs can play an even more pronounced role in the catching-up processes, compared with MNEs. In the past, technologies typically started diffusing to periphery regions only after they achieved a certain maturity. With increasing knowledge intensity and transformations of the world economy, commuting entrepreneurs can clearly mitigate this delaying mechanism and support an increasing number of regions worldwide in managing catching-up processes more successfully.

5.3 Summary of positive and negative effects of social networks

Social capital and SNA can help to create bridges between the human development and innovation and structural change approaches, by providing a theoretical and methodological framework to study the multiple effects of socioeconomic systems on human development and how positive and negative network affects may change over time. Networks have profound impacts on the agency and choices of the individuals – what, when and with whom they learn and in which sectors and occupations they work. Table 5.1 summarizes some of the main positive and negative effects of social networks. The list is certainly not complete, but aims to show some of fields of study where social network thinking can be beneficial for research on human development and structural change, and where positive and negative effects of social networks are often closely related to each other.

Table 5.1 The effects of social networks on human development

Positive and negative sides of networks	
Positive	*Negative*
Mutual help and capabilities expansion within social groups (e.g. friends, family)	Nepotism and corruption
Group capabilities	Lock-in effects and inter group prejudices
Division of tasks and social organization, making a system more than the sum of its elements	Hierarchies and inequality reproduction through network mechanism
Access to information and external capabilities	Inequality in the access to information and external capabilities
Interactive learning and collective innovation	Cumulative advantages/ disadvantages of different groups in the innovation race

Human development and innovation policies should take these multiple positive and negative effects into account. One key task for development policies is to prevent and overcome some of the negative effects of social networks and foster the positive ones. For instance, participatory approaches to development or providing the poor with the access and capabilities to make use of information and communication technologies can overcome some of the negative and foster the positive effects. SNA can help to reveal beneficial and pernicious social structures and dynamics. In the next section, some main SNA techniques are discussed.

5.4 Introduction to social network analysis

SNA studies the content, structure and evolution of networks of social relations. It provides a wide range of options for measuring and visualizing the structures of networks and the roles of individuals within them (Wassermann and Faust 1994; Albert and Barabasi 2002; De Nooy *et al.* 2005; Hanneman and Riddle 2005; Borgatti *et al.* 2009). SNA provides techniques to reveal the structural embeddedness and the roles of individuals, which common research methods tend to overlook (Borgatti *et al.* 2009). Network measures such as centrality, composition and cohesion can help to: (a) reveal the distribution of social choices across a population; (b) measure to what extent there is cohesion or fragmentation in a socioeconomic system; (c) find out how diverse the access of people to external capabilities is; and (d) gauge the equality of economic, political and social power distributed within a social system. Network analysis, furthermore, provides the means to make use of our geographical intelligence to see structures which influence human behaviour and can partly explain the inequalities between different people or groups. For these reasons, SNA offers valuable theoretical insights and analytical tools for understanding the interrelations between the network position of composition of individuals, their capabilities and functionings. The embeddedness of people within social networks has substantial implications for their freedom and the inequality of opportunities and power within complex socioeconomic systems. The following section explores some basic concepts and measures of SNA.

5.4.1 Basics of network analysis

A network is constituted of nodes (e.g. A, B, C in Figure 5.1) and ties between them. The network in Figure 5.1 has two ties – one directed tie from node A to node C, and one reciprocal tie between A and B.

We can distinguish between directed and undirected network graphs. A directed graph considers the directions of the relations between two nodes (e.g. information flow from A to C); an undirected graph assumes that all relations are reciprocal. SNA is based on mathematical graph theory and, to formalize network relations, relational matrixes are required, in which all the agents are recorded in rows and columns. The nodes in the rows could be considered as the transmitters, the nodes in the columns as the receivers. If all relations in a network are reciprocal, the underlying matrix is symmetrical; if not, the matrix is asymmetric. The example in Figure 5.1 can be recorded in a simple matrix presented in Table 5.2.

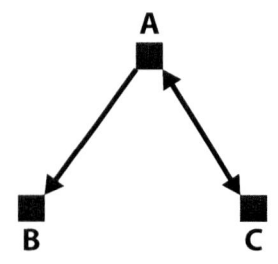

Figure 5.1 A simple network

Table 5.2 A simple network matrix

	A	B	C
A	0	1	1
B	1	0	0
C	0	0	0

Nodes A and B have a reciprocal relation with each other, whereas A and C do not. For example, information or money might flow from A to C, but not from C to A. B and C do not have a direct link with each other. The strength of the relations can be determined by giving the relation $x_{row} y_{column}$ different values and/or drawing the edges of the graph in different widths or colours. Attributes of the nodes (e.g. income, education, centrality) can be visualized by using different colours and/or making them different sizes. Therefore attribution matrixes can be created with the nodes on the vertical and the attributes on the horizontal axis; this is a familiar form known from statistical and econometric analysis, where the cases are placed in the rows and the variables in the columns. From this simple basis, we can produce complex applications with which to analyse: (a) the structure of entire networks; (b) the position and role of single nodes (or individuals) within networks; and (c) the composition of the ties and network partners of the individuals, the so-called ego-networks.

5.4.2 *Network structure measures*

The structures of networks in a socioeconomic system have decisive implications for the absorption and diffusion of knowledge and the distribution of power and social choices within the system. Theoretical and empirical evidence suggests that the topology and the evolution of real world networks are governed by robust organizing principles such as preferential attachment, small world phenomena and scale-free attributes (Watts and Strogatz 1998; Barabasi and Albert 1999; Albert and Barabasi 2002). Furthermore, as shown below, an analysis can be made of the cohesion and centralization of systems and to what degree subgroups and cliques within networks are found. This results in a set of standard measures of network structures, also shown below.

Network density (N_D) describes the overall level of linkages among actors. It is the number of actors who are connected to each other, expressed as a percentage of the maximum possible number of connected actors.

$$N_D = \frac{\sum_{i=1}^{n} \sum_{j=1}^{n} X_{ijk}}{n \cdot (n-1)}, \text{ for } i \neq j \neq k$$

where $n \cdot (n-1)$ is the total number of ties possible and k the relation being studied.

Network cohesion (N_C) is calculated as the number of ties between two actors compared to all possible dyads in the network. High network cohesion reflects a high degree of homogeneity within the network, since a high percentage of relations between two different actors are realized.

$$N_C = \frac{\sum_{i=1}^{n} \sum_{j=1}^{n} (X_{ij} + X_{ji})}{\dfrac{n \cdot (n-1)}{2}}$$

The average path length l_G measures the average of the length of the shortest paths (geodesic distance d) between all pairs of vertices v_i and v_j in a network graph G with n vertices (Albert and Barabasi 2002).

$$l_G = \frac{1}{n \cdot (n-1)} \sum_{i,j} d(v_i, v_j)$$

The average path length indicates how fast information can be spread within the system; in other words, it shows how many steps an agent needs on average to reach all other actors. As a result, it provides a proxy for the cohesion of the system. It can indicate the cohesion of a social network as well as the speed with which resources can be reached or information can be spread within a network. Innovation may change the average path length and speed of knowledge diffusion. For example, the ICT revolution led to significantly shorter path lengths for obtaining valuable information from and for the people who were connected. It opened up new opportunities but also created new potential threats for the poor. Being connected to the Internet provides an individual with access to valuable new information, the ability to access education from a distance and so forth. However, at the same time, not being connected (as a large percentage of people in developing countries currently are) means an individual may suffer further social exclusion and comparative disadvantages.

Clustering refers to the fact that in many larger networks there are subgroups bound together, forming groups (such as cliques and circles of friends) whose members frequently interact with each other. The degree to which nodes tend to cluster together can be measured by the clustering coefficient. This coefficient measures the extent to which tightly knit subgroups with dense and transitive connections exist within a network. The clustering coefficient for the whole network is the average of the clustering coefficients of all vertices.

$$C_{Network} = \frac{1}{n} \sum_{i} C_i$$

Watts and Strogatz (1998) illustrated that in many large networks (e.g. power grids, networks of movie actors) high clustering coefficients are found together with short average path lengths. In other words, 'we move in tight circles yet we are all bound together by remarkably short chains' (Strogatz 2003). This has fundamental implications for knowledge diffusion and the social capital of individuals. Information can be spread quite quickly throughout the network but in most cases the travel path of information depends on certain actors who connect the subgroups. These agents can be called brokers or hubs and have greater control and power over the flow of resources and knowledge than other members of the network. Clustering may have positive and negative implications for the freedom of actors and the groups of which they are members. On the one hand, it can provide the agents with valuable social capital which they can draw upon (e.g. Woolcock and Narayan 2000), but on the other hand it may lead to further inequalities and negative differentiation between different social groups and circles (e.g. Bourdieu 1983). Furthermore, brokerage between groups may provide the bridging agents with greater power and thus introduce interpersonal inequalities.

Degree distribution measures the difference in the number of contacts of nodes within a network. In a network, different nodes have different numbers of contacts, some having more or fewer than others (i.e. degree of the node). Barabasi and Albert have shown in several works that the degree distribution in large real world networks (e.g. protein and citation networks, power grids and several social networks) follows a power law distribution (Barabasi and Albert 1999; Albert and Barabasi 2002). This means that these networks have large numbers of nodes with few connections and a few nodes have many connections. Because there is no typical number of connections per node, these networks are considered to be scale-free or scale-invariant. This has crucial implications for inequality, as the actors with many connections have a larger set of opportunities to access resources and information than the actors with just a few links. Often the latter are dependent on the former, highly connected and bridging nodes, which have greater power over a system's resources and knowledge flows.

Barabasi and Albert (1999) argued that preferential attachment processes lead to the emergence of scale-free networks (a process that can lead to endogenous reproduction of inequalities). Preferential attachment refers to the understanding that new nodes (e.g. new webpages) tend to attach with a higher probability to nodes that have many links (e.g. established webpages) than to nodes with few links. This creates a 'rich-get-richer' mechanism, as the nodes which already have many linkages tend to receive exponentially more new linkages than the majority of weakly connected nodes. This is associated with a highly unequal distribution of power in the system, where a few nodes exercise considerable control over the network relations (e.g. information flows) and many nodes are dependent on them.

5.4.3 Node centrality measures

The structural analysis of networks provides valuable insights into systemic patterns and mechanisms of inequality and inequality reproduction. Nevertheless, these types of analyses say little about the impact of the type and strength of the relations and the position of single individuals within the network. Lin (1999, p. 36) points out that the network position is a key element of identifying the social capital of individuals. A principal technique for measuring the power and social capital of individuals in a network is to calculate their centrality (Borgatti *et al.* 1998; Hanneman and Riddle 2005). According to the concept of centrality, the actors who are most embedded in the network and/or most strongly control the flow of knowledge have a central role in the network. In contrast to the so-called ego-network measures (e.g. homophily and composition of ties), measures of centrality require complete samples (Borgatti *et al.* 1998). Four essential measures of centrality are degree centrality, eigenvector centrality, betweenness centrality and closeness centrality.

- *Degree centrality* measures the number of direct connections a node $i \in n$ has to the other nodes of the sample (C = centrality; n = node; d = degree).

$$C_D(n_i) = d(n_i)$$

  It is assumed that the more connections a node has, the more central it is. Hence degree centrality shows how well connected the individuals are and can be interpreted as representing the agent's direct influence (Borgatti *et al.* 2008).
- *Eigenvector centrality* measures the extent to which a node is connected to the well-connected. It can be considered as a measure of popularity and power and tends to identify centres of large cliques (Borgatti *et al.* 2008). A node has a high eigenvector score if it is connected to many nodes that are themselves well connected. In other words, a node has a high eigenvector centrality if it has many contacts with other central players. Given an adjacency matrix A, the centrality of node i (denoted c_i) is given by

$$c_i = a^* \sum (A_{ij} c_j)$$

  where a is a parameter. The centrality of each vertex is determined by the centrality of the vertices to which it is connected. The parameter a is required to give the equations a non-trivial solution and is, therefore, the reciprocal of an eigenvalue (Borgatti *et al.* 2002).
- *Betweenness centrality* measures the number of times a node i falls along the shortest (geodesic) path (g) between two other actors j and k.

$$C_B(n_i) = \sum_{j<k} g_{jk}(n_i)/g_{jk}$$

  Actors with high betweenness centrality link together actors who are otherwise unconnected, creating opportunities for the exploitation of information and control benefits (Borgatti *et al.* 1998). These actors are often called information brokers, intermediaries or gatekeepers. They are of great importance to the network because of their influence on the flow of information and the consistency of the network.

- *Closeness centrality* measures the distance between one node and all the others. To obtain a value for it, the sum of all the shortest (or geodesic) paths from node *i* to all other nodes in the network must first be calculated.

$$C_c(n_i) = \left[\sum_{j=1}^{g} d(n_i, n_j) \right]^{-1}$$

A node with a high closeness centrality can rapidly access information from the whole network. Conversely it may take a long time before that information arrives at nodes with a low closeness centrality. Hence closeness centrality also measures how long information takes to get to the node.

5.4.4 Characteristics of ego-networks

Ego-network measures can help to gain a qualitative insight into the composition (e.g. diversity, strengths and quality) of the contacts of a person. The standard network measures presented in the previous section provide us with knowledge of network structures and positions, but not with qualitative knowledge on the composition, types and values of network ties. Certainly the characteristics of the partners (e.g. education, income, health and literacy) are crucial to people's relational capabilities, choices and desires and the information they can access. Typical ego-network measures are the composition, heterogeneity and homophily of their personal network (see Hanneman and Riddle 2005; Borgatti 2009).

These measures can be used to infer the relational capabilities of quality of the personal network of the individuals. For example, the ego-network composition measures the proportion of the network partners with specific characteristics and the average values and distribution of those characteristics. These specific characteristics could be literacy, health, marital status, employment, age or income of the network partners. The ego-network heterogeneity measures the diversity of an actor's contacts and the ego-networks homophily the extent to which actors tend to have ties with actors who are similar to themselves (e.g. same sector, technology field, nationality, gender, age or education). Hence, SNA techniques provide a wide range of tools to scrutinize how capabilities and functionings are distributed across a social system, how they are influenced by network structures and how the composition of the individual's network contacts affects their agency, choices and well-being. The next empirical section gives an example of how social capital and innovation of peasant farmers can be measured. The case study illustrates how the network centrality of smallholder farmers in southeast Peru affects their capabilities to innovate and introduce structural changes into their villages.

5.5 Case study in Peru: Measuring peasants' social capital and innovation[1]

A substantial body of literature on technological learning and innovation networks of peasant farmers (e.g. Foster and Rosenzweig 1995; Monge *et al.* 2008; Conley and Udry 2010; Spielman *et al.* 2011) – which itself is based on the seminal work of Everett Rogers (1962) on the diffusion of innovation – has recently emerged. Taking social networks into account, it provides not just the means to understand how new technologies are adopted by the farmers and are diffused in the local system, but also opens up multiple opportunities of studying the relations between social networks, innovation and human agency. It must be highlighted that the capabilities to recombine a diversity of information and resources to innovate does not just matter for leading high-tech companies, but also equally for millions of smallholders and micro-entrepreneurs across the world aiming to make their living and expand their business success. In recent decades, significant progress and voluminous research has been made in the measurement and understanding of frontier innovation in highly industrialized settings. However, it is equally important to put emphasis on the processes of learning and the introduction of novelties in less developed regions. According to the World Bank (2008) approximately one in four people in the world, 1.5 billion people in 2007, live in smallholder households in developing countries. Urbanization and the percentage of the population living in cities are increasing, but nevertheless a large number of people make their living from small-scale farming and can benefit from having better capabilities to learn and introduce novelties. One key factor to advance in this respect is the access to information about technologies and the access to technical advice and finance through social contacts. Thereby both other farmers and agents in the region, external contacts and often NGOs or governmental institutions promoting agricultural development all play a crucial role.

This section, a collaboration with Atilio Arata (Hartmann and Arata 2011), aims to contribute to a better understanding of the social networks of farmers and their capabilities to innovate by addressing three crucial questions about the measurement and promotion of endogenous and local development:

1 How can we measure social capital and innovation in poor agricultural communities?
2 What is the impact of external agents (e.g. NGOs) on the local information flows and social structures?
3 Does centrality in local information networks correlate with the innovativeness of the smallholders?

SNA allows us to analyse the position, role and embeddedness of individuals in social structures and innovation networks and is therefore a suitable technique for investigating these questions (Giuliani and Bell 2005; Monge *et al.* 2008; Spielman *et al.* 2011). It helps to examine different dimensions of the social capital and innovative behaviour of wine producers in the local production and innovation system of Cháparra, a small agricultural valley in the south of Peru.

5.5.1 Social capital and innovation in smallholder agriculture

There is expanding interest in regional innovation systems in developing countries (e.g. Rabellotti and Schmitz 1999; Mytelka 2000; Cassiolato *et al.* 2003; Schmitz 2004; Giuliani *et al.* 2005; Arora 2009), and an increasing number of studies have investigated the role that agro-businesses and agricultural systems of innovation play in the development of economies (Hall *et al.* 2006; World Bank 2006). Several works, published by the International Food Policy Research Institute, demonstrate progress in measuring rural innovation networks, revealing the relations between social capital and innovation and studying the capacity of smallholders in less developed regions to introduce novelties into their local agricultural production systems (Monge *et al.* 2008; Spielman *et al.* 2011). It must be stressed that many innovative activities and high levels of creativity can be found in local agricultural communities all over the world (e.g. Mytelka 2000; Srinivas and Sutz 2008). Driven by scarcity, access to microcredit and external intervention (e.g. by development projects), many novelties are introduced into local agricultural systems, leading to new products, processes, inputs and new forms of organizing productive activities.

It has already been noted that social network structures are important in determining an individual's capacity to engage in entrepreneurial activity and innovation (Aldrich and Zimmer 1986; Hoang and Antoncic 2003; Grebel *et al.* 2003). In contrast to the common perspective that entrepreneurs are lone heroes, they are in fact embedded in social network structures which influence their desires and capabilities to introduce novelties into the local production system (Liñán and Santos 2007). Entrepreneurs need to form and draw upon social networks to have access to critical factors such as information and finance (Aldrich *et al.* 1987; Casson and Della Giusta 2007; Dahl and Sorenson 2009). This is true for developed settings, but even more so for underdeveloped regions, where people are still largely reliant on each other for help in their personal goals. Due to institutional weaknesses and instability in underdeveloped settings, strong ties (Coleman 1988, 1990) such as kinship and close friendship networks are essential features for an individual's success in any venture undertaken. Social networks profoundly affect the type and direction of individual learning activities and individuals' capacity to engage in entrepreneurial action and introduce novelties into their local innovation system (Rogers 1962; Mytelka 2000; Giuliani *et al.* 2005; Giuliani and Bell 2005). Studies on innovation systems and clusters have made increasing use of SNA techniques to investigate the structural features of development, learning patterns and the role of individuals within local and global innovation networks (e.g. Giuliani and Bell 2005; Cantner and Graf 2006; Pyka and Scharnhorst 2009). Network analysis allows for a better distinction and analysis of the importance of local and international network relations and the feedbacks between them (e.g. Giuliani and Bell 2005). A central point in these concepts is that knowledge is not evenly distributed and freely available within clusters and regional innovation systems, but is highly dependent on individuals and their specific skills (human capital) and social relations (Breschi and Lissoni 2001; Grebel *et al.* 2003; Giuliani and Bell 2005).

5.5.2 Cháparra

Our case region Cháparra is an agricultural valley in Peru. The Cháparra river valley lies in the dry landscape of southern Peru and descends from a height of over 3,500 metres in the high Andes towards the Pacific Ocean. As for the general level of socioeconomic development, Cháparra has a medium level of human development (0.6 on a 0 to 1 scale). Life expectancy is around 68 years and people can expect to learn to read and write and will earn approximately €130 a month (PNUD-Peru 2006). Most people are involved in agriculture, trading and informal mining activities (Arata and Toro 2005; Arata 2007; Arata 2008; MINAG 2007). Grape and wine production has been of great importance to the local economy for many centuries. Raimondi (1929), in his travel notes from 1863, mentions a prosperous wine industry in Cháparra and Caravelí, which commercialized its wines and pisco (a type of brandy) in the villages of the neighbouring provinces of Paucar del Sara Sara, Parinacochas and Lucanas. According to Arata and Toro (2005), the local wine industry continued to prosper until the mid-twentieth century, but declined in the following decades in size, importance and relative technological capabilities for various reasons: (a) the boom of cattle-breeding in the 1950s, which led to alfalfa being cultivated instead of grapes; (b) excessive taxation and state control of liqueur production; and (c) civil war and interventions from both the guerrilla group Sendero Luminoso and the government military, which cut the already deteriorated commercial links with the south of Ayacucho.

Today, the total area of land used in grape and wine production is rather small, but provides a living for a significant number of people in Cháparra. Many of those who left the valley during the civil war are now coming back, meaning that the population is increasing again, and with it agricultural production as well (INEI 1993, 2005; Arata and Toro 2005; Arata 2008). Cháparra is a useful case because it shares some features typical of many poor agricultural communities around the world, such as: (a) dominance of smallholder farmers; (b) scarcity of water; (c) small-scale production, in this case of grapes, pears, avocados and alcoholic products (wine and liquors); (d) incidences of civil war, negatively affecting levels of mutual trust; and (e) the presence of external agents who hold considerable influence over the local system.

However, there are also limitations to be considered: learning from the case of Chaparra has the same limitations as all local case studies – each case has its own peculiarities, path dependency and embeddedness in particular networks, providing rich in-depth information, but also making it difficult to compare them and develop something like best practice. For some years, NGOs and governmental institutions (such as SENASA, the Peruvian national state agency for agricultural health) have fostered technological upgrading and the prevention of crop plagues and diseases (Arata and Toro 2005). The innovative activities in Cháparra are fairly local and certainly not at the frontier of global research and technology, but they involve learning-by-doing, local adaptation and innovation and self-discovery processes. Cháparra will probably not develop completely new techniques for the global markets in the near future, but people have introduced (sometimes autonomously, sometimes with the help of external agents) a variety of new products, processes and organizational structures which have made beneficial and significant changes within region. The farmers, for example, explore new crop varieties, fertilizers and irrigation systems, design brand names, and explore new distribution possibilities. This might not be new to the world, but it is certainly new to the local market and innovation system. Although knowledge is often introduced by external agents (such as an NGO or a governmental development agency), the learning process is usually a matter of trial and error (with new crops, production techniques, etc.) and involves cooperation with local actors and external agents. There is no systemic analysis and adaptation of existing knowledge. However, to consider the innovative activities within this and other valleys in less developed or emergent settings as mere knowledge transfers, or catching-up, would ignore or underestimate the necessity of building endogenous capabilities in producing novelties and adapting existing knowledge to the local environment (Arocena and Sutz 2005).

5.5.3 Dimensions of social capital and innovation

To reveal the correlations between social capital and innovation of small farmers a questionnaire was designed to measure and visualize various facets of social capital and network structures and the innovative behaviour of the wine-producing community. As for any case study, close cooperation with the local population and experts during the questionnaire creation was crucial to prevent measurement errors, conceptual misunderstanding and data bias. The meaning of terms, especially regarding the evaluation of social contacts, can vary significantly across cultures, which makes it crucial to have close cooperation with local farmers and experts throughout the process of gathering data (pre-test phase, adaptation, final application and analysis).

The result was a comprehensive set of 89 indicators on the innovative performance, human capital, access to finance, social capital and other socioeconomic elements of the local wine farmers. Due to the relative ease in defining the spatial and social boundaries, within a total sampling method all 47 smallholder wineries could be examined. In other words, all wine farmers in the region who sell wine could be included in the sample. The final questionnaire was distributed and collected during February 2009. The questions on social capital focused especially on the ego-networks of the farmers; however, several indicators of other dimensions (such as access to information and communication technologies, collective action and mutual assistance) were included to draw a comprehensive picture of the social structure and patterns of cooperation within the village. The general purpose of the case study was to gain an in-depth picture of specific local conditions and, at the same time, to do this in such a way that the questionnaire could be easily adapted and compared with results from other cases. For this reason, the questionnaire considered diverse aspects of social capital and innovation in wine-farming communities in south Peru. Table 5.3 gives an overview of the questionnaire dimensions.

Our measurement of social capital is essentially based on the questions and indicators proposed by researchers from the World Banks Social Capital Initiative (e.g. Grootaert *et al.* 2004). It considered questions on social networks, group assistance, collective action, access to finance and to information and communication technologies and put an emphasis on questions that provided relational data on diverse types of overlapping social networks (e.g. kinship, friends and information networks, strong and weak ties). In addition, commercial ties were included more prominently, as both the information flow and the negotiating power of the local farmers are influenced by their ties to external traders, who buy their products and sell them to external wholesalers.

The first pre-test with farmers from Acaville, a neighbouring valley in the province of Caravelí, provided useful insights that helped to improve the final questionnaire design. Several farmers did not properly understand several of the questions on social capital (e.g. on groups, associations and collective action) suggested by a standardized questionnaire applied by the World Bank to local communities all over the world (Grootaert *et al.* 2004). This again demonstrates the essential differences in the significance and meaning of terms across countries, regions and cultures. For this reason, cooperation with experts and local farmers and the adaptation of the questionnaire to the local language and cultural concepts are crucial for this type of study.

For the dimension of innovation, the questionnaire drew upon Schumpeter's typology of innovation and the suggestions in the Oslo Manual (OECD 2005) and the Bogota Manual (Jaramillo *et al.* 2001) concerning their measurement. To measure innovation, several questions on innovation in products, processes, organizations and marketing were included. Furthermore, we introduced questions on what motives smallholder households have to innovate as well as on their capacity to deal with unexpected situations, such as droughts, crop disease and price

Table 5.3 Dimensions of social capital and innovation captured in the questionnaire

Social capital	Innovation
Social networks	Product and process,
Collective action	Organization
Group assistance	Marketing
Access to ICT	Desire to innovate
Access to finance	Motives for innovation
Commercial contacts	Flexibility and prevention of unexpected situations

Sources: World Banks Social Capital Initiative (Grootaert *et al.* 2004), Oslo Manual (OECD 2005) and the Bogota Manual (Jaramillo *et al.* 2001).

fluctuations. Flexibility in unexpected situations and prevention of exogenous shocks are vital for the survival and competitiveness of any agricultural business (Arumapperuma 2006). This is especially true for smallholders in developing countries, with their smaller range of options and resources to cope with crises. The question on the motives for innovation was designed to provide us with insights into the psychological dimensions of entrepreneurial action and innovation, and give us an idea of (a) what type of entrepreneurial actions were taking place, (b) whether the farmers innovate and engage in entrepreneurial action by necessity or by opportunity (e.g. Reynolds *et al.* 2001; Liñán and Santos 2007; Gries and Naude 2010), and (c) whether they are self-motivated or influenced by external agents, or even forced by internal and external pressure. It is worth noting that the farmers did not have that much difficulty distinguishing between different types of innovation (product, process, organization etc.). They intuitively understood what innovation is and had quite similar and converging ideas about its different types. Only in two cases did they seem to significantly underestimate their own innovative performance and only in one case was the own innovation performance highly overestimated. These three cases were not consistent with the observations made by Arata (2008) and development experts working in the region. For these reasons, the data from these three agents was excluded, while the aggregated innovation performance of the agents was estimated using the Arata (2008) comparative data on innovation and technological competences in the region. To initially identify the farmers as well as to complement our dataset, the study drew upon census data (INEI 1993, 2005) and recent survey data, produced by Arata (2008), on socioeconomic and production indicators in the region. The number of direct respondents (47 including the outliers) is rather small, but it still allows us to perform a comprehensive in-depth data-based case study on the local social structures as well as the individual farmers, their technological learning and innovative behaviour.

5.5.4 Local innovation networks and the role of external agents

SNA techniques were applied to analyse the role and position of the relevant actors in the local as well as in the external technical information networks, with a special focus on the influence of external NGOs. Having knowledge and control over information flows provides people with the capabilities to learn and innovate. In particular, for farmers to progress technologically in their business activities, it is vital for them to have access to information on production and distribution processes. For this reason, Cháparra's technical information network was analysed. To gather data on the technical information networks, the smallholders were asked who they had spoken most frequently with about technical issues and who they had received valuable information from in the last five years. This would provide the relational data required for the application of SNA and graph-theoretical measures (Wasserman and Faust 1994; Borgatti *et al.* 2002, 2009; Hanneman and Riddle 2005; De Nooy *et al.* 2005) and would allow a visualization and measurement of both the network structure (e.g. cohesion) and position of the farmers (e.g. centrality of the farmers) in the local technical network. Accordingly, the questionnaire asked about strong ties with frequent interactions, because high levels of trust are necessary for fine-grained information exchanges between people (Coleman 1988), and this is particularly important in a local setting that suffered in the 1980s and 1990s from guerrilla groups and civil war. Furthermore, the question about sources of technical information probed the recognition, knowledge and power of people the farmers consider important, reliable and valuable sources of technical knowledge – and of those who are not considered so reliable.

In the case of Cháparra, a total sampling technique (comprising all wine farmers in the valley) was made and hence it was valid to apply the standard centrality measures. To analyse the role of the farmers and external agents in the local system the degree, betweenness and eigenvector centrality of the interviewed and mentioned network partners were calculated. Furthermore, to analyse the social distance that information needs to travel within the system and what impact single actors have on the technical information network, the average path length and the centralization of the system (degree, eigenvector and betweenness) was also calculated. Based upon the calculation of each actor's centrality, the network centralization indicators measure to what extent the network is dependent on a single agent.

A striking fact revealed by the analysis is the dominant role of an external NGO in the local technical information exchange network. In relation to all centrality (and key player) measures, this external agent is the most central actor in the network. It has the most ties by far and is connected to a diverse range of people. Figure 5.2 illustrates the local technical information network. It clearly shows that the bright grey nodes on the left side are much more central and strongly connected with the well-connected than the rather peripheral black nodes on the right side of the graph, and that the NGO (node 1) is by far the most central and powerful actor in the technical network.

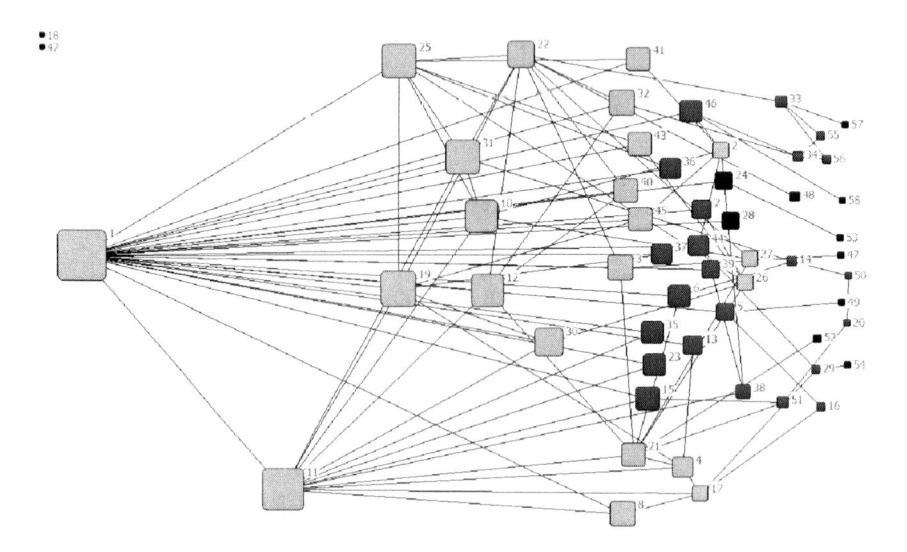

Figure 5.2 The technical information network[a] of Chaparra

Note

a The node size is according to the 2-Local Eigenvector centrality and declines from left to right. The node colour illustrates the k-core: bright grey indicates that the nodes have three or more contacts between each other, dark grey two links and black one or no link. The figure is visualised with Netdraw.

Furthermore, the NGO has a decisive impact on the local power distribution and plays a key role in the social cohesion of the system. If the network centralities are calculated first without and then with the NGO, significant changes in the centrality ranking of the individuals and the cohesion of the system can be observed (see Table 5.4 and Table 5.5). The NGO introduces centrality to the local system and shortens the average distance of the path length of the information flow (Table 5.4). Thus, due to the presence of the NGO, technical information can flow and spread faster within the local community.

However, the presence of the NGO also changes the ego centralities and the betweenness centrality of the farmers within the local community (Table 5.5). Between centrality measures how often an actor is on the shortest path between two other agents. The NGO changes the local power distribution with regards to knowledge and control over information flow. Some farmers gain and others lose in centrality and local power due to the presence of the NGO.

Of course, this finding is a hypothetical situation, because the fact is that the NGO works in the region and we cannot predict precisely how the system would change without this agent. Nevertheless, many common analysis methods (based, for example, upon census data) could have missed this central role of an external actor. Naturally, these results need further research, but a crucial point is that network analysis can help to reveal and analyse the social structures and power relations within local communities. This leads also to the question about the positive and negative effects of external interventions. This is beyond the scope of this book, but those interested can refer to discussion about the usefulness of international aid intervention (Patel 1974; Easterly 2001, 2006; Sachs 2005) as well as the literature on social network interventions (e.g. Valente 2012).

5.5.5 Relation between social capital and innovation

Fundamental to making network analysis work for development projects is an understanding of how different dimensions of social capital, human capital and innovation are related to each other. Human capital and social capital are considered to be core determinants and drivers of entrepreneurial action and innovation (e.g. Grebel *et al.* 2003). Conversely, entrepreneurship and innovative activities draw upon and also create social capital (Casson and Della Giusta 2007). Case studies such as that for Cháparra allow the exploration of several questions, such as whether the data confirms the theoretical considerations; whether external ties or the local network position are more important; and which network measures

Table 5.4 Centralization and cohesion of the local technical information network

Centralization and cohesion of the network	With NGO	Without NGO
Degree centralization	44.18%	18.73%
Eigenvector centralization	70.04%	56.89%
Node betweenness centralization	47.24%	28.11%
Average distance (among reachable pairs)	3.181	3.507

Table 5.5 Impact of the NGO on the betweenness centralities of the farmers in the local technical information network[a]

Nodes (N = 44)	Positive and negative changes in betweenness ranking position, when the centrality is calculated without the NGO	Position in the betweenness centrality ranking when NGO is not considered	Position in betweenness centrality ranking when NGO is considered
N17	+16	4	20
N2	+16	7	23
N25	+13	6	19
N10	+11	13	24
N12	+10	11	21
N19	+9	5	14
N11	+2	1	3
N21	+1	3	4
N22	0	2	2
N31	0	8	8
N32	−7	19	12
N3	−9	18	9
N15	−9	26	17
N46	−10	15	5
N34	−10	21	11
N8	−13	42	29
N44	−14	24	10
N5	−16	23	7

Note

a This table illustrates the betweenness centralities in the local technical information network and how these change when the NGO is considered in the calculation. It must be noted, though, that in other types of social relations such as friendship and kinship, the centrality rankings and the effects of the NGO are different, thus implying the need for careful interpretation.

seem to be more appropriate. To make a contribution to addressing these questions, this study analysed the correlations between different dimensions of social capital (local and external ties), human capital and the Cháparra farmer's innovative performance. In addition, the impact of selected control variables (age and desire to innovate) on innovative behaviour was analysed.

Social capital is a complex concept that includes a varied set of dimensions such as the agent's kinship and professional networks, collective actions or group assistance. In this partial analysis, emphasis was put on the position of the individuals within a local technical information network and their access to external technical information (related to their agricultural business activities). To measure the role and social capital of the farmers within the valley, their degree, betweenness and eigenvector centralities were calculated (see Section 5.4 for information on centrality measures). Furthermore, the participation and active roles of farmers in local associations, which are related to their productive activities, were considered.

To measure the external ties and social capital of the farmers, we asked for their external kinship networks and whether they frequently spoke with relatives living outside the valley about information related to business activities. Additionally, we asked about their participation in and attendance at fairs, expositions and other professional activities in cities as well as other valleys, as a proxy indicator for their access to external technical knowledge.

To measure the innovative performance of the smallholders a simple aggregated indicator was built. This was done by summarizing the values obtained from each farmer with regards to the various dimensions of innovation considered in the questionnaire: Innovation in Products, Processes, Marketing, Organization and Prevention (thus: *Innovation performance* = $Inno_{Prod}$ + $Inno_{Process}$ + $Inno_{Market}$ + $Inno_{Org}$ + $Inno_{Prevention}$). The reliability of this composed factor was controlled by a high significance level (0.003) of the Kendall-Tau correlations with another proxy indicator on the technical competences of the farmers, using expert evaluations (Arata 2008). Human capital was proxied using educational data and the amount of technical training a given farmer had received. Furthermore, we controlled for the effects of age and for the psychological variable representing the farmers' desire to innovate.

Based on these indicators, a correlation test was applied to analyse whether social capital and innovative performance are correlated with each other. In other words, to see whether farmers with more and better network relations tended to also be more innovative, as well as if more innovative farmers tend to have more social contacts and centrality in the local network. Due to the characteristics of the sample and the heterogeneity of the factors, a Kendall's Tau-b non-parametric correlation test was applied. Kendall's Tau-b measures the non-parametric rank correlations between paired observations (Kendall and Gibbons 1990). It provides a distribution free test of independence and a measure of the strength of dependence between two variables. In doing so, it calculates the number of concordances and discordances in paired observations. Concordance occurs when paired observations vary together and discordance occurs when paired observations vary differently. The Kendall's Tau-b coefficient is defined as follows:

$$\tau_b = \frac{C - D}{\sqrt{C + D + T_x}\sqrt{C + D + T_y}}$$

where C is the number of concordant pairs, D the number of discordant pairs, T_x is the number of tied pairs of x and T_y is the number of tied pairs of y. The values of Tau-b range from -1 (= 100 per cent negative association) to $+1$ (= 100 per cent positive association). A value of zero indicates the absence of association. In our case, the main reasons for using Kendall's Tau-b instead of Spearman's Rho or the Pearson correlation coefficient are: (a) the ordinal or non-normal distribution of several of the considered variables (e.g. network centralities, education data); (b) the rather small sample size; (c) the possible identification of outliers; and (d) the reduction of the random correlation probability.

Table 5.6 summarizes how the innovative performance of the 44 farmers correlates with their local network position, their external links and their level of education. It also shows the controls for the effects of age and the desire to innovate.

With regard to the correlations between the farmers centrality in the local and external technical information networks, it seems that a farmer with a high degree of eigenvector centrality and many external weak ties tends to be more innovative than a farmer with a weak local network position and few external linkages. However, the Tau values are comparatively small. While degree and eigenvector centrality appear to be highly significant in this case, betweenness centrality is not. The main reasons for this are twofold. First, an NGO dominates the network, interacting and connecting with a varied set of agents. It outweighs the betweenness centrality of many other agents. Second, within the close-knit local network of this case study, information can spread fairly fast to all other agents of the local system. In the case of Chaparra, the school education and the external kinship networks (which may provide access to external information) do not correlate significantly with innovation. One might suppose that education would lead to human capital and improve the absorptive capacities of the farmers and the

Table 5.6 Correlations[a] between the farmers' social capital and their innovation performance

Nonparametric Kendall's Tau correlations (N = 44) between different social capital dimensions and the aggregated innovation performance

Dimension	Indicator	Kendall's Tau	Significance level
The peasant's local network position	Degree centrality	0.345	0.003**
	Betweenness centrality	0.120	0.274
	Eigenvector centrality	0.297	0.006**
	Active member of local association	0.253	0.054
External ties of the peasant	Technical information exchange with relatives from other valleys, cities, countries	0.047	0.702
	Outgoing professional contacts and weak ties, (e.g. technical information exchange in fairs, expositions, business trips to other valleys and cities	0.424	0.002**
Human capital	Educational level	0.177	0.130
	Training in the use and processing of wine grapes	0.321	0.014*
Control variables	Age	−0.140	0.202
	Desire to innovate	0.211	0.082

Note

a Correlation:** = significant at the 0.01 level; * = significant at the 0.05 level.

kinship network access to external information and other resources. But specific training and practical learning seems to be more important in the case region than codified school knowledge. In addition, the school curricula and the interests of family members in cities are often disconnected from the needs and reality of life in agricultural communities (Hartmann 2006).

Regarding the kinship networks, it was found that all farmers have close family members living in other Peruvian cities and sometimes even foreign countries. However, during interviews it was discovered that most farmers see the activities of their family members in other regions as disconnected from their agricultural activity in the community, even when in several cases the children of the farmers studied issues such as marketing, accounting or completed internships in mechanics. Much more theoretical and empirical research is necessary on the causal relations between different network measures (e.g. centralities, composition, key player metrics) and the dimensions of innovation (e.g. inputs and outputs). The causal directions between social capital and innovation are unclear: it cannot be clearly determined whether social capital leads to innovation or innovation to social capital. It seems probable that there is a feedback mechanism between them. Social capital leads to better access to valuable information and innovative performance leads to a more central position and prestige (Akçomak and Weel 2009; Eagle *et al.* 2010). In addition, there is a need to research and study in more detail which network measures should be applied in local communities where virtually all people know each other. For instance, within the Chaparra network, there still is significant heterogeneity in the quality and type of ties and the role of the individuals.

5.5.6 *Interpretation of the results and research outlook*

Three crucial issues for research on smallholder innovation could be identified during the case study. First, it is necessary to differentiate between diverse dimensions of social capital and innovation when studying endogenous development. Second, it has to be assessed to what degree the modification of the existing social structures by external agents can be harmful or beneficial. Third, SNA can help to gain a better understanding of the complex relations between social capital and innovation and how these can contribute to fostering sustainable development projects. Methods of SNA and the increasing availability of detailed data enable advancement in the understanding of socioeconomic development in local communities and the efficiency of external intervention. Exploratory SNA (e.g. Wasserman and Faust 1994; De Nooy *et al.* 2005), in combination with econometric methods, can reveal the structural patterns and roles of agents which would otherwise be overlooked by common qualitative approaches, interviews and confirmatory analysis. In the case investigated here – which can be assumed to be representative of many other agricultural communities in developing countries – an NGO which is active in the region has become the key player in the local information network. By sampling the relevant data indirectly (i.e. available household data), this decisive actor and its influence on the network structure as well as on the individual indicators would have been missed.

The positive and negative issues concerning NGOs are highly disputed within the development community. However, this study suggests that external intervention and development projects might gain significantly from applying network-based analysis to the social capital and innovation capabilities within the respective communities both at the beginning and at the end of their projects. This would allow an identification and evaluation of endogenously grown social structures as well as the internal and external boundaries, which might hamper or promote the success of the project. Such information would help in the design of more efficient projects and minimize the negative impact of external intervention on endogenously grown structures and competencies. However, to develop best practices for network analysis and the promotion of endogenous development, a better understanding of the complex interrelations between the different dimensions of human capital, social capital and innovation is needed. The analysis here indicates that an individual's innovation capacity is determined by both internal and external linkages. It is important to note that investigating the network roles and position of local innovators, taking different types of both local and external ties into account, is still scarcely explored (e.g. Giuliani and Bell 2005). Indeed, although the qualitative importance of cooperation and participation as well as the role of innovation have been emphasized by the literature on local development (Mytelka 2000; Vázquez-Barquero 2002), knowledge of the measurement of different types of innovation and network positions in local agricultural communities as well as understanding of the feedbacks between the different types of innovation and the different roles in the local and extra-local networks, has still to be further explored.

5.6 Chapter conclusion

This chapter has focused on the positive, negative and ambiguous effects of social networks. There is a strong bias in the social capital and innovation network literature towards highlighting the positive aspects of social networks, such as the access to information, finance or mutual help and trust. However social networks can also impose constraints to the freedom and agency of the individuals or people outside the network and lead to inequality reproduction, social differentiation and levelling pressures. Human development and qualitative change policies need to promote the positive, and alleviate and prevent the negative effects of social networks.

The chapter also showed that social capital theory can function as a valuable theoretical bridge between the human development approach and structural economic change literature. Social capital plays a decisive role for both learning and innovation networks as well as group and external capabilities. The empirical application to a case in Peru revealed that diverse dimensions of social capital have a significant influence on the capabilities of peasant farmers (in poor agricultural communities) to be active agents of development and introduce novelties into their local production system. Finally, techniques from SNA can help to illustrate and measure the impact of social networks on the capabilities and freedom of the individuals. The next chapter on entrepreneurship shows that social networks are also crucial to the contribution that entrepreneurs can make to economic and human development.

Note

1 This empirical section is based on Hartmann and Arata (2011).

6 Entrepreneurship and human development

All across the world, from the micro-entrepreneurs in Bangladesh to the high-tech entrepreneurs in the Silicon Valley, people start new businesses or engage in self-employed work. Entrepreneurship has been an important field in economics and business science, at least since Joseph Schumpeter (1912) put forward the concept of entrepreneurs being the key drivers of innovation and economic development. Several scholars view differences in the frequency and quality of entrepreneurial actions as key factors which explain economic divergence in the global economy (Audretsch and Thurik 2000; Santos 2004; Szirmai *et al.* 2011). The key question in economics has been how entrepreneurship contributes to economic growth. Other questions have arisen as a result of the rise of microfinance and the concept of social-entrepreneurship, questions concerning issues such as what effect entrepreneurship has on people's social choices and human capabilities or what entrepreneurship means for the freedom and well-being of the entrepreneur and for society (Bornstein 2004; Yunus 2007; Gries and Naude 2010). Learning from the traditional approaches of Schumpeter (as well as taking recent network-based entrepreneurship research into account) can be helpful in addressing such questions.

As Schumpeter pointed out in his *Theory of Economic Development* (1912), entrepreneurship is a driver of creative destruction processes and the creator of new sectors and hence occupational choices. It therefore has positive and negative effects on the well-being and capabilities of people through its impact on structural change and economic diversification (Chapter 4). Recent approaches have added to the picture of entrepreneurship by focusing on the embeddedness of entrepreneurs in social networks, showing how they make use of and create social networks (Chapter 5). However, these insights do not sufficiently explain what entrepreneurship means from a human development perspective and do not provide a theoretical framework which is able to analyse, distinguish and evaluate the effects of different types of entrepreneurship, such as micro-entrepreneurship and/or social entrepreneurship, on human development and social welfare.

The human development approach pinpoints 'human agency' as a core objective of human development, alongside well-being and justice (Sen 1998a; Alkire 2010). Following this approach, people and groups should be enabled as agents rather than as patients of development. The agency goal is related to process freedom. Furthermore, systemic restrictions such as gender inequality, lack of democracy, problems with access to healthcare and education problems, or lack of access to resources need to be addressed to overcome unfreedom. The underlying goal of the human development approach is to overcome individual lack of freedom and external constraints and enable people to help themselves.

A large percentage of the poor in developing countries work as micro-entrepreneurs, engaged in activities such as selling food or clothing, or repairing small items. According to Banerjee and Duflo (2007), in Peru, 69 per cent of people in urban areas, who live on less than two US dollars a day, have their own business. In Indonesia, Pakistan and Nicaragua the equivalent number is between 47 and 52 per cent. Within the group of people living in agricultural areas on less than one US dollar a day, 25–98 per cent state they have self-employed agricultural businesses. Indeed, it seems that it is the rule rather than the exception that the poor own small businesses (Banerjee and Duflo 2007). The human development perspective shifts the emphasis, by asking whether micro-entrepreneurship means human freedom or unfreedom for the micro-entrepreneur, rather than merely focusing on its role in macroeconomic growth. In this way, entrepreneurship is not evaluated by the economic profit it creates, but by the extent to which it contributes to the human capabilities of the individual and the society.

This chapter introduces the approach of 'entrepreneurship as capability enhancement' as a complementary perspective alongside the classical approaches that view the entrepreneur as an innovator (Schumpeter 1912), risk and uncertainty bearer (Knight 1921) or arbitrageur and efficiency enhancer (Kirzner 1973). This approach evaluates how much entrepreneurship contributes to the agency of the entrepreneur and the welfare of society. This concept allows for the integration of social and micro-entrepreneurship within a theoretical framework that measures the effects on human development rather than the effects on economic growth. This allows for a combination of classical entrepreneurship theory and human development thinking. The chapter is structured as follows: Section 6.1 provides an overview on the various approaches to entrepreneurship. In the following sections (Section 6.2–6.4), the role of micro, social and destructive entrepreneurship for human development are explored. Finally, the 'Sen meets Schumpeter' perspective is applied to analyse feedbacks between micro-entrepreneurship, institutional change, and human development in north-east Brazil (Section 6.5).

6.1 Entrepreneurship theories

A number of different perspectives on entrepreneurship have been developed and discussed over the last centuries, beginning with the classical contributions of Richard Cantillon, Max Weber and Jean-Baptiste Say. Later Joseph A. Schumpeter, Frank Knight and Israel A. Kirzner introduced new concepts and theories regarding entrepreneurship and later still authors such as Peter Drucker, Marc Casson and David B. Audretsch further elaborated and developed different theories (for an overview, see e.g. Rickett 2006). In these series of theories and discussions of entrepreneurs, several definitions were posited. Some economists came to view entrepreneurs as risk takers or uncertainty bearers (Cantillon 1755; Knight 1921), while others argued that entrepreneurs are innovators and equilibrium destroyers (Schumpeter 1912; Audretsch and Thurik 2000), and still others argued that they are equilibrium-creating profit seekers (Hayek 1937; Kirzner 1973) or were simply anyone who is self-employed. No common consensus has emerged with respect to a series of basic questions about who might be an entrepreneur, what the characteristics and functions of an entrepreneur are, what the role of the entrepreneur is in the economic system and what the main factors and drivers of entrepreneurship are. The heterogeneity and complexity of human nature and socioeconomic systems, as well as capitalist progress and evolutionary transformation, makes it virtually impossible to develop a universally valid and consistent theory of entrepreneurship. Nevertheless, despite the impossibility of finding a 'one-size-fits-all' approach' to entrepreneurship, there are some principles common to most entrepreneurship theories, such as a focus on the entrepreneur as the central figure and driver of business creation and development. Most entrepreneurship researchers also agree that business development is a main driver of economic development, meaning that entrepreneurs are central agents of development. In the following paragraphs, the main differences between the dominant schools and approaches on entrepreneurship with regards to their definition of roles, characteristics and the functions of entrepreneurs are presented.

6.1.1 *The uncertainty bearer, the innovator and the arbitrageur*

The term 'entrepreneur' was introduced to economic theory by Richard Cantillon (1755). He viewed the entrepreneur as a risk taker who buys the output of the worker before the consumers have indicated how much they are willing to pay, and hence bears the risk caused by price fluctuations in the consumer markets (Casson *et al.* 2006, p. 3). Frank Knight (1921) refined and expanded this concept by distinguishing between risk and uncertainty. He regarded the entrepreneur as an uncertainty bearer (Casson *et al.* 2006). The heroic perspective of entrepreneurship was promoted by Joseph Alois Schumpeter's (1912) consideration of entrepreneurs as key agents of economic development: he considered real entrepreneurs as the equilibrium-destroying innovators who are able to introduce new combinations into the system, generating new surges of investment, growth and employment, the creation of new sectors and the destruction of old patterns (Schumpeter 1912; Freeman 1982; Grebel *et al.* 2003). Schumpeter identified (radical) innovations introduced to the marketplace by the entrepreneur as being the main driver of structural change and corresponding business cycles (Schumpeter 1939). Entrepreneurs are able to recognize and exploit market opportunities before others and reap the profits from their acts of creative destruction (Gruber 2007). Schumpeterian entrepreneurs can be found in the emergence of the cotton industry, the creation of railways, the chemical and electro industries, the automobile industry and more recently in ICT (e.g. Schumpeter 1939; Perez 2002; Acs and Audretsch 2003; Hanusch and Pyka 2007b). In his book *Capitalism, Socialism and Democracy* Schumpeter (1943) argued that corporate capitalism, driven by entrepreneurial action, cannot survive, but has to make space for a trustified type of capitalism in which innovation becomes a routine behaviour within large organizations. History has shown, especially with the upsurge of new technologies in the late twentieth century, that entrepreneurship has been thriving and that entrepreneurial capitalism still exists (Audretsch and Thurik 2000).

Whilst the concept of the Schumpeterian entrepreneur contributes to a better understanding of innovation, it does not help to understand the role of arbitrage entrepreneurs who do not really innovate, but rather use price differences between different regions. In contrast to Schumpeter's innovator-entrepreneur, Israel Kirzner highlighted the existence of the arbitrageur-entrepreneur. Kirzner considered that a common feature among entrepreneurs was an awareness of unexploited opportunities for arbitrage (Casson *et al.* 2006), meaning the mere exploitation of price differentials in different regions and social strata. From the perspective of the Austrian School, entrepreneurship is a natural process which brings the market back towards equilibrium. Kirzner recognized the fact that many entrepreneurs are neither uncertainty bearers nor innovators, but simply make use of the information they possess about price differences, and use the consequent opportunities to buy cheap and sell dear (Casson *et al.* 2006). Thus, in a similar vein to Hayek and Casson, the main function of the Kirznerian entrepreneur is the coordination and a more efficient reallocation of resources (Findeis 2007). Kirzner's theory of equilibrium-creating arbitrageur entrepreneurs, grounded in the thinking of Hayek, is considered especially relevant when it comes to explaining low-level entrepreneurship, such as textile trading at the local level (Grebel *et al.* 2003; Casson *et al.* 2006; Hernandez and Dewick 2011).

6.1.2 The network perspective on entrepreneurship

While entrepreneurs have often been viewed as individual heroes, modern approaches increasingly take into account that entrepreneurs rely on social networks. An entrepreneur's capacity to benefit from market opportunities depends on a range of factors, such as access to information flows, financial resources, well qualified and motivated employees and workers, technological capability and the presence of a socioeconomic environment which supports entrepreneurial action. All these factors heavily depend on the capacity of the entrepreneurs to access and manage social and physical networks. Chapter 5 of this book explored how social capital affects the capabilities of individuals to access different resources and to innovate. Whereas an individual's characteristics, skills and ideas are certainly crucial, without a prolific network of social contact scarcely any entrepreneurial action would be successful. Casson and Della Giusta summarized the network-based entrepreneurship literature as follows (Casson and Della Giusta 2007, p. 222):

> Although the popular perception of entrepreneurship is very much that of an individualist, there is ample evidence that entrepreneurship is, in fact, socially embedded in network structures (Aldrich and Zimmer 1986;

> Aldrich *et al.* 1987; Johannison 1988) ... modern theory affords a coherent view of the socially embedded entrepreneur advancing the coordination of activities in complex economic systems.

Hence, to become a successful entrepreneur requires not only individual conviction, motivation and ideas, but also more importantly the skill to make use of, develop and coordinate networks.

According to Hoang and Antoncic (2003), the content, governance and structure of networks are key factors influencing the success of entrepreneurs. Entrepreneurs use, for instance, interpersonal and inter-organizational relations for access to business information, advice and problem-solving. The precise content of a social network changes according to the stage which the business is at. Whereas at the beginning of a venture access to new information on markets and business opportunities are crucial, later, for example, access to distribution networks and qualified personnel with the ability to solve technical details becomes crucial. The structure of the networks (direct and indirect ties, density, cliquishness, structural holes) affects the speed of knowledge flow in the network and to what degree the entrepreneur has access to and power over the knowledge flow (see also Chapter 5). Additionally, entrepreneurs often have to rely on implicit and open-ended contracts that need to be supported by trust. This requires appropriate network government and coordination by the entrepreneur, who needs to create prolific social networks to successfully plan, found and establish a business. Creating networks of people trusting entrepreneurs is crucial to being able to acquire external help and resources and in making the company successful.

Additionally, social networks have a deep impact on the perception of the desirability and feasibility of entrepreneurial action – for example Liñán and Santos (2007, p. 447):

> Different contacts and experiences acquired by a person [e.g. through strong and weak ties, bonding and bridging social capital] can provide him/her with higher self-confidence so as to estimate whether becoming an entrepreneur is desirable and/or feasible.

The content, structure and beliefs of social networks are often also embedded within regions as well as in different social stratum. The institutions, norms and social networks of regions impact upon the entrepreneurial culture of social groups and regions. High quality entrepreneurship can often be found in regions with an established structure of large and small interacting enterprises that are deeply engaged both in cooperative behaviour and competition. Conversely, in regions where enterprises and institutions are weakly linked to each other and serve only the interests of external actors (e.g. as industrial satellites), low-level and subsistence entrepreneurship with little prospect for growth may be the dominant forms of entrepreneurship (Santos 2004). As the case studies in north-east Brazil in Section 6.5 show, a fertile network of institutions supporting the entrepreneurs is crucial, allowing access to important information about business opportunities, information and skills and allowing them to experiment with businesses to find out which ones work in their region.

6.1.3 The human capability enhancer

While there are different arguments as to whether entrepreneurs are best viewed as innovators, as risk and uncertainty bearers, as arbitrageurs, or network managers, the question on what entrepreneurship means for the freedom of the entrepreneur as well as for the human development of others has not been a core issue in the traditional economics perspective on entrepreneurship. To answer this question, Section 6.2 analyses micro-entrepreneurship in developing countries and Section 6.3 explores social entrepreneurship and business. This type of entrepreneurship focuses less on economic profit and more on expanding human capabilities and social innovation. The concept of 'entrepreneurs as human capability enhancer' creates a bridge between the main entrepreneurship approaches in economics and the human development approach (see Figure 6.1). It analyses both economic and social entrepreneurship and is intrinsically in the tradition of the 'Sen meets Schumpeter' paradigm presented in this book. Furthermore it departs from the common perception of entrepreneurs as being a rare class of people, but considers that a large number of people have the potential for entrepreneurial action. We can find examples of entrepreneurial actions all over the world, from the women micro-entrepreneurs in Bangladesh, to strategic movements of multinational enterprises (MNEs), from small agro-businesses in poor regions of Peru, to the high-tech ventures in Silicon Valley or Route 128 (Bornstein 2004; Yunus 2007). Of course, it is impossible for everyone to become a global business leader and introduce systemic changes to the global economic system, but many people are able to introduce changes on a local level and in their close social network.

If efforts in promoting highly educated and high-tech entrepreneurs in the economic realm are limited, the many possibilities in terms of human capital and the entrepreneurial spirit may be neglected. For this reason, every individual should be given the basic opportunity and social choices needed to engage in entrepreneurial action and be given active assistance in economic and social development processes. From a human development perspective it could be fruitful to understand entrepreneurial action as the active engagement of people changing the status quo of their lives, families, enterprises and socioeconomic environment, to achieve a higher level of social welfare for themselves and others. As Figure 6.1 illustrates, the concept of entrepreneurship as capability enhancement connects the main entrepreneurship approaches in economics with the human development approach. The value of entrepreneurial action is evaluated on the extent to which it upgrades the human capabilities of the entrepreneur and contributes to the welfare of the society.

Figure 6.1 Interdisciplinary view of entrepreneurship as capability enhancement

The concept of 'entrepreneurship as a capability enhancement' can draw upon several of the dimensions and roles of the classical economic entrepreneur, such as risk taker, innovator or efficiency enhancer (see also the case study in Section 6.5). The concept, however, considers the degree to which entrepreneurial action contributes to human agency and welfare. This enables the evaluation of, for example, the extent to which micro-entrepreneurship is born out of necessity or is a sign of agency and human capabilities.

6.2 Micro-entrepreneurship in developing countries: Obligation or capability enhancement?

Micro-entrepreneurship is often driven by a lack of reasonably paid and stable employment; hence it is driven by necessity (Bosma and Harding 2006; Banerjee and Duflo 2007). The literature argues that most micro-ventures in developing countries will not be able to upgrade to small or even medium sized enterprises, because they generally lack the necessary resources, such as human capital or technology, and/or because they are not based on innovation or really new market opportunities. The existence of large numbers of micro-entrepreneurs in very poor countries clearly illustrates that micro-entrepreneurship alone is not enough for economic development. Yet this may just be part of the story. Some micro-entrepreneurs certainly do foster local innovation. They are not always merely forced into business and, furthermore, many micro-entrepreneurs are proud of the successes they are able to achieve for themselves and their families through their own small businesses. Overall, we cannot make broad generalizations; rather, we must look case by case to see whether entrepreneurial action provides better choices and more freedom than other occupational choices.

For this reason, entrepreneurial action should not merely be measured in terms of economic turnover. For example, the recent microfinance boom is not so much about macroeconomic development, but more about poverty reduction and providing meaningful assistance to encourage actors to help themselves (Hartmann 2011). To view micro-entrepreneurship from a human capability perspective, the following must be determined: (a) when entrepreneurship is a functioning (Gries and Naude 2010) and when it is an obligation; (b) how it affects the capabilities of the entrepreneur; and (c) how it affects the capabilities and functionings of other people. The next section will review the literature on necessity-based entrepreneurship. It will then address the question whether the distinction between necessity and opportunity-based entrepreneurship is the right framework from a human development perspective. Finally the 'entrepreneurship as functioning approach' of Gries and Naude (2010) will be discussed.

6.2.1 Necessity versus opportunity-based entrepreneurship

Entrepreneurship does not necessarily imply human agency in the sense of freedom expansion. Large numbers of people in developing countries are forced to engage in informal micro-scale enterprises to survive, as either the formal economy does not provide jobs, or the people do not have the skills required by the formal (and informal) job market. The Global Entrepreneurship Monitor (GEM) therefore distinguishes between opportunity and necessity-driven entrepreneurship (e.g. Bosma and Harding 2006; Bosma *et al.* 2008, 2009; Kelley *et al.* 2011). Necessity-based entrepreneurship refers to those entrepreneurs who have entered self-employment because they have no better opportunity to work and generate sufficient income for themselves and their families. Opportunity-based entrepreneurship refers to those who have chosen to start a business as a result of opportunities, despite having other valuable employment possibilities. The GEM furthermore includes questions on the motivation of the entrepreneurs: whether they desire independence in their work, or engage in self-employment to maintain or increase their income. As Figure 6.2(a) shows, the percentage of the population working in early-stage entrepreneurial activities tends to be very high in many developing countries (such as Ghana, Zimbabwe or Peru), substantially lower in more developed countries (such as Japan, Belgium or Germany) and rises slightly again in the richest countries (such as Norway or the US). In other words, far more people are entrepreneurs and have their own business in developing countries than in most developed countries.

However, Figure 6.2(b) shows that a high percentage of the entrepreneurial action in developing countries is necessity-based. The necessity-based entrepreneurial activity drops substantially when the average income level of the country increases. This implies that the slightly rising level of overall entrepreneurial activity in the very richest countries (e.g. the US, Sweden or Norway in Figure 6.2(a)) are not due to necessity-based but to opportunity-based entrepreneurship.

Figure 6.2(b) implies that entrepreneurship does not necessarily result in human freedom and agency. Indeed, the decline of early-stage entrepreneurial activity can even be an indicator of a positive development in developing countries. It can indicate that more people are able to find a reasonable job and fewer people are obliged to engage in necessity-based self-employment. Moreover, studies in less developed countries with high rates of entrepreneurial action have also revealed high entry and exit rate for newly founded businesses. One good example is Peru. The GEM 2006 (Bosma and Harding 2006; Serida *et al.* 2007) indicates that in Peru, two out of five people of working age are engaged in entrepreneurial actions, one of the highest rates in the world. The fact that an extremely large percentage of workers engage as entrepreneurs in Peru has little to do with qualitative or

(a)

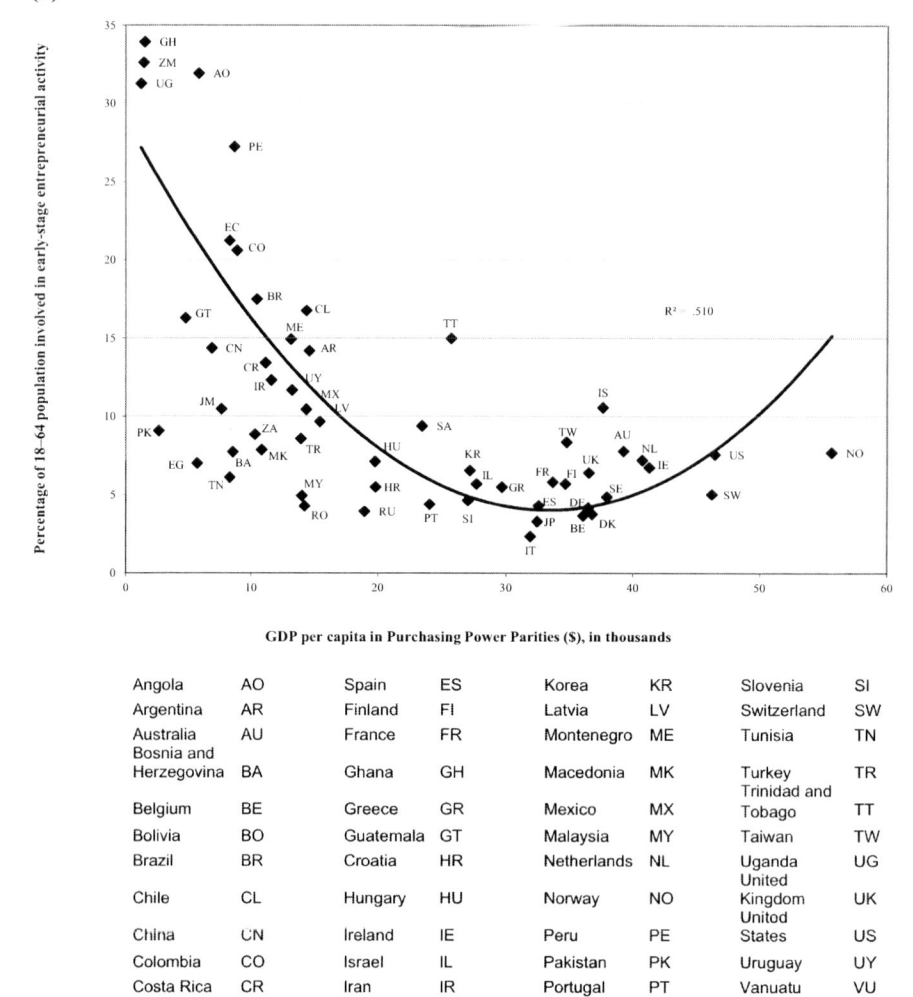

Angola	AO	Spain	ES	Korea	KR	Slovenia	SI
Argentina	AR	Finland	FI	Latvia	LV	Switzerland	SW
Australia	AU	France	FR	Montenegro	ME	Tunisia	TN
Bosnia and Herzegovina	BA	Ghana	GH	Macedonia	MK	Turkey	TR
Belgium	BE	Greece	GR	Mexico	MX	Trinidad and Tobago	TT
Bolivia	BO	Guatemala	GT	Malaysia	MY	Taiwan	TW
Brazil	BR	Croatia	HR	Netherlands	NL	Uganda	UG
Chile	CL	Hungary	HU	Norway	NO	United Kingdom	UK
China	CN	Ireland	IE	Peru	PE	United States	US
Colombia	CO	Israel	IL	Pakistan	PK	Uruguay	UY
Costa Rica	CR	Iran	IR	Portugal	PT	Vanuatu	VU
Germany	DE	Iceland	IS	Romania	RO	South Africa	ZA
Denmark	DK	Italy	IT	Russia	RU	Zambia	ZM
Ecuador	EC	Jamaica	JM	Saudi Arabia	SA		
Egypt	EG	Japan	JP	Sweden	SE		

Figure 6.2 (a) Total early-stage entrepreneurial activity rates and per capita GDP 2010.
(b) Necessity-based early-stage entrepreneurial activity rates and per capita GDP 2010

Source: Kelley *et al.* (2011): GEM Global Report 2010, p. 28.

Note
Permission to use figures from Global Entrepreneurship Monitor 2010 Global Report by Donna J. Kelley, Niels Bosma, José Ernesto Amorós, which appear here, has been granted by the copyright holders. The GEM is an international consortium and this report was produced from data collected in, and received from, 59 countries in 2010. Our thanks go to the authors, national teams, researchers, funding bodies and other contributors who have made this possible.

(b)

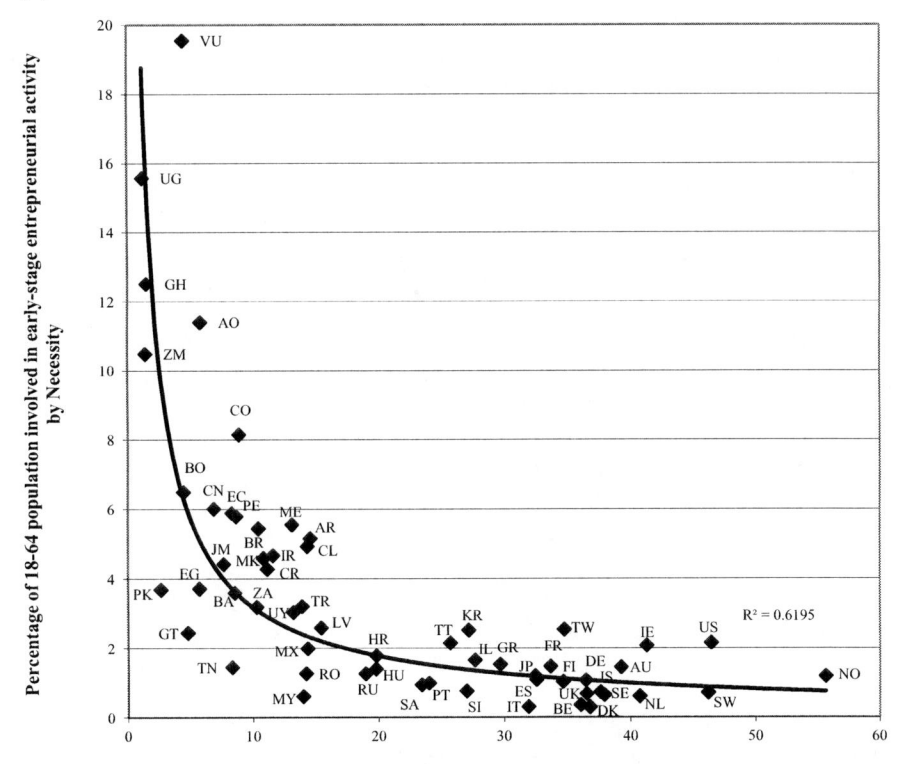

GDP per capita in Purchasing Power Parities ($), in thousands

Angola	AO	Spain	ES	Korea	KR	Slovenia	SI
Argentina	AR	Finland	FI	Latvia	LV	Switzerland	SW
Australia	AU	France	FR	Montenegro	ME	Tunisia	TN
Bosnia and Herzegovina	BA	Ghana	GH	Macedonia	MK	Turkey	TR
Belgium	BE	Greece	GR	Mexico	MX	Trinidad and Tobago	TT
Bolivia	BO	Guatemala	GT	Malaysia	MY	Taiwan	TW
Brazil	BR	Croatia	HR	Netherlands	NL	Uganda	UG
Chile	CL	Hungary	HU	Norway	NO	United Kingdom	UK
China	CN	Ireland	IE	Peru	PE	United States	US
Colombia	CO	Israel	IL	Pakistan	PK	Uruguay	UY
Costa Rica	CR	Iran	IR	Portugal	PT	Vanuatu	VU
Germany	DE	Iceland	IS	Romania	RO	South Africa	ZA
Denmark	DK	Italy	IT	Russia	RU	Zambia	ZM
Ecuador	EC	Jamaica	JM	Saudi Arabia	SA		
Egypt	EG	Japan	JP	Sweden	SE		

Figure 6.2 Continued

opportunity-based entrepreneurship, but is rather due to self-employment survival strategies and a lack of formal employment opportunities (Serida *et al.* 2007). However, a very good and expanding microfinance infrastructure also contributes to a high level of micro-entrepreneurship (Economist Intelligence Unit 2008). There are a comparatively large number of domestic and international microfinance institutions (MFIs) with a considerable array of products in the Peruvian credit market. Nevertheless, while there is certainly a widespread engagement in entrepreneurial actions within the Peruvian population, the capabilities and opportunities for innovative and successful ventures are rather limited. Most of the entrepreneurs engage in fairly saturated markets (e.g. commerce, retail, accommodation, restaurants or handicrafts) with low knowledge intensity and low potential for expansion. Indeed, according to the GEM Peru 2006 (Serida *et al.* 2007), only around 2.9 per cent of all enterprises have an elevated potential for market expansion, which take into account the supply of new products, the use of new technologies and the competition in the market. Most of the ventures and small and medium-sized enterprises (SMEs) only focus on the local market and do not export; the companies that do export are predominantly large enterprises (e.g. in the mining sector). There are also problems with high entry and exit rates of firms in the market, owing to a low survival rate of ventures. In other words, a large number of micro-ventures are made every year, but a large percentage of them fail to become established in the market. One out of ten people of working age indicated that they had closed a business within the last twelve months. Three out of four Peruvian enterprises have recently been created, while only 12.4 per cent of the enterprises can be considered to be established (Serida *et al.* 2007). In addition, 68 per cent of the ventures are able to create a job for the entrepreneurs themselves alone, meaning it will create no employment opportunities for other people. Most of the newly founded businesses will fail within a few months or years and its owners will go on to open up another business soon thereafter, fail again, try another business and so on.

6.2.2 *Entrepreneurship as a functioning approach*

Gries and Naude (2010) introduced the concept of entrepreneurship as functioning. They argue that in economics, entrepreneurship is mostly viewed as a productive factor leading to economic efficiency (Kirzner 1973) or innovation and structural change (Schumpeter 1912). Management research focuses on the 'whom', 'how' and 'what' rather than on the impacts of entrepreneurship on social welfare. Gries and Naude (2010), on the other hand, ask what impact entrepreneurship has on human development. They suggest that when the entrepreneur has also the choice/opportunities to 'not be an entrepreneur', entrepreneurship is a functioning that indicates human agency. Conversely, if the entrepreneur does not have decent employment opportunities, entrepreneurship is often undertaken out of necessity and likely can mean unfreedom.

This implies that labour market policies are crucial to promote high quality entrepreneurship: '... promoting labour intensity and wage employment, and creating social security are pro-entrepreneurship because they turn entrepreneurship from a potential functioning into an actual functioning' (Gries and Naude 2010, p. 4). Thus, economic diversification (that provides new occupational choices), labour market policies and a good social security system can contribute to good quality entrepreneurship and social welfare. Entrepreneurship based on economic and social opportunities contributes to human development, while entrepreneurship as a necessity can often be considered a symptom of unfreedom and deprivation. This perspective focuses on the implications of entrepreneurship for the freedom of individuals. It allows for a better theoretical integration of entrepreneurship into the human development framework. It also demonstrates the necessity of analysing the extent to which entrepreneurship is a functioning based on a positive choice, or an obligation due to a lack of choice (Gries and Naude 2010). While entrepreneurs in developed settings often deliberately choose self-employment in order to fulfil their desires, in many cases in less developed settings it is a sign of unfreedom and/or risk diversification (Banerjee and Duflo 2007). On the other hand, if we look to highly developed settings such as the United States or Germany, low-paid self-employment is also increasingly becoming an obligation or a coping strategy for people unable to find a decent job.

The implication of the work of Gries and Naude is that entrepreneurship as a functioning tends to make a greater contribution to human development than entrepreneurship as necessity. The reason is that when entrepreneurship is based on entrepreneurs' intrinsic motivation and a true economic or social opportunity, it has a much greater likelihood of contributing to efficiency, structural change and human development. Conversely, entrepreneurs, out of necessity, may be based on human unfreedom and hence require a systemic socioeconomic development policy on the meso, macro and meta levels of the economy (Esser *et al.* 1996). One could criticize a strict distinction between entrepreneurship as necessity and entrepreneurship as a functioning, because in reality an entrepreneurial action can be both at the same time or change over time. An entrepreneurial action based on free choice may become a necessity or an obligation, limiting the freedom of the individual. Conversely, necessity-based entrepreneurship can change into a true functioning if the venture excels. Entrepreneurial action can lead to applied learning processes and open up new contacts and opportunities for the formerly necessity-based entrepreneurs. In addition, the accumulated knowledge through trial and error in different businesses may enable an individual to find an activity which they are good at and can enjoy. Last, but not least, both individuals and the environment can change over time. Understanding these dynamic features could help the understanding of what contributions entrepreneurship make to the agency of the individual. Approaching economics in this way can provide a more dynamic picture of how positive and negative effects can change over time. One form of entrepreneurship deliberately aims to enhance the welfare and human capabilities of other people: social entrepreneurship.

6.3 Social entrepreneurship

Over the last few decades around the turn of the century, social entrepreneurship has become a key concept for development practitioners and has also received attention from companies, managers and academics. Social entrepreneurship refers to entrepreneurial actions that do not focus on economic profit generation, but address social problems (e.g. regarding health, gender equality and education) and improvements to welfare. Social entrepreneurship, social business and social innovation are overlapping concepts, which bring together the understanding of entrepreneurship research with human development and capabilities.

A social business can be defined as a financially auto-sustainable type of social entrepreneurship (Yunus 2007). Hence, theoretically, social business is a sub-category of social entrepreneurship. Nevertheless, there is also an implicit distinction; the term 'social entrepreneurship' is often connected to changes in social and public domains, such as democracy, health, education and training, whereas the term 'social business' refers to entrepreneurial actions and changes in economic domains, such as microcredits or economic goods and services adapted to the needs of the poor. Typical examples are making microcredits available, launching a micro-entrepreneurship, or providing economic goods and services adapted to the needs of the poor. The term social business often overlaps with social corporate responsibility or new approaches by MNEs to address the markets at the bottom of the pyramid that do not solely exploit market opportunities but also empower the poor.

Microfinance is the most famous example of social innovation: providing micro-entrepreneurs with more resources to run their businesses, which can in turn contribute to the agency of the people, as well as to social development. As the case study in Section 6.5 shows, microfinance is also a good example of areas where a combination of Schumpeter's approach on innovation and structural changes and Sen's human capabilities and freedom approach can be very useful for theoretical advance and policy-making. The new technologies of microfinance have led to a structural change in the way the poor access finance, enabling them to lift themselves out of poverty. The crucial outcome therefore is not so much the effect on the aggregated income of the national or global economy, but rather the positive impact on poverty reduction and providing the individuals with agency.

Muhammad Yunus (2007) emphasized that one shortcoming of mainstream economics is that it assigns people and their entrepreneurial action only to the economic sphere of life, and assumes that each individual exclusively focuses on maximizing their profit. Entrepreneurship research (e.g. Acs and Audretsch 2003; Casson *et al.* 2006) has shown that there are many other motives for entrepreneurial action. Due to this variety of human motives, incentives and desires, entrepreneurship and structural change are not limited to the economic sphere, but occur in all domains and levels of socioeconomic systems. Social entrepreneurs such as Muhammad Yunus and Bill Drayton[1] have shown that entrepreneurship is not reserved to the economic sphere of life, and nor does it necessarily mean the use of great resources or produce large macroeconomic impacts (Bornstein 2004). Social entrepreneurship is crucial not only for poverty reduction and social welfare, but also for the introduction of novelty and change in the social, political and environmental spheres of socioeconomic life (Schumpeter 1912; Bornstein 2004).

Beyond the academic sector, the concepts of social entrepreneurship, social business and social innovation have received increasing attention from society and private companies. For example Ashoka and the Schwab Foundation for Social Entrepreneurship identify social entrepreneurs and provide them with scholarships allowing them to dedicate themselves to realizing their ideas and fostering social change. Arguably the best-known social entrepreneur is Muhammad Yunus, who together with the Grameen Bank won the Nobel Peace Prize in 2006. The Grameen Bank provides small loans to micro-entrepreneurs in developing countries, without requiring guarantees (that the poor do not have), but instead introducing innovative models such as mutual help and control within borrower groups. Its establishment has enabled a microfinance revolution across the world, with millions of poor people now having access to microcredits at far lower rates than on the informal credit markets, and with repayment rates of over 95 per cent (far above the conventional repayment rates of small, medium and large sized companies). Significantly, most of the clients of microfinance are women, utilizing their organizational skills and tending to place more emphasis on the future and well-being of their families and children. Many MFIs have reached operational and financial sustainability and are no longer dependent on donations. The next section explores what social entrepreneurship is and what distinguishes it from economic entrepreneurship: it is followed by an outline why social entrepreneurship is a growing sector which increasingly receives public attention. The concept of social business is then explored in more detail, including how multinational companies can also help to address the needs and the means to empower the income-poor in developing countries

6.3.1 What are the goals and actions of social entrepreneurs?

According to Ziegler, '…social entrepreneurs act as social change agents who imagine and carry out new combinations of capabilities' (Ziegler 2010, p. 267). The goals of social entrepreneurs are not directed towards economic profit maximization, but towards expanding the capabilities of other people; therefore social entrepreneurs need to recombine existing human capabilities. Social entrepreneurs recombine and improve existing human capabilities (such as civic engagement, human rights, nutrition and health, civil laws, use of technologies and education). Furthermore, social entrepreneurs have to struggle against established routines and norms to establish social ventures. While there are some similarities between economic and social entrepreneurs, such as their deep convictions and their capacity to influence and change routines and social networks, there are also important differences between economic and social entrepreneurs in relation to their means, obstacles and goals for change. For example, the routines and methods of doing things in social and political spaces are often different from the logic of economic markets. Additionally, simultaneous changes in different spheres of socioeconomic life have to be made. For example, social entrepreneurs typically need to speak with and create bridges between people from different social backgrounds (e.g. between illiterate people, local administrations and private companies), to convince them of the usefulness of the recombination of new capabilities to achieve new or improved functions for other people or the socioeconomic system. Ziegler suggests that social entrepreneurship can be better understood with an approach that synthesizes Sen's human capabilities and Schumpeter's innovation as a recombination (Ziegler 2010, p. 256):

> …first, social innovation is the carrying out of new combinations of capabilities. Second, social entrepreneurs can be characterized by their capacity to imagine and carry out new combinations of capabilities.

Consequently, entrepreneurs need to establish '…effective links, for example, between being able to participate effectively and being in good health…' (Ziegler 2010, p. 256) to create a social association that solves health problems together. This shows again the crucial role of social networks. To realize their entrepreneurial venture and to recombine human capabilities, entrepreneurs often require the help and support of others, such as friends, or government officials, or in many cases the people (i.e. potential clients) that the entrepreneur aims to help. Of course social networks (outlined in Section 6.1 and Chapter 5) do not just matter to economic entrepreneurs but also to social entrepreneurs. For instance, David Bornstein (2004) analyses the success stories of social entrepreneurs in various countries, and while he does not explicitly highlight the crucial role of networks, it becomes obvious that all of the successful social entrepreneurs he discusses managed to build up a network of social relations with different agents in the public, private and civil sectors. Most of the entrepreneurs had a comparatively good educational background and later drew on contacts from their time at school and university. Each of them had to deal (and often struggle) with public institutions and bureaucracy, and most of the agents relied on contacts and financial resources from the private sector. Virtually all the social entrepreneurs dealt with and were helped by people from the civil sector. Most of the social ventures have had a deep impact on the economy by promoting the education and health of the workers, opening up new social businesses and providing people with new capabilities and opportunities. It becomes obvious that social entrepreneurs are embedded in, and build up, a network of social relations. Entrepreneurs need to build up and draw upon a fertile and potent social network to make ventures and success possible, and change existing structures through acts of creative destruction. This is true for economic but even more so for social entrepreneurs, whose goals are to deliberately promote social change and build new social structures.

6.3.2 *Reasons why social entrepreneurship is a fast-growing sector*

Bornstein (2004) points out that in the last two decades of the twentieth century, the civil and social sectors have been the fastest-growing sectors in occupational terms. Numerous new foundations, social ventures and NGOs spread across the world. However, there is a need to examine the reasons for this rapid growth in the third sector. Although it is beyond the scope of this book to answer this question, the following four possible factors seem to be important, at least as a way to open up discussion.

The first factor is an *increasing individual motivation* for social action. The rise in social innovation and civil sector engagement is partly due to the changing motivation systems in the highly developed countries. Once individuals have all their basic needs met, they often aim to realize their full potential in terms of achievement and job satisfaction. This interest in self-realization in combination with the struggle for social recognition by their social networks makes social entrepreneurship an attractive option for many people. Other incentives for social entrepreneurship are perceptions of inefficiencies and a mismatch between the supply side and the demand side of public goods. Further drivers are personal experiences (e.g. problems in education, health centres, etc.) or a deep religious and ethical conviction of the human duty to help other people.

A second reason for the fast-growing civil sector seems to be the *rising complexity of economic and social organization*. Governments are not able to oversee all the influencing issues and interrelations in a highly diversified socioeconomic setting. There is a growing demand for civil and private sectors to tackle manifold socioeconomic issues, such as the ageing population, labour mobility, or cultural diversity management. Governments are not able to handle all the social problems, coordination and market failures. However, the government has to provide incentives for social action created by the private and civil sectors. The government, therefore, should establish adequate regulation and standards (such as environmental standards or healthcare standards in companies) or make direct subsidies for social businesses and entrepreneurship.

A third factor, strongly related to the complexity issue, highlights the ability of social innovation to *deal with budget constraints of governments*. The provision of public goods is supposed to contribute to individuals' sets of choices. In a similar vein, merit goods (in particular concerning education and the acquisition of capabilities) are considered to improve individual decision-making (Pyka 2011). Budget constraints and increasing efforts to reduce public debt, however, constrain the possibilities of providing public and merit goods. At the same time, the amount of GDP located in the public sector is extremely high. As the funds to the public sector increase, it is not surprising to see claims of improvements in the efficiency of the public sector, as well as more contribution from the private and civil sector for the creation of public goods. With regards to the need of more effective and efficient government spending and the provision of public good, it is worth noting that innovation is not confined to the private sector alone, but is also required in the government and civil sector (Hanusch and Pyka 2007, 2007b; Pyka 2011).

A fourth factor seems to be *increased individual and social learning*. Most of the conditions and requirements for improving the quality of public goods are closely connected to decentralized information processing. Networks of local and international social entrepreneurs willing to take on the risks of embarking upon new ventures are well suited to offering a diversified bundle of public goods as well as exploring and exploiting the opportunities for innovative and creative solutions (Pyka 2011). In this sense, the social entrepreneur resembles the venture entrepreneur in some respects and faces similar problems and difficulties. The application of modern entrepreneurship theories (such as the network or the capability enhancing perspective) will therefore be likely to generate new insights that improve our understanding of social innovation.

6.3.3 Social businesses

A social business is a financially auto-sustainable type of social entrepreneurship. In other words, a social business tackles a social problem and enlarges the capabilities and well-being of individuals, but runs (at least after an initial financial push) without the help and finance of external actors. A new NGO that provides lifelong learning courses to elderly people with the help of private donations is a social entrepreneurship, not a social business. A social business could be, for instance, a financially auto-sustainable microcredit institution or a project of an MNE to provide high-quality clothing and food to the poor at low prices. Or a social business could be a consultancy company run by and for elderly people, drawing upon the skills and experiences of elderly people and helping other people.

The term 'social business' implies the existence of types of policies, financial resources and incentives other than mere donation-driven social ventures. The combination and importance of the cooperation partners from the public and private spaces can also be quite different. Social business may provide more options for civil-private ventures and win-win situations for private companies and society in general, for example through the sustainable production of products and services that match the needs, demands and acquisitive power of the poor. While an NGO and a social business both address societal problems, their functioning and daily business activities can be quite different. A key business activity of most NGOs throughout their lifetime is to raise funds to keep it running. In contrast, a social business thinks about how to advance processes, technologies or organization – in summary, how to innovate – to provide more services to the people who need them. Accordingly social businesses can contribute to social change and welfare in a financially auto-sustainable manner.

This idea finds many supporters in science, politics, and the civic and private sector. For example, the microcredits revolution show that this type of contribution is possible, but several multinational companies do as well. It is worth mentioning that making market forces work for human development is in line with Amartya Sen's thinking, which first follows the basic ideas of Adam Smith (and John Stuart Mill) that markets and the division of labour are crucial for the economic wealth of nations (Smith 1776), but so too are the moral implications of economic development and the well-being of people (Smith 1759, 1776). Naturally, many politicians (finance ministers in particular) like the idea that social problems can be addressed by markets which do not require money from the government budget. And arguably most people working in enterprises would like the idea that they are not just expanding the turnover and profits of the company, but are simultaneously doing something useful for society as a whole. Of course, in many cases enterprises may act in this way because they are obliged to, or to foster their long-term economic profit; however, many people within the company would probably like to work in social corporate responsibility, or in social business and not just for economic profit. Indeed, enterprises are increasingly engaging in corporate social responsibility and social business and trying to explore the potential fortune at the base of the income pyramid. Prahalad (2004), Yunus (2007), Hart (2010) and others show that companies, especially multinational companies, can indeed work with and have positive effects for the two-thirds of the world's population living at the base of the income pyramid. Both sides can profit from proper integration. MNEs can enter into a trillion dollar market, expanding their turnover and profits as well as benefitting from reverse and frugal innovation (Immelt *et al.* 2009). On the other hand, the poor can gain access to markets, improve their standard of living and well-being and become active agents of economic development. For some this may sound utopian, while others may despise the idea of capitalist enterprises penetrating into social sectors and addressing social needs. However, it is happening and it often has a positive influence on standards of living, job creation and human agency. Maybe it is better to focus less on the 'if' and more on the 'how', because most simply state-driven development models have turned out to be economically inefficient and have in many cases negatively affected people's levels of freedom and self-determination.

It is crucial to address how people can be empowered to be able to create positive social changes through market forces. Continued polarization and polemic-driven discussions about state against market, capitalist companies against human welfare, and knowledge and innovation in industrialized countries against poverty and backwardness in developing countries all miss the opportunities that exist between these extreme positions. Demonizing the enterprises and blind belief in market forces both seem to oversimplify or else miss the complexity involved in these issues. Market forces and private companies can indeed help the poor, in the same way that the poor can also contribute to economic development and innovation. In this vein, Prahalad and Hart (2002) make a plea for the exploitation of the major opportunities for new markets and social welfare through MNEs focusing on the bottom of the pyramid:

> It is tragic that as Western capitalists we have implicitly assumed that the rich will be served by the corporate sector, while governments and NGOs will protect the poor and the environment. This implicit divide is stronger than most realize. Managers in MNCs, public policy makers, and NGO activists all suffer from this historical division of roles. A huge opportunity lies in breaking this code – linking the poor and the rich across the world in a seamless market organized around the concept of sustainable growth and development. Collectively, we have only begun to scratch the surface of what is the biggest potential market opportunity in the history of commerce. Those in

the private sector who commit their companies to a more inclusive capitalism have the opportunity to prosper and share their prosperity with those who are less fortunate. In a very real sense, the fortune at the bottom of the pyramid represents the loftiest of our goals!

(Prahalad and Hart 2002, p. 14)

Addressing the bottom of the pyramid and creating win-win situations between MNEs and the poor offers large opportunities for economic development and social welfare; however, several challenges have to be tackled first. Prahalad and Hart (2002), Prahalad (2004) and Hart (2010) show that assumptions impeding the focus of MNEs at the base of the pyramid (BoP) are wrong, for various reasons. First, the BoP is indeed an enormous market; second, it is possible to produce goods and services that the BoP can afford; third, the poor are interested in technologies and novelties; fourth, managers can be very excited by businesses with humanitarian dimensions and fifth, the BoP can contribute to innovation and business development. However, to reach the BoP, MNEs have to introduce new business models and invest in the commercial infrastructure of the BoP. Many Indian and Chinese enterprises (as well as some MNEs from income rich industrialized countries) have impressively shown that the BoP can indeed be a source of innovation and a market which facilitates firm growth, turnover and profits (Prahalad 2004; Immelt *et al.* 2009). For example, Lenovo would never have grown so fast without adapting its products and services to the local needs and demands in China (Lu 2000). India is the springboard for several reverse innovations and frugal innovations and large MNEs such as General Electric are changing their business models and winning through attending to and learning from the BoP (Immelt *et al.* 2009; The Economist 2010). Reverse innovation refers to innovations (e.g. new products, designs, services and business models) that are developed or first used in developing countries and then are spread to the industrialized countries, such as for instance a battery-driven, portable electrocardiograph machine that was first developed for doctors in India and China. Frugal innovation refers to reducing the complexity of a good or service and deleting non-essential features, thereby lowering the costs of production, as well as reducing the complexity of usage for the clients – and although these frugal goods and services are often originally designed for clients in development countries, consumers in the industrialized world also desire more simplicity and easy handling.

These factors show that the markets at the BoP can actively contribute to the innovation and introduction of new products and services by MNEs. The BoP should not just be considered as made up of passive clients for whom companies try to provide lower quality and price products, but rather as a source for new ideas and innovation. To facilitate economic win-win situations between the MNEs and the BoP, investment in local areas is necessary. MNEs have the resources to contribute to sustainable economic development in less developed and rural regions of developing countries. However, enabling the poor to become clients, business partners and innovators requires the creation of institutions and a commercial infrastructure that can foster human agency and development. According to Prahalad and Hart (2002), focus on the following particular measures is necessary to accomplish this goal.

1 The creation of buying power through access to credit, and income generation through jobs.
2 Shaping aspirations, for example through consumer education.
3 Tailoring local solutions, through bottom-up development and targeted product innovations.
4 Improving access through communication links and distribution systems.

There are many practical examples that show these measures can help to make the attendance of the markets at the BoP viable and profitable for MNEs, while at the same time opening up new economic opportunities for the local population. For example, Tata, Nestle, Novartis, Starbucks, Hewlett-Packard, Unilever, Citigroup, Johnson and Johnson, Lenovo, Avon and the Grameen Bank all engage successfully with the BoP and often create win-win situations. Serving the bottom of the pyramid requires new business and distribution models as well as new finance and cost structures that can contribute to local and human development and lead to a wave of new technological, organizational and institutional innovations. This in turn requires business strategies ranging from frugal innovation, cost reduction and a focus on the core characteristics of the products, to localization of the production and distribution to the integration of the BoP as an innovator and business partner. Each approach leads to different challenges, but also enormous opportunities for innovation and business competitiveness. It is noteworthy that top-down frugal innovation is not enough; localization and zero-based innovation are also required for prolific access to the local knowledge basis, client binding and business competitiveness. This requires companies to deal with structural changes to their routines and power structures. Companies that succeed in this venture can open up new markets and opportunities for their corporate innovation system. The government, however, must also in turn ensure that multinational companies do not abuse modern words such as frugal and reverse innovation merely to gain market power. To address several potential issues and problems proper regulation and control by the state is necessary to:

• impede the exploitation of the labour force, money and ideas of the poor by MNEs; prevent rent-seeking by MNEs;
• create incentives for MNEs to empower the poor;
• invest in local business development; and
• impede the crowding out of local nascent industries.

A regulatory framework can help to prevent the exploitation of the poor and contribute to the sustained economic development of poor regions and enhance the human capabilities of the BoP. In this way social businesses (as well as socially responsible economic businesses in poor regions) can be significant contributors to human agency and development, providing new innovative ideas, services, goods and organization models that empower the poor and contribute to human welfare. But social entrepreneurship should not be abused by companies to legitimize economic exploitation and crowd out local economies. Nor does it free government from its responsibility to address market failures and social problems. Social entrepreneurship is an important concept and has contributed to the improvement of human agency and welfare, but sometimes provision within an institutionalised framework, for example of high quality public education provided by the state, arguably is the final goal. Social entrepreneurs can be important actors who introduce new ideas and solutions. They often address problems that result from other shortcomings, such as the lack of public goods, technology, competitive companies and well-paid jobs, or institutions that do not empower the people and do not provide minimum acceptable standards of human rights and access to social services. So far this chapter has discussed entrepreneurship that has a positive or productive aim, but some entrepreneurial actions are deliberately destructive.

6.4 Destructive entrepreneurship

The term 'entrepreneurship' has a strong positive connotation, at least for most economists. However not all entrepreneurial ventures aim to produce something (productive entrepreneurship) or to improve the welfare of society as a whole (social entrepreneurship). It is important not to forget the destructive side of the creative destruction processes. Innovations that entrepreneurs introduce in the market and society can destroy some competences, capabilities and jobs by making them obsolete. Although these short-term negative effects can end up contributing to economic and human development in the long term, there are also many entrepreneurial actions that create an advantage only for the entrepreneurs and their close social networks at the expense of others, or else maintain the status quo and impede new competitors.

Destructive entrepreneurship can have strong negative effects on economic and human development. The history of humanity is full of examples of people showing great ingenuity when engaging in unproductive or even destructive entrepreneurship (Baumol 1990). Typical examples are military operations, conflicts and wars, rent-seeking, corruption and organized crime. These activities are entrepreneurial actions, as they require leadership, a business goal and/or conviction by the entrepreneurs, the capacity to push things through, and the ability to organize networks and make profits. From a historical perspective it is a comparatively new phenomenon (since the Industrial Revolution) that people become rich through productive activities of their own labour, rather than merely subsist. For example in ancient Rome, the primary sources of income for the rich were military conquests, landholding, usury and political payment (Baumol 1990, p. 899). In medieval China the wealth created by private enterprises was often confiscated by the monarchy and the path to wealth and prestige was instead through success in the imperial examination for a position in the bureaucracy or government (Baumol 1990, pp. 901–2). In both cases exploitation and corruption was widespread. In Medieval Europe, warfare and conquest were key sources of economic profits and social prestige (Baumol 1990, pp. 903–4). With the coming of law and order, rent-seeking and the attempt to gain property rights, monopoly became a primary source of income (Baumol 1990, p. 907). In modern times, much energy is put into litigation and lawsuits between companies as they can generate massive gains or losses of wealth and power (Baumol 1990, p. 915). Furthermore crime and drugs can also be sources of individual wealth. All of these activities are of an entrepreneurial nature, but they are highly unproductive and even destructive. By no means do these activities add to human development, apart from the enrichment of the individual entrepreneurs and their close network or following. In fact, they have a strong negative effect and even impede innovation and structural change. This implies that it depends on the 'rules of the game' whether people's entrepreneurial spirit adds to innovation and social welfare. As Baumol (1990, p. 897–8) has argued:

> If entrepreneurs are defined, simply, to be persons who are ingenious and creative in finding ways that add to their own wealth, power, and prestige, then it is to be expected that not all of them will be overly concerned with whether an activity that achieves these goals adds much or little to the social product.

For this reason, policy makers and society need to change the rules of the game to reward productive and pro-human development entrepreneurship. Institutional changes are required to prevent enrichment and the achievement of prestige through unproductive activities such as rent-seeking, betting on the financial markets without any productive claim, corruption, war and crime. Instead, wealth and prestige should be achieved through productive and/or pro-human development activities. This is possible, as the strong growth in initiatives and employment in the social and civic sectors show.

6.5 Case study in the north-east of Brazil

This section applies the 'Sen meets Schumpeter' perspective to a case study on micro-entrepreneurship in the city of Patos in the interior of the Federal State of Paraiba in north-east Brazil. From October to December 2009, more than eighty semi-structured interviews were conducted with micro-entrepreneurs, microfinance employees, business consultants, social entrepreneurs and researchers to try to (a) understand whether the micro-entrepreneurs in the case region are efficiency enhancers, innovators, capability enhancers or necessity-based, and (b) get an in-depth picture on the contribution of microfinance to human development.

An independent consultant in Joao Pessoa (the capital city of the Federal State of Paraiba in which Patos is located) introduced the author to participants in the finance and consultancy market in Paraiba and facilitated the participation in workshops of the Brazilian Service of Support for Micro and Small Enterprises (SEBRAE). Subsequently, over a period of six weeks, the team of the microfinance institute 'Estrela' provided an in-depth insight into their daily business with the clients in Patos, facilitating direct access to the suburbs and surrounding villages.

Additional interviews were made with several scholars at the universities in Patos, Joao Pessoa and Campina Grande and the information supplemented by secondary data on entrepreneurship and general socioeconomic dynamics in Paraiba and Brazil (Campos *et al.* 2010; GEM-Brazil 2012; UNDP-Brazil 2013). Of course, the results and findings do not support broad generalisations. Nevertheless, they show the practical relevance of the Sen meets Schumpeter perspective in understanding and evaluating the complex relations between social innovations, human agency and local economic development, and illustrate how qualitative case studies can provide useful insights for both academics and practitioners. In addition, the topics addressed affect millions of micro-entrepreneurs in Brazil and similar regions.

6.5.1 Patos and the microfinance institution 'Estrela'

Patos is located in the 'Sertão', a semi-arid region in the interior of north-east Brazil, covering some 18,000 km². With about 100,000 inhabitants, Patos is the biggest city and a major trading hub in this part of the Sertão in Paraiba. According to UNDP-Brazil (2013), in 2010 Patos had a medium HDI score of 0.701. Though this represents an improvement from previous years (from an HDI of 0.678 in 2000), Patos continues to be one of the poorest regions in Brazil. While some people, in the centre of the city, live comparatively well and have a good standard of education and health, there are also serious levels of poverty, deprivation, crime and human unfreedom in the suburbs and the villages. In recent decades, millions of people have emigrated from the Sertão to the economic centres in the south of Brazil in search of economic opportunities. According to UNDP-Brazil (2013), 18.86 per cent of the population live on less than US$1.25 dollars a day; just 49.27 per cent of the over 18 age-group completed their primary education; and 62.06 per cent work in the informal sector. Poor families often depend upon the money from the retirement income of the older family members and/or recently the contribution from Bolsa Familia (Brazilian cash transfer program). Though they are still very high, poverty and economic inequality have declined considerably in Patos as well as in Brazil in general – partly as a result of economic growth and political stability and partly thanks to Bolsa Familia, microloans and a variety of other social policy measures (Duarte *et al.* 2009; Neri 2009; Campos *et al.* 2010; Sicsú 2013).

The Estrela Institute, founded in May 2005 in Patos, is contributing to this positive dynamic and is a successful case of a financially sustainable and innovative social business. After the third year, the MFI has reached both operational and financial sustainability, expanding from its starting base in Patos to several neighbouring villages. Recently it even founded two smaller branches in two other small cities in the Federal State of Paraiba (in Sousa, a city in the Sertao with around 65,000 habitants, located about 127 km from Patos, and in Guarabira, a city with approximately 55,000 habitant and about 243 km from Patos). At the time of the study, 23 people worked for the Instituto Estrela and it had served over 9,000 clients so far. As it states on its webpage, the promotion of human freedom is the explicit founding mission of the Instituto Estrela.

> Mission: Develop the market for microcredits with a focus on contributing to the expansion and assurance of individual freedoms (Sen), and treating people as agents of change and not as passive recipients. Expand the freedom with regards to economic opportunities of potential entrepreneurs deprived of the possibility to access credits through the conventional banking system, and offer our scope of activities as a vehicle for social change, financial emancipation and environmental sustainability. (www.institutoestrela.com. br, own translation[2])

The Estrela Institute has played an important role in Patos and its surrounding area in helping hundreds of micro-entrepreneurs to help themselves and in contributing to local economic development by enhancing local efficiency and sometimes even innovating.

6.5.2 Semi-structured interviews

Three main issues were analysed during the field research in Patos: first, to what extent the micro-entrepreneurs contribute to local economic dynamics and human development; second, the reasons for success or failure of the micro-entrepreneur; and third, the success factors and constraints of the social venture 'Estrela Institute'. The interview questions were guided by a list of central issues regarding the socioeconomic dynamics in the region, the capabilities and motivations of the micro-entrepreneurs, the business model and learning processes of a local micro-finance institute as well as the local innovation and business support system. More than eighty interviews were held with micro-entrepreneurs, a social entrepreneur and her microfinance employees, business consultants, university researchers and others (see Table 6.1).

The specific content of the interviews was adapted to the situation, interests, knowledge and language of each particular interviewee. For example,

Table 6.1 Type and number of interviewees

Type of interviewees	Number of interviews[a]
Micro-entrepreneurs	43
Micro-finance employees	11
University researcher	10
Micro and small company consultants	9
Externals: Journalists, NGO employees, professionals	8
Social entrepreneurs	1
Total	82

Note

a The interviews were held between October and December 2009 in Patos and surrounding villages, Joao Pessoa, Campina Grande, Guarabira and Souza.

micro-entrepreneurs were asked about their motivations, desires, problems and plans regarding their businesses, but also about their opinions on societal changes and their satisfaction with education, health and the government. Microfinance agents and business consultants were asked specifically about local market opportunities and dynamics, as well as the problems and strengths of the micro-entrepreneurs. Local researchers and journalists were consulted on the sectoral, institutional and historical development of the regions. University researchers were asked about education and research in the region, institutional changes in the region and the interactions between university, industry and government. Table 6.2 provides an overview of the main interview topics, according to the interviewee group.

Table 6.2 Interview topics

Interview topics	Main interview partners[a]
General questions (to all respondents)	
• Perception of institutional changes and improvement of human development (e.g. education and health)	
• Perception of market opportunities and sectoral dynamics (which markets)	All respondents
• Desires for the professional lives of their children and themselves	
General questions (mainly to microfinance and SME consultants)	
• Typical factors of success and failure of the entrepreneurs	Micro-finance employees; business
• Dynamics, improvements and problems in the microfinance market in Paraiba	consultants; university researchers
Particular cases (asking the micro-entrepreneurs and cross-checking with the microfinance employee and/or consultants)	
• Motivation and crucial steps of the venture, including: idea generation, expansion, establishment, future plans	Mainly micro-entrepreneurs;
• Evaluation of competitors	Cross-check with
• Use and implementation of new technologies	micro-finance
• Information seeking: access and use of training possibilities (e.g. Sebrae)	employees and business consultants;
• Cooperation with persons from other micro-ventures and institutions	
• Coordination and motivation of the employees	
• Learning and innovation within the venture (e.g. organisational novelties)	Social entrepreneur
• Evaluation of the success, constraints and potential of the ventures	
• Impact on other persons and the local area	

Note

a The interviews were made between October and December 2009 in Patos and surrounding villages, Joao Pessoa, Campina Grande, Guarabira and Souza.

The questions were also adapted to the age and education of the individuals. In a country and region with such profound differences in people's education, income, interests and experiences, it is important to adjust to these differences to gain a comprehensive picture from the different perspectives.

6.5.3 *Local innovators and capability enhancers*

Economists often criticize micro-entrepreneurship for its inability to overcome larger economic and institutional problems, arguing that few micro-entrepreneurs have the potential to expand into innovative SMEs able to promote sustained technology upgrading and structural change for their region. However, it should not be forgotten that the main purpose of microfinance and micro-businesses is not macroeconomic growth, but immediate poverty reduction and provision of the means to enable people to start helping themselves. There is no doubt that long-term structural change and economic development require a series of other factors, such as thriving SMEs, institutions, investment, R&D, and demand, but micro-entrepreneurship can contribute to poverty reduction and increase human agency. The interviews with the micro-entrepreneurs and microfinance consultants indicate that micro-entrepreneurship can contribute to economic efficiency and qualitative change on the local level. Several micro-entrepreneurs did indeed introduce structural changes into the local markets and can be considered local Schumpeterian innovators, but naturally, as a general rule in an economy, most entrepreneurs function more as efficiency enhancers, or in other words Kirznerian entrepreneurs. For example, many micro-entrepreneurs exploit price differentials by shortening transportation costs and offering products and services directly to the clients. Several business consultants argued in the interviews that there are virtually no saturated markets in the region, such as those in highly developed settings, so there is not necessarily a need to design radically new products, processes, organization, inputs or marketing to be competitive and survive, but that determination and business skills (such as appropriate accounting and selling skills) matter. Strikingly, all interviewed consultants of micro- and small enterprises in the region agreed that there are still significant business opportunities in all the existing sectors.

Most of the activities of micro-entrepreneurs in Patos are certainly not very innovative from a global perspective, but some of them introduce new products, processes, organizational structures, ways of marketing and inputs that are new to the local markets. Several micro-entrepreneurs have come up with indigenous innovations based on their local conditions and available inputs. If they are successful, they can inspire other micro-entrepreneurs who subsequently try to enter into these markets and adopt their strategies and business models. The micro-entrepreneurs in Paraiba engage in learning-by-doing and learning-by-solving activities and make incremental innovations. This can be seen in the way local micro-entrepreneurs explore and discover which technologies, products, processes and organizations do work, what endogenous capabilities and inputs are available and what the demand is. For example, a very poor man in Patos, having lived for some time on the street, started to sell meat from a small self-constructed grill on a street corner with the help of a small micro-loan. He took quality and customer satisfaction seriously and saved a fixed percentage of his income to invest in the improvement of his assets. Then he diversified into new products, first offering beverages and later sandwiches. Finally, he managed to open the first small pizza restaurant and delivery service in his fairly underdeveloped district of the small town, with some employees and a delivery service. Owing to his motivation at the beginning and business success later, the MFI gave him first a microcredit 100 Reais (about US$48, exchange rate 24 August 2013), then 360 Reais (US$152), later 1,500 Reais (US$635) and finally 6,000 Reais (US$2,540). Without the help of microfinance, this man would have never had a chance to get his microbusiness started, much less expanded into a competitive and profitable small business. He constantly invested in new assets and various types of organization. Due to his success, several other entrepreneurs have tried to enter these markets and copied the strategies of this entrepreneur. The microcredits helped him to gradually expand and improve his company.

Another good example is a successful entrepreneur in Patos who started to collecting and selling used goods from an old supermarket trolley. He recognized that local products were held in much higher regard in other districts and regions than they were locally. With the help of microcredits he bought local shoes and travelled to a neighbouring region where he found a much greater demand for these shoes. Now he owns a local shoe company and exports shoes to twenty states in Brazil.

Many similar cases can be found in a variety of other sectors such as food production, textiles, and retail or local marketing. These cases may not sound like innovation and structural change to someone living in a rich industrialized setting; however, for the economically poor population, these entrepreneurs introduce considerable changes. First, new sectors and jobs are created; second, the local product portfolio of the poor becomes diversified and affordable; and third, the composition of economic activities changes.

6.5.4 *Reasons for business failure*

Although the microfinance boom in recent years has made it easier for poor people in north-east Brazil to obtain loans and invest in micro- to small businesses (Neri 2009), many of the micro-ventures fail to become sustainable small businesses: the microbusinesses fail to create a sustainable income source for the micro-entrepreneurs. Why does this happen? The interviews indicate that reasons for these failures are not a lack of motivation, market opportunities or demand, but rather individual inability and lack of management skills to deal with the complexity of business processes. Many micro-entrepreneurs fail to upgrade to small or medium enterprises and become bankrupt when complexity rises. The agency of several micro-entrepreneurs in the region often becomes constrained by growing indebtedness and the lack of the required organizational skills, due to the access to various sources of microfinance and the assistance from several different lending groups, with different financial institutions and different lending conditions. Today, a number of NGOs as well as state-run and commercial banks hand out microcredits. Many small-scale entrepreneurs have become clients of several lenders, often as members of different groups with different payment terms and interest rates. The director of the Estrela Institute, Edinalda Lima, has warned that some small entrepreneurs overreach themselves and become insolvent. She said (during an interview in October 2009) that some micro-entrepreneurs are very successful at first, and quickly take out more loans from different banks. But they lose focus, and if their business runs into seasonal problems or fails to perform as anticipated, they fall behind with repayments and find themselves unable to pay the loans back. In light of the growing competition, some MFIs have lowered their requirements for credit. All too often, MFIs measure staff performance in terms of the generation of new customers. For some clients, however, the extra micro-loan is really just an additional burden. Lima insists that MFIs and their employees must not lose sight of the core idea of microcredit, which is to give people the chance to escape poverty themselves.

The effectiveness of MFIs, however, also depends on institutional support. The government needs to play a role in creating an appropriate environment in which borrowers are able to generate more successful business. On the whole, Brazil has made advances in the promotion of small-scale entrepreneurship. Increasing funds for micro-loans, forming new laws to formalize businesses, and providing social insurance to small entrepreneurs all aim to give the people the means for self-help. The Micro and Small Businesses Act in Brazil, for example, is specifically designed to motivate small-scale entrepreneurs to leave the informal economy and join the social security system. Micro- and small entrepreneurship is advancing in Brazil, and has a positive impact on self-determination and human development. Most of the microcredits are provided by a regional branch of BNDES, the national Brazilian development bank; nevertheless, some innovative small MFIs are emerging. In addition, there are also improvements regarding the basic access to education and health recognizable in Brazil (IPEA 2009; Sicsú 2013). There is certainly further need and great potential for improvement in infrastructure, education and health.

Besides these factors, the micro-ventures failure rate could be reduced by promoting a better systemic learning between the various groups of micro-entrepreneurs, the small and medium enterprises and the local institutions, such as the government, education centres, universities, MFIs and micro- and small enterprises' support services. While there are a considerable number of support institutions for micro-entrepreneurs, it can be argued that the systemic cooperation between these institutions is not as strong as it might be. Many opportunities for synergies and a great deal of know-how are not utilized. For instance, the employees of MFIs often have an in-depth understanding of local markets and prices, profit margins and market opportunities as well as small entrepreneurs' strengths and weaknesses. Public and private institutions could make use of this rich source of knowledge and more mutual learning and concerted action between the agencies involved in the microcredit business could contribute to clients' business success. For example, SEBRAE arguably does not interact with the local MFIs in Paraiba as much as it could, even though they have overlapping and often complementary skills: both sides could learn from each other and move forwards in their task of promoting small enterprises. While interested entrepreneurs currently use the knowledge and services of both institutions, cooperation between the different institutions would increase the quality and power of the aid they receive by creating better services and developing local tailor-made solutions.

Another difficult constraint to address is the comparatively low levels of trust between different groups. While the ties within social groups in the case region are very strong (for example, within family and friendship clans or within different public and private organizations and institutions), the ties between such groups are often weak in north-east Brazil. This causes new information on problems, strengths and opportunities for jobs, entrepreneurial action and innovation to be diffused fairly slowly. Instead, learning and incremental innovation in the case studies in Paraiba are mostly triggered by competition, access to common suppliers (e.g. of leather or equipment for the production of shoes and clothes) and shared infrastructure (e.g. local markets). Within cliques, kinship or close friendship networks, there is considerable knowledge exchange and mutual help.

6.5.5 *Success factors and constraints of the social business 'Estrela'*

The Estrela Institute is a good example of a successful social business venture that works closely together with its clients and aims to improve their human capabilities. The success of the venture seems to be mainly driven by the motivation and engagement of microfinance agents, most of whom are women who do not necessarily only want to sell their microcredits, but in many cases also want to see their clients excel, provide meaningful help for self-help and improve the welfare of the people. The close relation between the Estrela Institute and its clients allows it to adapt its financial products to the needs of the local population and entrepreneurs, such as by considering the seasonal fluctuations of different sectors, setting appropriate repayment and credit rates and creating group and individual credit models. Furthermore, it enables knowledge transfers about market opportunities, best practices and business administration skills, such as basic accountability, costs and prizes, location, marketing and so forth.

The main growth constraint for the Instituto Estrela is related to the problem most MFIs face: they struggle to obtain more operational money through credits from larger private or state-owned banks with acceptable rates and conditions, a difficulty similar to that of their clients. BNDES provides the largest financial support for microcredit in Brazil, working through its regional branches. In a way, this approach conforms to the logic that economies of scale can be realized through large-scale production, internalization of transaction costs and a comparatively large demand. However, it also seems that enabling institutional self-determination, agency and competition on the micro and local levels is critical. The Instituto Estrela and other small MFIs in Brazil should be able to compete for government funds or privileged tax rates because of: (a) their good performance in both financial and operational sustainability; (b) their contribution to local economic efficiency and economic development; and (c) their contribution to human development.

In a similar vein, incentives and access to finance for entrepreneurial action by the poor should be provided by the public and private banking sector. Furthermore, it is important to deal with the current situation in which most of the leading private and public banks have a strategic interest in not providing possible competitors with money (for instance new MFIs).

6.5.6 Lessons from the case study

The case study on human development and microfinance in the north-east of Brazil illustrates that combining the perspectives of innovation economics and the human capability approach can be very helpful in getting a more comprehensive analysis of the strengths, problems and challenges of micro-entrepreneurs and social businesses. The analysis of the social business Instituto Estrela shows how interactive learning between clients and microfinance agents as well as systemic learning within an MFI can lead to business success and better adaptation to the demands and needs of the clients. It also shows that the desire to empower other people and provide them with economic freedom certainly has the potential to be a driver of economic competitiveness and support sustained success of a business. The Estrela Institute can be considered a successful social business which manages to provide microcredits (with comparatively low interest rates) and business advice to the poor in a financially auto-sustainable way, helping the micro-entrepreneurs to help themselves.

The study also indicates that once people are provided with the basic capabilities and opportunities to be active agents of development they are able to innovate and make qualitative changes in their lives and those of their families. Many micro-entrepreneurs function as local efficiency enhancers and some can even be seen as local Schumpeterian entrepreneurs, introducing local innovations into their city or villages and changing their lives for themselves, their families and their district. Microfinance and innovation at the BoP can and actually do foster human development, as seen in the case region. Microfinance expands the human freedom of people by opening up new occupational choices and providing the opportunities to realize their own businesses. However, also a set of institutional challenges and problems must be addressed to make the microfinance work for the poor and expand human development. First, there is a threat that the competition between MFIs for the business of micro-entrepreneurs may burden people with debt as they accept various different credits from different groups and from different institutions. Second, although the population has broader access to education and health services, the quality of these services is still in need of substantial improvement. Third, the inability of micro-ventures to upgrade into small and medium enterprises is not rooted in a lack of market opportunities, demand or entrepreneurial motivation, but is rather due to the lack of organizational skills, finance and information. Fourth, better coordination between the MFIs, the Brazilian small business promotion programmes and the local government is necessary to facilitate learning processes between the various agents in the local production and innovation systems and to help the micro-entrepreneurs excel. Of course, these findings cannot be generalized to all less developed regions in which microfinance is applied. Each region, its agents and networks, problems, strengths and opportunities are different. However, interviews with experts from regional development agencies and SEBRAE confirm that analysing the relations between human development and local innovation is highly relevant and applicable for many other parts of north-east Brazil.

6.6 Chapter conclusion

This chapter has presented the concept of 'entrepreneurship as capability enhancement,' as a complementary perspective to the traditional entrepreneurship theories (see Section 6.1). Typically, economics views entrepreneurs as an input factor for economic growth that enhances efficiency, solves coordination problems, or introduces innovation and new dynamics into the system (Gries and Naude 2010). However, entrepreneurship can also contribute to the human development of the entrepreneur and other persons. The evaluation of entrepreneurial action is then not based on its contribution to economic efficiency and growth, but on its contribution to human development and welfare.

Micro-entrepreneurship and social entrepreneurship are two of the key areas of interest for the 'entrepreneurship as capability enhancement' approach (see Sections 6.2 and 6.3). Micro-entrepreneurship is widespread in less developed regions, often as a result of the lack of decent employment choices and the need of the poor to gain more money: it is often an indication of unfreedom and a lack of choices rather than human agency. Nevertheless, if a person cannot attain a decent job, micro-entrepreneurship can be an option by which to become active, to raise the standard of living for the family and perhaps even introduce qualitative changes into their local environment. Furthermore, becoming a micro-entrepreneur – even when initially an obligation – can change into a valued functioning role. This is why the approach of entrepreneurship as capability enhancement can provide a useful evaluative framework for the role of micro-entrepreneurship in poverty reduction and human development, beyond the mere judgement of its role in overall economic development. Social entrepreneurship deliberately aims to increase the human capabilities and/or well-being of other people. This approach matches the concerns and ideas of the Sen meets Schumpeter paradigm, as social entrepreneurs create networks and introduce innovations leading to qualitative change in socioeconomic structures.

These theoretical concepts have been tested within a case study on micro-entrepreneurship and microfinance in north-east Brazil. Most importantly from a theoretical perspective, the study reveals that microfinance and entrepreneurship can be understood from the 'Sen meets Schumpeter' perspective. Social innovations, such as access to microfinance, together with entrepreneurial spirit, can lead to qualitative change in the lives of the poor and their immediate socioeconomic environment. The success stories of some micro-entrepreneurs lead to demonstration effects and imitative behaviour by their neighbours and friends, and consequent changes in the entrepreneurial culture and local economy. The case study also illustrates that technological learning and innovation is not significant only for the high-tech level in industrialized settings, but is also crucial for the success of micro-entrepreneurship and social businesses in less developed regions. But co-evolutionary institutional changes and concerted policies are also necessary to promote the success of the local entrepreneurs and allow them to engage in trial and error activities. This implies the need to create a prolific network of supportive institutions, diffusing information, promoting interactive learning and also competition between the different agents and enabling high quality entrepreneurship that contributes to both economic diversification and human development.

Notes

1 In 1981 Bill Drayton founded the non-profit organization Ashoka which identifies and supports leading social entrepreneurs through a social venture capital approach. Currently [December 2011] Ashoka operates in over 60 countries and supports over 2000 social entrepreneurs; http://ashoka.org.

2 Original version: 'Desenvolver o mercado de micro-crédito com foco em sua contribuição à expansão e à garantia das liberdades individuais (Sen), compreendendo os atores integrados como agentes de mudança e não como beneficiários passivos. Empoderar a liberdade de oportunidades econômicas dos empreendedores podados de possibilidades de crédito por meio do sistema bancário convencional, tendo nosso escopo de atividades como um veículo para mudança social e financeira, emancipação cidadã e ambiental.' (www.institutoestrela.com.br, retrieved on 21st October 2011).

7 Policy dimensions for structural change and human development

Previous chapters have shown how the human capabilities of people are deeply affected by economic diversification within their country and the networks they are embedded in. One key achievement of the basic needs and the human development approach has been to convince policy-makers that focus of development policies should not be on economic growth as an ultimate goal of development, but should rather focus on empowering people, making them agents instead of patients of development. But neither should politics focus on human capabilities and neglect economic development and competitiveness. Paul Streeten, one of the most influential proponents of both basic needs and the human development approach, wrote:

> [W]e should never lose sight of the ultimate purpose of the exercise, to treat men and women as ends, to improve the human condition, to enlarge people's choices. …[A] unity of interests would exist if there where rigid links between economic production (as measured by income per head) and human development (reflected by human indicators such as life expectancy or literacy, or achievements such as self-respect, not easily measured). But these two sets of indicators are not very closely related.
>
> (Streeten 1994, cited in Ray 1998, p. 7)

This statement implies that there is a certain disconnection between economic production and human development. This book has addressed this divide and shows various possible ways that economic and human development can be integrated, both theoretically and methodologically. The main political implications are that sustainable human development policies must go hand in hand with proper economic and structural change policy. Several examples of direct and indirect links between economic and human development have been illustrated. The theoretical proposition has been to introduce structural features linking both dimensions, rather than concentrate on the role of income or production expansion for human development. Taking entrepreneurship, social capital and economic diversification into consideration enables a better understanding of the complex feedback between economic and human development. The theoretical analyses and empirical applications described in this book have shown the profound effects of these factors on human development. The human development approach correctly identifies the purpose of development: to expand people's well-being, quality of life and agency. However, to correctly identify the means of development, it is necessary to do more than merely focus on increasing individuals' capabilities, for example, through health and education expenditure, or income redistribution. Individuals are immersed in networks of social relations and economic systems that change over time, providing different economic choices, opportunities, demands, specific capabilities and skills that affect their decisions. The human development approach rightly moved the focus to the supply of human capabilities, but in doing so, it neglected the economic demands for such capabilities. Merely expanding basic capabilities may not necessarily lead to the systemic creation of economic development, such as employment opportunities. Indeed, many human development researchers are aware of the importance of economic development for human development. For instance Ranis *et al.* (2000, p. 203) state:

> It is not enough to create a larger pool of educated people; there must also be opportunities for them to be productively employed or it might simply increase the number of educated unemployed. Relevant to the demand side are the savings and investment rates, technology choice and the overall policy setting.

Amartya Sen also reiterates the importance of economic opportunities and income (Sen 1999). Nevertheless, the practical policy implications and research interests of the Human Development and Capability Association has tended to focus on basic needs, justice and human rights. Their policy focus is based on covering basic needs (health, education, income, etc.) as a means to bolster development processes. However, this does not automatically lead to long-term development and poverty reduction. Structural features of economic systems (such as networks, or sectoral composition and interrelations) deeply affect economic production and human development and can lead to the reproduction of structural inequality, as discussed in previous chapters. Development policy approaches have focused on macroeconomic stability, economic efficiency, good governance, redistribution of income and the provision of social services and public goods, yet little focus has been applied to understanding the economic meso-structures and how the dynamics at a more disaggregated level affect people's choices and capabilities. To facilitate pro-poor structural change and to design proper industrial policies, in-depth knowledge of individual behaviour at the micro-level, as well as learning processes, sectoral linkages and dynamics at the meso level is required. These are decisive issues in the emergence of new sectors and the creation of jobs, with important implications for the design of industrial policies and institutional architecture. This is where innovation economics can help. Innovation and (economic) structural change may not be the primary goals of development, but certainly they are the key drivers of development; not just of economic development but also human development (see Chapters 4, 5 and 6). This is why development policy must not only focus on providing actors with basic capabilities, but must also, in parallel, engage in the promotion of fertile and inclusive network structures, as well as horizontal and vertical economic diversification and integration. A greater structural embeddedness and diversification can provide more actors with opportunities to participate in, contribute to and benefit from the development processes of their socioeconomic environments. This is why structural intervention and incentives are needed to provide people with the opportunities to apply and increase their knowledge through learning-by-doing activities (Arocena and Sutz 2005; Lundvall 2007) and promote fertile creative destruction processes. To design policies that simultaneously promote structural change and human development, the following theoretical and practical questions need to be addressed.

1   Why is state intervention necessary? (Section 7.1)
2   Should industrial policy focus on specialization or diversification? (Section 7.3)
3   What are the essential policy dimensions and measures needed to make structural change work for human development? (Sections 7.3 and 7.4)
4   How can the labour market and human agency policies contribute to structural change? (Section 7.5)

Consideration of these questions is essential when designing development policies. However, there are no one-size-fits-all practical answers. Indeed, evolutionary economics and human development theorizing highlights the fact that all people and regions are different and hence require solutions that can be adapted to their specific constraints, demands and possibilities. Nevertheless, theoretical frameworks, methodologies and empirical studies are needed to provide decision makers with the tools to fully take into account economic complexity and the interrelations between structural change and human development.

7.1 The need for state intervention

The role of the state in structural economic transformation processes has been strongly debated in development economics. The different schools of thought have tended to place themselves into two radically opposing camps, either pushing state-planned development or full market liberalization. Today, an increasingly more balanced position between free markets and state intervention is seen both in academia and policy (Rodrik 2004). Both market forces and strategic intervention by the state are required for sustained economic development and social welfare. There is a consensus in modern development economics that systemic action in economic, social and political spaces is required to achieve structural change, employment creation and poverty reduction in a sustained manner (e.g. UNRISD 2010).

The Washington Consensus (Williamson 1989) represents the strand of development thinking that focuses on the importance of privatization and liberalization in overcoming government failures and improving economic efficiency. However, economic history has shown that the rise of entirely new sectors has virtually never been achieved solely by free market forces. In most cases, government interventions, subsidies and incentives together with private investment have been required to encourage the emergence of new sectors. A notable example of this is Silicon Valley, which would probably never become the global high-tech cluster in semiconductors, information and communication industry that it is today without funding from US government agencies such as NASA and the US Air Force. It was similar interaction between governmental and private investment in railroads and roads that allowed the Industrial Revolution, mass production and consumption, such as the automobile industry, to spread effectively. We can also see this in the role of government subsidies in the Chinese government, which were passed onto the Chinese Academy of Sciences and Free Trade Zones, enabling the rise of companies such as Lenovo and attracting direct foreign investments.

There are a huge number of public–private cooperation ventures that have established the viability of new sectors; in fact it is so commonplace that it seems impossible to support the notion that any of the radical new technologies that trigger significant creative destruction processes have been driven by market forces and trade alone. It seems difficult for radically new sectors to emerge and to establish solely on the basis of neoliberal policies, liberalization and privatization (UNRISD 2010; Lin and Monga 2011). Of course, market forces and liberalization can be an important efficiency driver (Krueger 1985), but the emergence of new sectors often requires a critical mass of agents, infrastructure and services to achieve the economies of scale and agglomeration effects needed to make the sector profitable. This is where state subsidies and incentives, for instance installing infrastructure or providing tax incentives, can be helpful or even necessary. Once it has achieved critical mass, the sector can grow, upgrade and diversify through self-organization and market forces. Supporters of the polarization theory have argued that these economic reactions require an initial push (Rosenstein-Rodan 1943; Nurkse 1953; Myrdal 1957; Hirschman 1958). Market forces, along with educated, healthy people, are crucial but often insufficient; this is especially true for radical innovations and completely new sectors which require several co-evolutionary processes and initial investments. This is where industrial policy and a future-oriented public sector come into play (Rodrik 2004; Hanusch and Pyka 2007a). However, this requires a proper institutional architecture, based on cooperation and competition that overcomes market failures, government failures, technological lock-ins and the negative effects of polarization. What is vital is that governments have knowledge available to them concerning the market failures they have to address and the mechanisms which bring about polarization and inequality reproduction (see Section 7.2). Furthermore, qualitative diversification requires a proper combination of related and unrelated variety growth, concentration and de-concentration, and regional and national policies (see Section 7.3).

7.2 Market failures and polarization effects

Market failures make strategic industrial policy necessary to promote positive feedback mechanisms, achieve a more efficient allocation of economic activities, facilitate innovation and expand social welfare. Market failures can lead to underinvestment in R&D, a lack of entrepreneurial discovery processes and insufficient social protection and cohesion.

One reason for market failures is uncertainty and the bounded rational behaviour of agents. Uncertainty and bounded rationality, in which no economic agent alone is able to have a perfect comprehensive view of the system and its agents, interactions, technologies and causal relations, are key features of economic life. The representative rational agent, constantly making optimal decisions based on total information, does not exist. Rather the world is dominated by routines and satisficing behaviours, market failures and rigidities. Simon (1947, 1957) pointed out that people and companies are rarely able to maximize their profits, but rather try to at least satisfy their minimum standards. He argues that usually people do not know all the relevant probabilities of outcomes and can rarely evaluate all outcomes with full information to make perfect decisions; therefore, he presents the term 'bounded rationality' as a more realistic approach to human behaviour, taking these limitations into account. Bounded rationality refers to the idea that the rationality of the individuals is constrained by the quality and amount of available information, and the cognitive limitations of people and time. Due to these constraints people in many cases do not behave optimally but rather apply satisficing strategies. Another effect is that rational choices for entrepreneurial actions are often dismissed. Furthermore, qualitative entrepreneurship often does not emerge (without government subsidies or incentives) because of the uncertain returns from inventions and the risk of failure from innovations.

Another key reason for market failure is the natural tendency of market forces towards short-sighted profit maximization instead of long-term social welfare maximization. Of course, market forces can be and often are an essential contributor to welfare and provide a powerful mechanism to deal with complexity and uncertainty through specialization, the division of labour and trade. However, drawing the best out of market forces requires capable institutions and strategic state interventions to tackle market failures caused by uncertainty as well as externalities. Technological externalities are probably the best known types of externalities in economic; however, Rodrik (2004) outlines the fact that technological externalities are not the only, and perhaps not even the most important, factor impeding structural change and economic diversification, especially in less developed settings. Information and coordination externalities are also crucial problems. Underinvestment in R&D and lack of search mechanisms and trial and error behaviour is demand-side problem as well as being a supply-side problem. A proper institutional framework and strategic collaboration between the private and public sectors need to enable market forces by creating the demand for entrepreneurs, for R&D, invention and innovation.

The three types of market failure – technological, informational and coordination externalities – are outlined in further detail below, together with an explanation of why they can either prevent or foster the supply and demand of R&D, entrepreneurship and innovation.

7.2.1 Technology externalities

Technology externalities refer to the indirect effects that the creation of new technologies by one economic agent has on the consumption and production opportunities of others. New technologies can have positive effects on society as a whole, but often creators of new technologies cannot appropriate all the benefits created by their investments in R&D, and therefore they tend not to invest sufficiently in R&D, but instead wait for others to solve the technological problems. To a certain degree, technology has the non-rivalry and non-excludability characteristics of public goods. First, technical knowledge can be used simultaneously by various producers. Second, inventors or property owners cannot entirely prevent the use of their knowledge by other firms. As a result of this non-rivalry and non-excludability, the creation of technical knowledge by one firm has positive effects, not just for that firm, but also for other firms. This leads to the freerider problem and underinvestment in R&D and technology. Investment in R&D is costly and the outcomes are uncertain. However, if the investment is successful, then the outcomes cannot be appropriated entirely by the inventor/innovator, and thus, as noted earlier, many companies wait for other companies to innovate and solve technical problems. This leads to underinvestment in R&D as well as costly formal and informal measures to protect intellectual property. Both mechanisms impede the creation and diffusion of innovation, a higher labour productivity and the emergence of new sectors. This is especially damaging in settings where there are weak legal enforcement of property rights and high risk-aversion. Underinvestment in R&D is even more pronounced in technologies that are important for human development and well-being, but that are not expected to provide high-economic profits in return. For example, many diseases (such as malaria) are predominantly located in areas with comparatively low economic purchasing power. The cost of systemic R&D is high, the outcome for private companies uncertain and the expected potential economic gains comparatively low. In addition, the probability of copycats producing generic drugs is quite high. Generic drugs would be extremely positive for social welfare, but not for the inventing company's profits. A prisoner's-dilemma type of situation can emerge, where the companies do not invest enough in R&D even though this would be in the common interest for the economy and society.

7.2.2 Information externalities

Information externalities are another factor crucial to structural change, which might (especially in less developed regions) be even more important than technology externalities (Rodrik 2004). Especially in the case of new technologies and sectors, there is often a lack of information about which businesses are involved, and where they are located (Caplin and Leahy 1993). Information externalities appear, for instance, when companies try to produce new goods and services in locations where it has not been done before. These first movers create information about market risks, opportunities and best practices from which other economic agents can learn and imitate, reject or change their behaviour. Whereas this information can be very valuable, the first movers are typically not remunerated for providing it and take the risk alone; therefore companies are often reluctant to invest in new locations and prefer to wait until other competitors have tried it first to see if it works. The result is that many possible sectors never emerge. This is especially true in less developed settings, where it can be very risky for entrepreneurs to test which technologies, products and services work. Whether the potential success will be appropriate is highly uncertain and the risk of failure is huge, especially for SMEs. Failure may lead to bankruptcy, and even success may be appropriated by large companies or the state.

Often the constraints on innovation and structural change come not just from the lack of R&D, but also from an institutional framework that hinders qualitative entrepreneurship and self-discovery processes. There is also a general lack of knowledge about the true costs of production and which products could be efficiently produced, and where. As pointed out by Hausmann and Rodrik (2003, p. 9):

> Producing a good that has not been locally produced previously requires learning about how to combine different inputs in the right way, figuring out whether local conditions are conducive to efficient production, and discovering the true costs of production

Information externalities hinder the ability of companies and organizations to discover by themselves which products and technologies work and which do not, and which can be produced at lower costs than in other regions (Hausmann and Rodrik 2003; Rodrik 2004). The authors, furthermore, argue that this lack of self-discovery processes is a major obstacle for economic development in poor regions. The information externalities constrain the exploration of cost structures and of '... learning what one is good at producing' (Hausmann and Rodrik 2003, p. 4).

In many developing countries the situation is aggravated by economic inequality, structural heterogeneity and power imbalances. On the one hand, large companies in developing countries can often draw upon monopolies, create high formal and informal barriers to entry and generate large profits through resource exploitation. They have little reason or incentive to change the situation. On the other hand, impoverished individuals, in most cases, are not able to engage in qualitative entrepreneurship due to financial constraints, lack of access to information and inadequate education. In the meantime, the small middle class is searching for stability and security and seeking to minimize risks. All this leads to weak self-discovery processes regarding the types of technologies and innovations that could work. The study of micro-entrepreneurship in north-east Brazil (Section 6.5) revealed that the poor explore business possibilities, but unfortunately their search radius for technologies is rather limited. It is the lack of freedom of the poor, but also the constraints on the agency of the middle class and SMEs together, that have strong negative effects on self-discovery processes and structural transformation. This is the reason why human development policies, institutional reforms, as well as the promotion of knowledge flows, are necessary to deal with information externalities, to trigger self-discovery processes and to allow innovation.

7.2.3 Coordination externalities

Coordination externalities is the third important factor influencing the ability of a region or country to promote economic diversification (Rodrik 2004). The emergence of new sectors often requires concerted action and coordination between a variety of different agents from public and private institutions. 'Coordination externalities' refers to the simple understanding that concerted action allows the attainment of achievements and profits that each agent alone could hardly generate. This is also very true for the emergence of new sectors. Often large investments in infrastructure and services and a critical mass of companies are required to enable the creation of a viable cluster or sector. Many technologies, new products and new sectors need to reach certain levels of economies of scale before they become profitable (Rodrik 2004). In some cases, the necessary investments and self-organization can be created by private enterprises alone. But in many cases large-scale initial investments are required, which requires the cooperation and concerted action of several agents, such as different small and large companies, research institutes, landowners and society. Often the different involved actors cannot (easily) reach an agreement. This is where the state must come in and provide the initial structures that make self-organization and economies of scale possible. The emergence of new sectors is dependent on a varied set of inter-related factors such as matching supply and demand, necessary infrastructures and institutions, interactive learning, cooperation and competition for profits and innovation races among the agents involved.

Several different research communities have outlined the crucial role of concerted action and prolific coordination among agents necessary to achieve economies of scale and promote knowledge spillovers, interactive learning, innovation and growth. For instance, polarization theory, which will be explained in more detail below, showed that systemic coordination effects are necessary to make a lead sector excel and create linkages which can translate into overall growth (Perroux 1955; Hirschman 1958). Literature from economic geography has shown the crucial role of agglomeration effects, competition and cooperation at the spatial level (Porter 1990, 1998; Glaeser *et al.* 1992; Brenner 2004). The innovation system approach has highlighted the role of interactive learning (Freeman 1987; Lundvall 1992; Malerba 2002; Cooke and Memedovic 2003). Governments need to facilitate the establishment of learning institutions able to provide incentives for proper coordination among agents. A sustained fertile knowledge flow between the private and public sectors is necessary to help to understand the constraints and potentials of each side (Rodrik 2004). Coordination failures are especially pronounced in activities where we find different maximization rationales in opposition to one another. Profit maximization versus social welfare maximization can lead to coordination failures and a lack of mutual learning about social goals and economic possibilities and necessary policy measures among companies, civil organizations, NGOs and the state. Proper institutions need to be created that promote mutual learning and understanding on all sides. If it is organized well, this can provide enormous incentives and possibilities for innovation, economic diversification and human development.

Other factors aside from the market failures outlined above can lead to low levels of diversification. For example, LASA has shown that centre-periphery positioning in global trade patterns can lead to the periphery specializing in primary resource exploitation (Prebisch 1949, 1964; Furtado 1961). In this way, network and agglomeration effects can lead to income concentration. In these cases, strategic intervention is necessary to counter the negative effects and facilitate virtuous circles of investment and economic diversification in the periphery.

7.2.4 Polarization effects

Around the 1950s the so-called development pioneers, such Rosenstein-Rodan (1943), Nurkse (1953), Hirschman (1958) and Myrdal (1957), showed that without appropriate government interventions free-market forces can lead to increasing polarization into poor and rich regions. They argued that a governmental push strategy is necessary to start positive systemic feedback mechanisms between supply and demand, investment and capital accumulation, and horizontal and vertical sectoral linkages in less developed regions. In sharp contrast to the neoclassical theory, they pointed out that the incomes of rich and poor regions do not automatically converge, even if they form part of the same country with similar governmental regulations and free trade between the regions. In the neoclassical theory, market mechanisms lead to the reconciliation of negative events and scarcity through the price mechanism. For example, the bankruptcy of a company and consequent rise in unemployment and production losses in a region will be reconciled through lower labour costs and higher prices for the scarce product(s). Free market forces are assumed to lead to income convergence between regions.

In contrast, polarization theory takes the view that initial positive or negative dynamics can reinforce themselves through selective migration, demand multipliers, positive or negative expectations or knowledge accumulation. Nurkse (1953, p. 5) noted that '... a country is poor because it is poor'. The lack of purchasing power, demand and savings create high barriers, impeding the creation of virtuous circles of savings, investment and capital accumulation. Through self-reinforcing effects, initial inequalities in knowledge, capital, infrastructure and institutions can lead to different speeds of innovation and diversification. This leads to centre and periphery structures, in which the periphery is systemically dependent on the dynamic diversifying centre (Prebisch 1949, 1964; Furtado 1961; Friedmann 1972). While the periphery (such as Latin America or Africa) specializes in the provision of primary goods and inputs that have a low income elasticity of demand, the centre (such as Europe, Japan and North America) is innovating and creating new (manufactured) products that show a higher income elasticity of demand (Singer 1949; Prebisch 1950). This means that, as income rises, the demand for the centre's manufactured products increases more rapidly than the demand for the periphery's primary products. For instance, the demand for sugar and coffee beans does not grow at the same speed as the demand for new medical products or electronic devices. The primary input of the periphery constantly loses more and more of the global consumption basket, leading to systemic inequality reproduction between the centre and the periphery of the world. Indeed, the global trade system does have a centre-periphery structure (e.g. De Nooy *et al.* 2005; Hidalgo *et al.* 2007). There are numerous linkages among the countries of the industrialized centre of the world economy. Furthermore, there are many linkages from the semi-periphery to the centre, but few linkages among the countries of the semi-periphery. Ultimately, the poorest countries at the periphery have virtually no linkages among them, but are dependent on the linkages towards the centre. Of course, this leads to asymmetries in price negotiations, global information flows and political power.

Polarization is not just limited to the country level, but can be perceived in many different spheres, such as between the countryside and the cities, or lead and dependent sectors. From the 1950s to the 1970s, many countries in the developing world, particularly in Latin America, saw the solution to polarization as leaving systemic dependence and inequality production by closing their markets and promoting industrialization, thereby substituting imports from foreign countries with the establishment of their own national production facilities. In some countries with large national markets, such as Brazil, this strategy – called ISI – indeed encouraged industrialization. However, closing economies deprives companies of critical inputs, in terms of primary resources, upstream products, services and knowledge (Krueger 1985). This has often led to inefficient and expensive production systems, especially in the smaller countries with small markets. Other possible side effects of closing the markets are the lack of internal competition and the threat of corruption, nepotism and rent-seeking, leading to economic inefficiencies and a lack of human freedom. Whereas today a strategy to close entire markets is considered very harmful, there is nevertheless a basic understanding that often policy intervention is necessary to facilitate the emergence of value added new sectors, accumulate the necessary knowledge and reach the level of competitiveness needed to compete in the global markets. These targeted interventions are crucial for economic diversification, the prevention of the reproduction of the systemic inequality and underdevelopment, and the fostering of social cohesion.

Modern mainstream growth approaches consider some of the arguments of polarization theory in their growth models. The endogenous growth theory (Romer 1986, 1990) and new economic geography (Krugman 1991a, 1991b) provide models that show how economies can diverge due to knowledge accumulation and agglomeration effects. However, neither mainstream economics nor polarization theory has dealt properly with understanding the promotion of economic diversification. Mainstream economics strongly believes in the power of comparative advantage and free trade and thus suggests the need for specialization. In contrast, polarization theory highlights the importance of innovation and diversification, but does not provide a proper understanding of how these can be realized. This is where innovation economics and evolutionary economic geography can reveal the way qualitative diversification requires proper support and phasing of specialization and diversification, concentration and decentralization, and related and unrelated variety growth (Saviotti 1996; Boschma and Martin 2010).

7.3 Specialization and diversification in the process of structural change

Specialization and diversification are both contradictory and complementary aspects in the process of structural change. Without the division of labour and specialization, economic diversification would probably not be possible. New activities, products and services often require new specialized skills. Conversely, without the diversification of products and the demands, specialization would come to an end. Additionally, specialization on the local level often allows for the diversification of activities at a higher level of aggregation. This poses difficult questions for the policy maker and the design of structural change policies, such as whether a particular or several sectors should be promoted, if concentration or decentralization, and if related or unrelated variety growth should be encouraged, and what level of government intervention (regional, national or supranational) is appropriate. All these questions address the complex interrelations between specialization and diversification. They help to design an appropriate institutional framework that facilitates both specialization and the creation of comparative advantages within particular industries (e.g. electronics) as well as diversification into several different competitive sectors (e.g. electronics, machinery and chemistry).

7.3.1 The nexus between specialization and diversification

Specialization at a lower level often goes together with diversification at higher levels of aggregation. The division of labour allows for the efficient production of more goods and services, leads to higher productivity and saves time and resources that can be invested in other activities (Smith 1776). Saviotti (1996) and Saviotti and Pyka (2004) have shown that specialization and diversification are complementary forces of structural change. It is the interaction between specialization and diversification that leads to long-term competitive upgrading, the division of labour, knowledge accumulation and innovation. For this reason, economies and companies need to find a fertile balance between specialization and diversification. However, while specialization can free up resources through efficiency, growth and accumulative learning effects, it can also bring with it a high risk of rigidities and failure in times of crises. Both Pasinetti (1981, 1983) and Saviotti (1996) also show that economies need to diversify in the long run to overcome constraints on the demand side. If merely the efficiency of an existing sector rises, less and less labour is necessary. This then tends to create unemployment and underemployment and can have very negative effects on the demand side and social stability (see also Chapter 4). Nevertheless, initial specialization is necessary to achieve later qualitative diversification in related or unrelated sectors. This why regions and countries need to both specialize and diversify to stay competitive in the long term: indeed, Imbs *et al.* (2011) argue for the need for economic integration at the national level to foster regional specialization and national diversification. They argue for economic integration at the international level to foster national specialization and a competitiveness upgrading process.

It is not only countries, regions or companies that need proper diversification strategies; people also need to combine a broadly diversified general knowledge base with specialized knowledge and expertise. This makes them (a) less dependent and more flexible, as well as (b) less substitutable. A good education and training system is needed to provide people with the capabilities to be active agents and choose their lives. A good general knowledge helps people in a number of ways. It helps them to:

- actively participate in the political, social and economic processes of their countries;
- exercise their civil rights and be less prone to exploitation;
- choose the fields in which they are most interested (but also to be aware of the value and need of other topics and ideas); and
- change their life styles and occupations if they desire to do so.

However, as Banerjee and Duflo (2007) show, specialization of skills is equally important. This is especially important during adulthood and in employment. Often, the poor engage in multiple jobs to diversify their risk, such as making bread for customers early in the morning, hemming clothing in the before noon, then working in subsistence farming and/or other activities, and finally collapsing to sleep. This is particularly true for women, but also for men living under the US$1.25 poverty line, who tend to engage in several parallel activities. Often men also migrate temporarily to other places to earn more money (e.g. to the next-door cities or to mining locations), but do not become more specialized in these activities, because they return home to continue to engage in many of the same varied activities. However, these multiple jobs do not allow the poor to build up the detailed and complex knowledge required to access good jobs (Banerjee and Duflo 2007). Increase in expertise makes people less substitutable. Due to their sheer abundance in numbers, workers with less specialized knowledge tend to receive lower remuneration. The poor often do not have the specialized knowledge necessary to work in more stable and better paid jobs, such as in the accounting, controlling, marketing or finance departments of medium to large companies. To allow this specialization of skills to be possible, a strong social security system is also required. The poor need social security to be able to engage in the specialization required for value added activities and higher income opportunities. Both specialized and general knowledge are necessary to allow people to become agents of development. For instance, to upgrade from a micro-business into an SME often requires further general and specialized skills. Beyond the skills needed in activities such as making food, shoes and working in agriculture, this also implies the need for organization, accounting and marketing skills. As mentioned in Chapter 6, entrepreneurship in developing countries is often an indicator of the lack of other employment choices, rather than an indicator of agency, motivation and skills of the entrepreneurs. A more diversified economy provides people with more choice of activities to engage in; thus there is a need for the combination of a general and specialized knowledge base, together with a diversified economic structure, if people are to become agents of development. The types of education and balance of general and specialized knowledge available (and demanded) depends also on the economic structure and sectoral strategy of the companies and the government. This leads to the question of whether policy makers should promote related or unrelated variety growth.

7.3.2   *Unrelated and related variety growth*

Innovation is not predictable. By definition, innovation is something new. If we knew all the details about something new, it would no longer be an innovation. In the words of Arrow (1991, p. 473): 'We cannot, of course, predict a surprise; that is a contradiction in terms. But we can predict the kind of surprises that might occur.' This rather obvious point has enormous implications on economic policy-making. It implies that optimal planning is not possible. However, the policy and incentive framework can influence the direction of the search mechanisms and trial and error procedures and thereby increase the probability of innovation. For this purpose, a distinction between unrelated and related variety growth must be made (Frenken *et al.* 2007).

Unrelated variety growth is based on radically new innovations and competences for the company or spatial unit under consideration. It requires the creation of radically new ideas and competences through a combination of completely different knowledge bases and competences. In contrast, related variety growth is based on incremental innovations and the creation of slightly different products and services. These diversification types have different implications for welfare and people's choices.

Related variety growth creates employment in related sectors and increases regional and sectoral productivity through knowledge spillovers (Boschma 2004; Frenken *et al.* 2007). It creates systemic linkages and promotes the quantity and quality of production and labour. Incremental innovations and the emergence of complementary products increase the competitiveness, coordination and market power of a region or country in a specific sector. This can trigger economies of scale and enable further investment and positive agglomeration effects. Related activities allow for faster knowledge flows and, therefore, facilitate incremental innovation. The subsequent systemic competitiveness in the relevant sector allows for the generation of profits that, once again, can be invested in production and innovation and/or in higher wages and demand. All this leads to a virtuous circle of supply, demand, innovation and related diversification. However, it can also make a region very dependent on a core sector and hence, vulnerable to external asymmetric shocks. For example, a steep increase in input prices or a steep fall in demand in the core sector (e.g. owing to new competitors offering lower prices or new products) can lead to severe economic crises and unemployment (Frenken *et al.* 2007).

For this reason, unrelated variety growth is crucial in diversifying the risk of asymmetric shocks and dependence on a few core activities. The portfolio or risk-spreading effect of unrelated variety growth dampens regional unemployment (Boschma 2004; Frenken *et al.* 2007). From a human development perspective, unrelated variety growth opens up completely new choices and activities from which people can choose. Unrelated variety also enables the possibilities and capabilities of radical innovation through the recombination of different knowledge bases, technologies, services, inputs, and marketing or product characteristics. In addition, it may favour a more democratic regime by diversifying economic power (see Chapter 4).

The importance of related and unrelated variety growth leads to another question: on which type of variety growth should policy makers focus? A practical example of this question can be found when governments face the decision on whether emphasis should be put on further developing existing sectors (such as agriculture or textiles) or on creating entirely new sectors (such as nanotechnology). Studies have shown that, despite the need for unrelated variety growth in long-term economic development (Saviotti and Frenken 2008), it is not possible to become competitive in very different sectors in the short term (Hidalgo *et al.* 2007). Take the example of a country that merely produces and exports some rather simple and standardized agricultural products. Theoretically the government could generate a considerable amount of money by establishing a competitive automobile industry, but in practice this would be very difficult and could not be achieved in the short term. The reason for this is that unrelated variety growth requires co-evolutionary processes and the establishment of productive capabilities that are difficult to achieve, very time-consuming and/or expensive. Unrelated variety often requires completely new institutions, infrastructures, inputs, specialized supplier networks, education and skills of the workers, new research institutions, new regulations and standards, etc. Economic development is a path-dependent process leading to routines that have proved valuable in the past and are difficult to change for the future. This path-dependence characteristic of the economic development process makes routines immutable in the short/medium-term, since this is the only way that agents can guarantee for themselves a minimum amount of the expected outcome (Nelson and Winter 1982). Policy makers and companies may stop looking for changes in the internal routines and power structures and/or they may not be able to identify viable unrelated activities or sectors, making regional and national policy makers, companies and workers much more comfortable with and capable of engaging in diversification into related sectors. For this reason, related variety growth is much more viable for short to medium-term employment creation, productivity enhancement and growth, even though unrelated variety is crucial for long-term economic and human development.

The decision to foster related or unrelated variety growth should also take into consideration different levels of economic complexity. At low levels of diversification, focus on related variety growth in a set of different key sectors and regions is required. In the medium to long-term, unrelated variety growth is vital in accelerating the recombination of knowledge, diversifying against the risk of external shocks and creating positive feedback mechanisms of demand and supply. However, the resources for such a strategy are very limited, especially in less developed countries and regions, still, though it is important to achieve long-term unrelated variety growth. This can be accomplished by focusing on related variety growth in different regions and core sectors. Proper diversification strategies must be based on endogenous productive capabilities. Variety growth is path-dependent and large jumps in the product space (e.g. from simple agriculture to complex chemical and electronic products) would require enormous amounts of investment and the upgrading of large-scale systemic capabilities. Most countries do not have the resources or the ability for such an expensive and complex task. For this reason, the simultaneous promotion of different related variety growth patterns in different regions of the countries, according to their comparative advantages and latent productive capabilities, appears to be the better strategy. Specialization and related variety growth within different regions can constitute unrelated variety growth at a national level.

At high levels of complexity and diversification, proper selection processes and customer-friendly innovations are necessary to prevent the negative effects of related variety growth on human well-being and agency. For example, extensive product proliferation (such as a hundred different types of just slightly different cornflakes, or a multitude of slightly different mobile phones, or internet providers adding no significant new functions) may not necessarily lead to an overall positive effect on social welfare. Schwartz (2004) shows how sometimes more is less and how the explosion of choices can lead to decision paralysis and unhappiness (see also Chapter 4). As outlined above, a proper trade-off between unrelated and related variety growth can contribute to both economic growth and human development. It was also noted that, owing to market failure and polarization effects, policy interventions are necessary. However, this leads to the question of who should make these interventions: is it in the domain of national or regional policy makers to foster economic diversification? And which type of diversification should be promoted?

7.3.3 *Spatial concentration and decentralization*

When it comes to economic development, each region follows its own evolutionary path, with specific routines, socioeconomic setups, diverse implied agents, systemic intra and extra- regional linkages and sectoral structures and dynamics

(Boschma and Martin 2010). For this reason, a proper innovation and structural change policy has to take interregional variety and regional specificity into account (Boschma 2004). In most cases, national policy makers are not able to acquire an overview of the whole complexity of intra and interregional structures, dynamics and socioeconomic setups. It is simply too much information to process. Thus national policies need to be deeply sustained and complemented by prolific regional institutions that understand regional specificities and path dependencies and create powerful bottom-up development. Proper decentralization can help by taking into account regional demands and possibilities and creating tailor-made regional solutions. Regional specialization allows for complexity and uncertainty to be dealt with. Decentralization can provide a counter-balance to the inequality reproduction that stems from power imbalances and dependence. Mere centralized planning is not the solution because no central government is able to understand the complexity of intra and interregional relations. Again, there is simply too much information to process and plan on the national level. Regional agents have more in-depth knowledge and information of regional cases. This is decisive for the institutional ability and legitimacy of promoting evolutionary learning and trial and error processes, as outlined in Boschma (2004, p. 3):

> …policy makers are not optimizers, but adapters: that is, they learn and adapt in the light of experience. Regional policy-making is a process of trial and error: we have to accept that policy-making may fail, especially policies that are innovative... [the] potential impacts of public policy may be the larger the more the policy objectives and features are embedded in the local environment... policy makers are more inclined to embrace a policy that is focused on localized change: there is less risk involved, local support will be much stronger, and the guarantee of success may be higher.

Regional public polices can adapt better to local conditions, deal with specific problems and reduce uncertainty. For this reason, a bottom-up development strategy is required that enables each region, company and person to make the best of their history and capabilities. Each region, along with its inhabitants, has different experiences, knowledge and desires. Regional diversity can make innovation and interactive learning flourish (Van Zwanenberg *et al.* 2009). Naturally, regional diversity must be complemented by national institutions and regulatory frameworks, such as national laws and regulations, social cohesion and labour market policies (see also Section 7.5), and the promotion of interregional knowledge transfers (Boschma 2004). Nevertheless, structural change and human development expansion are not only driven at the national or international level, but crucially depend on efforts at the regional and local level. Innovation takes largely place on the local level, where competences are located in R&D departments of firms and research institutes and where collective learning through spillovers occurs. Regions, villages and towns are also the places where people meet, learn from each other and where companies and associations originate. Regions are home to local populations, who first start to search for job possibilities and a good quality of life close to their friends and family circles; in other words, they start looking for work in their own regions first. It is wrong to view human development, as well as industrial policies, as comprising top-down tasks for which only national government and international regulations must take responsibility. National and international institutions are of central importance, no doubt, but endogenous capabilities must also be built up at the local level. For this reason, future-oriented regional institutions that promote sustained information flows among the variety of regional and supra-regional agents, local, national and multinational companies, local banks, administrations and civil associations are necessary. Regional governments need to foster regional strengths, tackle regional problems and prevent regional lock-ins and rigidities. Regional systems need to be open to new ideas from inside and outside and promote interregional knowledge flows. This is crucial to preventing institutional lock-in and fostering the flexibility of the region.

National institutions need to promote social cohesion among the regions through national regulation and redistribution. In addition, they need to help regions to overcome market and/or government failures that they might not be able to overcome alone. For example, reaching the critical mass of basic infrastructures and services required to make a new cluster or a sector take off might be beyond the financial scope and technological capabilities of one region alone. It is, therefore, the task of the national government both to identify and support globally competitive clustered and advanced regions, as well as to promote development in weaker regions. Proper linkages among the regions must be established to facilitate an adequate composition of interregional related and unrelated variety growth. The identification of economic potential and social needs must take place in close cooperation between regional and national institutions from the private and public sectors. However, national government needs to identify and facilitate the emergence of strategic activities and sectors, such as general-purpose technologies or sectors with great potential for human development expansion. This leads to further relevant policy questions: should the focus of national policy be on activities or sectors, and how can national governments identify and facilitate unrelated variety growth in strategic sectors?

7.3.4 *Should the national policy emphasis be on activities or sectors?*

Establishing entirely new sectors requires the ability to overcome diverse information and coordination failures, to make huge investments and to build up extraordinary organizational and management skills. It is important to take into account that sectors are typically constituted of a large set of related activities (such as particular kinds of technologies, training goods and services) within the sector and in relations with other sectors. Exporting, for example, high-quality coffee beans, requires competences in a varied set of technologies and skills, such as agricultural technologies, logistics, measurement, marketing and organization. As Rodrik (2004) argues, the promotion of specific new technologies and activities is more appropriate than trying to plan and incentivize whole new sectors.

While theoretically this seems to be correct, in practice national governments may not always be able to identify and address the set of key activities or technologies that hamper sectoral development. The pre-selection of future-oriented sectors in accordance with the demands and desires of consumers and producers can be an essential task for governments in promoting unrelated variety growth, identifying possible constraints and initiating learning and trial and error processes. The rationale of the policy emphasis on activities or on regions instead of sectors is crucial for related variety growth. Due to the fact that large jumps in the product space are extremely difficult (Hidalgo *et al.* 2007), the main policy emphasis should be on related variety growth. To overcome coordination and information externalities, it is certainly more efficient, effective and viable to deal with particular activities and constraints than it is to try to change the entire system. Nevertheless, governments also need to be receptive to new possibilities for entirely new sectors and proactively promote unrelated variety growth to prevent structural dependence or technological lock-in of the national production structure. Furthermore, key sectors for human development often need broader systemic actions on, for example, renewable energies, the education system or the health sector. This leads to the difficult question of how national governments can identify potential areas of unrelated variety growth.

7.3.5 Concerted policies for variety growth

To enable prolific related and unrelated variety growth, proper coordination between regional and national policy makers is necessary. There is a need for national policy makers to promote regional competition and cooperation for economic and social development, as well identifying and supporting successful companies. This should also extend into policies that encourage social cohesion and create a need for social contracts (Hanusch and Pyka 2007a). Owing to the high degree of uncertainty of innovative activities, which may lead to underinvestment and lack of trial and error activities in new technologies, governments must provide support to companies and entrepreneurs. But governments also should claim social responsibility from the companies for their innovative success, by incentivizing and partially obliging them to diffuse the knowledge and gains of their new technologies (Hanusch and Pyka 2007a; Acs 2007). Regional governments need to work in collaboration with private and research-oriented firms to promote framework conditions and technological learning processes in activities and technologies that are related to the core competencies of the firms and research institutions of their regions. There is also a need to promote knowledge transfers and concerted action by the agents involved. Useful instruments might be the subsidizing of collaborative public–private innovation networks or the promotion of new institutions linking agents to venture capital, or the establishment of knowledge transfer agencies, or running dedicated trade fairs. The creation of specialized and properly integrated/coordinated finance and consulting institutions is necessary at both the regional and national levels. Dedicated institutions should address the diverse needs and demands of micro-, small-, medium- and large-sized firms from different sectors. Furthermore, key activities and technologies that connect different activities with each other should receive priority. For instance, metrology and materials engineering are fundamental to advances in several sectors and create linkages between sectors and promote the upgrading of systemic competitiveness. Another example is industrial design, which can connect different suppliers, technologies and distributors with each other and create added aggregate value. The creation of clusters and business incubators can be incentivized or subsidized by national governments (e.g. by cluster planning competitions or complementary investments), but they must be implemented by local and regional agents. Specific policy interventions for related variety growth at the regional level, such as the promotion of one sector through infrastructure and incubation parks, must be complemented with generic interventions and technologies, such as the promotion of information and communication infrastructure at the national level (Frenken *et al.* 2007). Regional policy emphasis on related variety growth must also be complemented by the promotion of general-purpose technologies and legal frameworks put in place by national policies. National governments must also enable knowledge exchanges and concerted actions between public and private agents from different regions. One specific task is proper niche management. While in-depth discussion at this point is beyond the scope of this book, it is worth noting that proper niche management of both declining and rising sectors, as well as the promotion of spin-off enterprises, can close structural holes and trigger new innovations and economic dynamics (Frenken *et al.* 1999, 2007). Saviotti (2000) argues that each country needs to find a proper mix of niche entry strategies. This could involve early or late entry into niche markets. In addition, niches arising from the specialization of mature markets, as well as entry into locally specific niches, can be a successful strategy; however, this requires proper entrepreneurship and innovation policies both at the regional and national level.

7.4 Institutional architecture for structural change and human development

Strategic private-public collaboration is necessary to overcome both market and government failures. Policy must create a proper institutional framework and provide incentives for self-discovery processes, interactive learning and trial and error processes. From a human development perspective, entrepreneurial search efforts should not only be governed by profit maximization, but also by the maximization of human agency and social welfare. Governments should foster innovation that addresses societal needs and leads to more and better jobs. For human development to take place, it is essential to create institutions that promote the positive aspects while simultaneously minimizing the negative aspects of creative destruction processes. Strong social protection and cohesion are necessary to counter the negative effects of creative destruction processes and endogenous inequality reproduction. This is not just imperative for ethical and human development reasons, but also for maintaining fruitful interactive learning, trust and system cohesion. It all requires state intervention and concerted actions between the public and private sectors: there is a need to design an adequate combination of economic and social policies. To meet these needs, it is essential to analyse what type of institutional architecture is required to promote entrepreneurial search and innovation processes that do not just focus on mere production expansion, but also address social needs. A crucial task necessary to accomplish this goal is to establish an institutional framework that enables agents from the private and public sectors to learn from each other about their problems, constraints and potentials. This also contributes to the prevention of institutional rigidities and technological lock-ins, and maintains the future orientation of the economy.

7.4.1 Embedded autonomy and innovation systems

Key factors in promoting qualitative change of the economy are the embedded autonomy of the state and an institutional framework that facilitates the entrance of new agents and enables trial and error processes. The state should frequently interact with the private sectors (hence, be embedded) as well as being autonomous and independent. An embedded autonomy of the state can help to overcome information and coordination externalities and promote self-discovery processes (Evans 1995; Hausmann and Rodrik 2003; Rodrik 2004). Information exchanges between the public and private sectors can help to design adequate subsidies and incentives that enable self-reinforcing organizations and realize economies of scale in new activities.

Close cooperation and intensive information exchanges between the private sector and the state are also required to overcome the lack of knowledge of the constraints and potentials on both sides (i.e. information externalities). However, to prevent lobbying, corruption and rent-seeking the state also needs autonomy and internal control. Lobbyism and corruption can be used for rent-seeking activities by obtaining monopoly power and demanding higher prices than necessary; subsidies and favourable tax regimes could go to sectors which no longer require them. Occasionally massive subventions can also lead to rent-seeking behaviour into heavily subsidized sectors without improving the technological processes and quality. For instance, energy conglomerates could merely enter into renewable energies, only to skim off the profits allowed by government subsidies instead of promoting the technological efficiency and effectiveness needed to make the country truly independent from fossil fuels and nuclear and coal power plants. For these reasons, both knowledge exchange and institutional autonomy are necessary to establish learning institutions that promote in a sustained manner innovation, self-discovery processes and economic diversification.

The embedded autonomy of the state needs to be sustained by strong mechanisms of transparency and accountability for both private and public action. A critical task of the government is to prevent the economy both from staying in an economic activity for too long and also from discarding promising activities too early (Eliasson 2000; Hanusch and Pyka 2007a). This, though, is a complex task and leads to some complicated questions. Should a government, for instance, invest in an established automotive industry or redirect its attention to new sectors, such as renewable energies or software? Is it possible that other countries are able to produce cars at a far lower cost and thus there is little chance of maintaining the sector in the country anyway? Or could new developments in the automobile industry, such as hybrid motors, give a new push to the sector? Even more important is giving economic agents the opportunity to learn which activities, goods and services could work efficiently in different locations. This is why 'carrot and stick' policies should be applied to overcome information externalities (Hausmann and Rodrik 2003; Rodrik 2004). This means that both entrepreneurial action and innovative trial and error processes must be promoted, although such initiatives at some point should be able to show some results, or else be declared a dead-end and closed (e.g. subsidies cut). However, this in turn implies the need for prolific taxonomies and constant discussion on how success or failure can be measured in both economic and social terms.

The institutional framework should promote trial and error, and self-discovery processes, but also include mechanisms for discarding unprofitable or exhausted trajectories. Rodrik (2004) emphasizes the need for institutional design principles that facilitate trial and error process and enable the system to renew itself, incentivized by the state, but driven by endogenous market forces, entrepreneurship and innovation. It must be noted that no general strategy for all regions and countries is possible. There are certainly some economic activities that provide higher profits than others. However, each country or region follows a unique historical development path leading to a unique set of agents, social networks and socioeconomic structures. This is why policy makers need to promote innovation systems that enable the generation, implementation and diffusion of technologies according to their own productive capabilities and demands (Freeman 1987; Lundvall 1988, 1992). Interactive learning, flexibility and future orientation must be the guiding policy principles in the creation of innovation systems that facilitate the diffusion of knowledge, deal with new demands and find new solutions; therefore, concerted action and interactive learning among the public, industry and finance sectors are necessary (Hanusch and Pyka 2007a). Achieving the right institutional setting and policy process might even be more important than thinking about appropriate policy choices (Rodrik 2004). For example, the goal of investing in a certain future-oriented sector might be highly necessary, but if concerted action between the public and the private sectors is not effective, the emergence of the sector will probably never happen.

7.4.2 Re-directing the search mechanism towards societal needs

Market mechanisms and technological innovations can be powerful drivers of human development expansion, but search mechanisms, entrepreneurial actions and innovations do not automatically address or foster human development. The concerted action of the private, public and civic spheres is required to promote variety growth, not just towards profit maximization, but also towards welfare maximizing activities. Industrial and social policy need to go hand in hand to facilitate entrepreneurial actions addressing societal needs and demands.

The government should incentivize the creation of institutions identifying and promoting social entrepreneurship and innovation. Towards this end, 'coopetition' (meaning a proper mix of competition and cooperation) between social entrepreneurs should be promoted. Furthermore, in cooperation with the private and science sectors, governments need to identify and promote activities and technologies that lead to high direct and/or indirect social outcomes, such as education, health and environmental technologies. Governments need to foster innovation in these strategic sectors; thus, for example, entrepreneurial activities by private companies can be complemented by public R&D and private-public partnerships. Additionally, companies should be provided with incentives and regulations to address the markets at the BoP, with business models, products, services and jobs that foster their agency and the life quality of the poor. This, for example, could be a requirement that MNEs produce or design a certain percentage of their products in the countries where they aim to sell (a large number of) their products. For instance Brazil is obliging car producers such as Mercedes to do this (or to build a local R&D facility, create good jobs etc.). This strategy is not without its problems, but has sometimes been successful. Another possibility is complementary investments in infrastructure and/or training facilities if the companies invest in the region.

Not only is the promotion of close interactions and knowledge transfers between agents from the public and private sector required, but so is the promotion of the inclusion of society and social policy groups in industrial policy-making. Industrial policy-making must not merely focus on the ex-ante maximization of economic output and then the ex-post redistribution of outcome. Ex-ante redirection of search mechanisms that promote social welfare is possible; therefore social interest groups, for example from education, health, labour and migration, gender, environment and development ministries should be included in the industrial policy-making process. The integration of social groups and society in general can help in thinking about potentially negative effects and take possible constraints and demands into account. It can also provide legitimization to the policy and economic development process and foster social cohesion between agents. It follows that the role of social cohesion and human development in the process of structural change must be further studied, to create policies that help to alleviate the negative and promote the positive aspects of creative destruction processes, preventing human unfreedom and ensuring human agency during the course of economic development.

7.5 Labour market and human agency policies

According to the human development approach, every person should be provided with the basic capabilities they need to lead a self-determined life. One underlying aspect of the approach is the idea of distributional justice, in the sense of an initial equality of opportunities (Rawls 1971; Sen 1998a, 2009). As such, not only the achieved outcomes, but also the capabilities and process freedoms of the individuals are important. This means that the state and/or concerted public–private action must provide a minimum standard of living for everyone, guarantee universal access to education and health services, establish transparent democratic structures, and prioritize the reduction of poverty and social exclusion. All these measures increase people's social choices and capabilities and provide them with the possibility for self-determination and agency.

A large amount of research generated by the human development community (e.g. Streeten *et al.* 1981; UNDP 1990, 2010; Sen 1999; Ranis *et al.* 2000) has shown that policy emphasis on human development not only fosters human well-being and justice, but also triggers economic development. A healthier and better-educated labour force is capable of higher labour productivity, increased entrepreneurial action and better economic decisions, and thus can contribute to technological progress and economic growth (Streeten 1979; Ranis *et al.* 2000). Moreover, diversity of ideas and allowing the people to have individual desires and multiple group identities can expand human agency and trigger economic diversification. The implicit assumption is that if the people are supplied with the basic capabilities, they can become active agents of development and help themselves to be full members of the society. For example, it is argued that the empowerment of women and gender equality are key contributors to human development (Sen 1999; Ranis *et al.* 2000; Gray Molina and Purser 2010). Indeed, analysis of panel data from the period 1970–2005 reveals that the empowerment of women has been a key driver of positive tendencies in human development in recent decades (Gray Molina and Purser 2010). Better access to education and to finance for women in developing countries increases social welfare. This results not merely in improving the women's human development indicators, but also in improving the education and health of their children and bringing about the emergence of innumerable successful micro-enterprises across the world.

Certainly, the theoretical framework of human development includes systemic interaction between human development and economic opportunities (e.g. Sen 1999). Nevertheless, the main policy implication of the human development approach is social protection and attending to people's basic needs and rights through government intervention and expenditure. This book, however, shows that focusing on basic needs and social protection alone may not overcome structural economic heterogeneity or the reproduction of structural inequality. Human development policies need to go hand in hand with structural economic policies, such as the promotion of social capital or congruent employment policies. Proactive labour market and education policies must deal with the increased economic complexity in a globalized world. People need to be prepared for an economic environment that increasingly requires flexibility and lifelong learning; therefore, labour market policies must go hand in hand with education and social cohesion policies to promote the positive and alleviate the negative effects of creative destruction processes and business cycles. The prevention of structural crises through economic diversification, flexible labour markets, education and social protection are interrelated policy dimensions to make structural change work for human development. While in-depth consideration of specific labour market and education policies is beyond the scope of this book, it is nevertheless useful to highlight some key points on why flexible labour markets, strong social security systems and targeted labour market interventions are crucial in promoting structural change and human development.

7.5.1 Crisis prevention and flexible labour markets

During economic crises, government interventions in the labour markets might be necessary to create incentives and the regulatory framework to create employment or alleviate job losses. This, of course, is a difficult task that must be solved by cooperation between private companies and the state agencies. For instance, whereas the complete collapse of entire sectors and subsequent unemployment should be prevented and alleviated, it is important to prevent promotion of inefficient sectors. Economic crises are often seedbeds of innovation and renovation, in which inefficiencies are addressed, cost reductions are made and new ideas are developed and then realized in the new recuperation phase. Nevertheless, deep economic crises also have profound negative effects on human development and well-being, because of massive bankruptcies and job losses and the creation of structural unemployment. Deep crises can stifle demand and the founding of promising projects and economic dynamism, making state intervention and public–private collaboration necessary to alleviate the negative effects of crises, but also to make use of the possibilities for renovation. But prevention is certainly the best measure; thus there is a need for governments to place strong emphasis on education and the flexibility of the labour force. Moreover, strong incentives for diversification in times of economic expansion and maturity must be provided to make the economy more flexible and less vulnerable. This requires proper coordination between industry, finance and the public sectors (Hanusch and Pyka 2007a), to redirect entrepreneurial actions away from rent-seeking and arbitrage towards investment in the real economy and the creation of new sectors. Equally, large bubble bursts, as well as rigidities and stagnation, must be prevented, and this requires proper regulation of speculation, incentives for real investment and the enabling of entrepreneurship, and innovation policies.

Appropriate labour market policies, such as flexible working time regulations in combination with (re-)training measures, can help to deal with structural change and the recurrent economic crises. Reduced working hours over a limited period of time can prevent the dismissal of workers or bankruptcies of companies in times of crises. However, the periods of reduced working hours need to be actively used for training and retraining measures. Reduced working hours has in general been a measure that companies (e.g. in Germany) have justifiably applied in the case of extraordinary cyclical movements in demand and the prospect of an imminent recovery of demand. However, simultaneously, institutional mechanisms must be installed to prevent the erosion of worker's rights, since reduced working hours or short-time contracts can be used for massive exploitation. Collaborative action between companies, workers and the public sector is required to provide sound training possibilities.

Flexible and dynamic labour markets create the need for the better coordination of the process of switching from one employment to another. Managers often receive outplacement assessments before they leave a company or a branch of the company. Something similar should also be promoted for all employees and workers. Instead of labour contract wars, companies and labour agencies should investigate the possibility of helping people to find alternative jobs in the same or other companies when labour reduction or outsourcing in the sector and/or company is necessary. This is why well-informed and dynamic labour agencies (which transfer information on employment opportunities and trends) must be created. Better usage of ICT will be necessary. This means learning institutions are required that frequently revise and improve the opportunities they provide and elaborate tools for tailor-made individual solutions, as well as training programmes for their clients. Naturally, physical assessment will also be required, but better usage of ICT can open up new possibilities, such as information on job availability and trends, learning materials and e-courses and so forth.

7.5.2 Education and social services

Education is essential in preparing individuals for a life where there will be a variety of different jobs to choose from. More than merely general broad academic knowledge will be needed; they will also need to learn social skills and the ability to treat different groups, ethnicities and religions with respect and understanding. It also means educating individuals to be able to meet changes in the world with confidence. Managerial training, when addressing these issues, increasingly uses the term 'change management'. Indeed, the ability to deal and adapt to an increasingly complex, diverse and changing environment is increasingly important for all individuals. To address the increasing flexibility and changes in the skills demanded in the labour market lifelong learning needs to be promoted. Adequate courses for older generations must be designed and made available. Life expectancy has massively increased and people may need to change their jobs more frequently and refresh their formal knowledge to continue finding a job and be able to engage in the societal discussions (e.g. about ICT technologies and online voting systems). Interactive learning between different generations can help. Indeed, a large number of opportunities for mutual learning exist. For example, interchange programmes between the old and the young from different ethnic and social backgrounds could be very beneficial for both sides. Older people can teach language and grammar to migrant children, and in return they can teach the older people computer skills. Well-designed educational measures can promote social cohesion, information flow and trust within society: in principle, the creation of jobs and the establishment of a good education system are some of the best methods of ensuring social security. However it is impossible to completely eradicate economic crises and transition or (re-)training phases in a market economy. This creates the need for strong social security systems, not just for ethical reasons, but also to minimize the risk-aversion inherent in qualitative entrepreneurship, as well as giving people time to retrain. Social protection is crucial for the creation of trust and social capital in society, the disposition of qualitative entrepreneurial action and the alleviation of the negative effects of economic crises.

7.5.3 *Taking social networks into account*

A promising additional area for the promotion of social cohesion, the fostering of structural change and understanding the embeddedness of individuals in socio-economic systems is social network research and policy-making. Social relations are crucial for promoting people's agency and their well-being. People are not isolated individuals, but are embedded in socioeconomic structures. Networks of contacts determine individuals' capabilities, and their choices, opportunities and agency. Furthermore, these networks decide the value which people attach to different functionings and capability upgrading processes, as well as deciding what individuals perceive as feasible and socially desirable. Human development policies should therefore take into consideration the key role of social networks.

Some human development researchers have pointed out the importance of group and external capabilities (e.g. Foster and Handy 2008; De Herdt and Deneulin 2007). For example, the capabilities of the illiterate can be improved by literate family members; self-help groups can upgrade the individual capabilities of their participants. However, despite extensive research into social capital and the general agreement on the importance of trust and cooperation (e.g. Granovetter 1973; Coleman 1988; Woolcock and Narayan 2000), network indicators have not yet found their way into the HDI. A good network position has a strong positive influence on the human development of people, regions and countries. A weak position in the network may lead to dependence and lack of freedom. It is worth noting that being excluded from a network (e.g. having no production facility in the country) is often even worse than being in a dependent position. For this reason, appropriate and careful network interventions need to be designed. Expert commissions are required to discuss how to analyse social networks and make proper network interventions to foster social cohesion and information access. Participatory development approaches and promoting the capabilities to access and use ICT are just the first steps.

7.6 Chapter conclusion

This chapter has shown that to foster structural change and economic policies must go hand in hand with social policies. Market failures such as technology, information and coordination externalities, as well as the negative effects of polarization create the need for state intervention as a means to trigger learning and innovation processes, impede social instability and foster human agency. Concerted action by national and regional policy makers is necessary to promote prolific related and unrelated variety. Innovation, labour market, social cohesion and human development policies should be designed complementarily to promote the positive and prevent the negative effects of structural change. Promoting the emergence and establishment of new sectors requires the combined forces of industrial policies, labour markets and companies that can adapt to the new demands. Social instability, economic inequality and lack of cohesion and trust, may (a) hamper the possibility for concerted actions and (b) lead to a lack of incentives and risk-taking to engage in innovative activities. Without a free and active population, diversity of ideas, cooperation and competition cannot excel. Without cooperation between the government, private sectors and society in general, many huge social projects and the establishment of investments to enhance human development (e.g. in education and health) may not be possible. It is important for all elements of the economy and society to complement each other to form prolific innovation systems promoting both structural change and human development.

8 Conclusion
Key ideas and research outlook

This book has synthesized modern perspectives in innovation and development economics which emphasize the role of networks, diversity and entrepreneurship for human agency. It stresses that economic systems and social relations are not static but change over time, leading to different sets of capabilities that people need to be free and active members of the society. Within dynamic socioeconomic systems, access to various social networks can increase people's choices, but fixed roles and dependent network positions can also be a root cause of inequality and poverty. Economic diversification can increase the number of potential social choices, but can also lead to increasingly difficult decision processes and economic inequality between different regions. Due to the structural and dynamic features of development, emphasis of development policies on individual capabilities (e.g. education and health) is a necessary but not the only factor needed to empower people and promote social inclusion. Congruent innovation and human development policies are also necessary, to encourage entrepreneurship and diversification not just simply for the sake of production expansion, but also to create valuable new choices and to promote human agency. This book contributes to emergent approaches (such as social entrepreneurship, systems of innovation and development, and evolutionary welfare economics) which aim to contribute to a better understanding of the dynamic relations between innovation and human development. These approaches (e.g. Arocena and Sutz 2005; Binder 2010; Ziegler 2010; Capriati 2013) combine the following two complementary perspectives on development:

1 Amartya Sen's perception of development as expanding human freedom, emphasizing the need to provide every human being with the basic capabilities and opportunities to determine their own life and to be active agents of development; and
2 the Schumpeterian concept of development as a historical process of endogenous structural changes and pattern formations, driven by the introduction of innovations and co-evolutionary processes.

Combining these complementary perspectives on development helps to gain insights on how to address poverty by promoting growth, by gaining a better understanding of the dynamic relations between economic development, human agency, social networks and inequality. This book contributes to this emerging field of evolutionary welfare economics by putting emphasis on the multiple positive, negative and ambiguous effects of economic diversification and social network on social choices and human agency. In practice both perspectives (human development and structural change) form part of the daily life of billions of people around the world, who live in a complex and changing economy and who are in search of a better life. A good job is still a key factor for the life quality of people and the structural changes and cyclical crises of the economy deeply affect human agency and well-being.

The social networks we are embedded in deeply affect our social choices and capabilities in the many different spheres of human life, such as work, consumption, family planning or lifestyles. Certainly, far more research needs to be carried out to develop a more fully developed evolutionary welfare theory or a dynamic, complex perspective on development. Nevertheless, modern interdisciplinary research, methods and data availability allows us to advance in this respect. Such research facilitates the study of the complex feedbacks between normative goals of development and structural changes in the society and economic systems, and shows how the embeddedness in socioeconomic systems affects people's choices and capabilities. For a considerable period of time mainstream (neoclassical) economics has taken the normative goal of economic growth in terms of production and consumption expansion for granted and has highlighted aggregated indicators such as capital accumulation, labour growth and a third black-box factor called 'total factor productivity' as being the key drivers of development. It is noteworthy, however, that many classical economists such as Adam Smith, Karl Marx and Joseph Schumpeter, as well as many other development economists and researchers in development studies, have drawn a more complex picture of development that highlights dynamic factors such as increasing division of labour, technical progress and changes in the composition of the economic system, as well as taking sociological, historical and ethical aspects into account. Modern interdisciplinary approaches and data availability enable researchers to enter empirical study and qualitatively explore the complexity of development, considering qualitative aspects, such as life quality and human agency, analysing the role of social networks and interactive learning for innovation and future orientation, and creating a more detailed view on structural changes in the composition of economic systems. It is now methodologically possible to empirically study the theories of the classical scholars (such as Smith or Schumpeter) and combine them with new insights (such as Sen's capability approach and new data availability). In contributing to this goal, this book shows that a varied set of traditional and modern research technologies can be applied to understand the relations between innovation, economic complexity and human development. It also illustrates that there is no single correct approach or method to achieve this, but that theoretical research, case studies, qualitative and quantitative research can and should complement each other.

Chapter 2 has given an overview of the main ideas and concepts of three core perspectives in development economics: economic growth, innovation and progress, and human development. The human development approach argues that there are problems with the belief that economic growth automatically translates into social welfare and the expansion of human freedom. Conversely, structuralist and evolutionary approaches to economic development argue that mere focus on basic human capabilities (such as health or education) may be equally insufficient in overcoming structural and dynamic effects that lead to economic inequality reproduction and an unequal distribution of job opportunities, such as agglomeration effects, recombinant growth and network effects. A cluster analysis of the Latin America systems of innovation and human development illustrates that none of the three approaches (neoclassical growth, the human development approach and Neo-Schumpeterian economics) alone are able to provide a comprehensive picture of the strengths and weaknesses of countries. Whereas in some countries knowledge is the main bottleneck for future-oriented development, other countries suffer from having inefficient economic structures or large parts of their population excluded from economic life. This illustrates the fact that having one single approach to development may neglect essential strengths and weaknesses in other realms of development.

While it is essential to take into account that multiple factors are involved in development, extensive lists of influencing factors and goals of development are also not sufficient to elaborate comprehensive policies. What is even more important – though also complex – is to have a better understanding of the relations and effects between different drivers and goals of development. This is what makes interdisciplinary approaches necessary. To contribute to this goal, Chapter 3 has discussed theoretical pillars of a 'Sen meets Schumpeter' perspective, which allows for an analysis of the relation between individual capabilities and structural economic changes. It argues that a complexity perspective, highlighting networks and diversity, can help to create theoretical links between the two approaches and draw a more dynamic picture of development. A common element of both approaches is the emphasis on individuals and diversity. Complexity research puts emphasis on the structure of interactions of heterogeneous agents and the diversity of outcomes resulting from these interactions. An agent-based perspective, highlighting the diversity of individual's capabilities, social networks and normative goals, can contribute to a deeper understanding of innovation and structural change processes, and evaluate and understand it with regard to its foundation and effects on normative aspects of development, such as human agency and life quality and not merely according to its contribution to production expansion and technological progress. It also facilitates an exploration of how the evolution of the economic system and its increasing complexity, in terms of higher diversification in production and consumption as well as more complex social network structures, has multiple positive, negative and changing effects on human agency and welfare over time. Consequently the following chapters have synthesized a variety of theoretical and empirical approaches that have the ability to reveal the structural and dynamic effects of economic complexity, in terms of the diversity of sectors, entrepreneurial search and recombination processes and social interactions, on the choices and capabilities of the people.

Chapter 4 has illustrated that economic diversification has the ability to make a fundamental contribution to social welfare, providing people with occupational choices and income, distributing economic and political power, and making the economy more robust against asymmetric shocks. Yet diversification can also lead to the loss of former capabilities, the decline in the capabilities of certain groups and increasingly complex choice processes. To provide policy makers with insights about how to promote structural change for human development, being able to differentiate between the effects of different types of economic diversification is crucial. Whereas the emergence of entirely new sectors, services and products has the potential to provide significantly new and valuable choices, it also tends to demand new and changing capabilities, product proliferation of very similar products may increase choice complexity and can be used for exploitation of economic benefits, without really adding substantive new functionings or capabilities for the people. An empirical study of 121 countries and 772 sectors shows that unrelated economic variety growth has a marginally increasing positive return on both human development and GDP per capita. Yet as predicted by the theoretical analysis, the positive effect of related economic variety on human development is marginally decreasing.

Interestingly, the empirical study also shows that economic diversification seems to be even more relevant for human development than mere aggregate income. However, much more empirical research is necessary to understand the complex relations between economic diversification and social welfare.

Chapter 5 proceeded to examine the effects of social networks on human development, drawing upon insights from social capital theory as well as insights on innovation networks. It illustrates that whereas social networks can provide people with valuable information, new choices and social support, they can also be a root cause of social exclusion, lock-in effects and systemic inequality reproduction. An empirical case study on the innovation networks of smallholder farmers in a Peruvian valley shows how modern structural data analysis techniques can be used to study how the embeddedness in social networks affects the capabilities of people. The case study illustrates that the capabilities of the farmers to innovate are more substantially correlated with their position in local information networks, access to training measures and external knowledge sources then with more traditional capabilities measures such as the extent of their formal education or their age. In addition, network analysis can help to understand how development projects affect the information flows and power distribution within villages.

Chapter 6 has shown that entrepreneurship can be viewed by its contribution to human development. Whereas traditional approaches in economics focus on the contribution of entrepreneurship on efficiency, technological progress and income generation, modern concepts such as social entrepreneurship or entrepreneurship as functioning focus on the contribution of entrepreneurship to the capabilities of the entrepreneurs and other persons. A qualitative case study in north-east Brazil shows how social innovation microfinance enables many micro-entrepreneurs in the region to help themselves, but also reveals that appropriate institutional support and improvement of management skills are necessary to prevent over-financing or bankruptcy when the complexity of business rises during the business expansion phase. Most importantly, the case study shows that combining human development and innovation economics thinking can provide practical, relevant insights into the relations between social networks, human agency and structural change. It can, for instance, help the understanding of the success factors and constraints of micro-entrepreneurs and social businesses.

Chapter 7 has discussed development policies that help to make structural economic change work for human agency and welfare. The main thesis is that a future-oriented policy to foster individuals' capabilities and choices goes hand in hand with prolific industrial and innovation policies that promote qualitative economic diversification and fertile social network structures. Human development and structural economic change policies need to complement and reinforce each other, to facilitate social progress and spread welfare more equally in the long-term. Policy emphasis on the improvement of human agency through the provision of better social services, democracy building initiatives or gender equality policies, must be complemented by providing access to social networks as well as concerted economic policies, enabling the emergence and competitiveness of sectors which provide new valuable choices and opportunities for the people. This requires an appropriate institutional framework to facilitate the cooperation between different agents involved in the development processes (e.g. government, companies, academia and society in general), allowing for the joint elaboration of structural change strategies promoting sectors which provide valuable new choices and improve the agency of the people. The positive effects of diversification must be enhanced, but also possible negative effects, such as increasingly difficult choices, need to be considered. An appropriate mix of related and unrelated variety growth, selection and variation mechanisms is necessary. This implies that learning processes and innovation must be promoted in such a way that the emphasis is on qualitative entrepreneurship and knowledge exchange between the many people and institutions involved in the generation, application and diffusion of knowledge. Beyond emphasis on individual capabilities, the poor need to be provided with network access to information, finance and social services if they are to become active agents of development. However negative effects of networks, such as levelling pressures within closed groups or the tendency of inequality reproduction in large networks, must also be properly addressed to prevent structural inequality reproduction or the inflexibility of the system. In addition, labour market policies are necessary to connect the people to information networks, and provide the training and flexibility required to enable people to deal with changing capability requirement within complex and dynamic socioeconomic systems.

An enormous number of further exploratory and confirmatory applications are possible and are currently being made by researchers in the fields of evolutionary welfare economics, complexity and development economics. It is worth noting that we are only at the beginning of the information age (which is accompanied by new research methods and possibilities such as big data and democratic innovation) that allows us to analyse in detail structural economic transformations (e.g. distinguishing between thousands of different sectors), network structures (e.g. of the global production system or the international development aid network) and different dimensions of human agency and life quality (such as multidimensional poverty, global entrepreneurship, or life satisfaction in the different regions across the world). New data analysis techniques and infographics allow us to transform huge amounts of data into knowledge, prove previous theoretical reasoning and explore new areas of ignorance. Advances in complexity research and econophysics, for instance, have shown the importance of economic complexity for the income level an economy achieves (e.g. Hidalgo *et al.* 2007) as well as the importance of network structures for the well-being of people (e.g. Eagle *et al.* 2010). Of course these quantitative approaches need be complemented by and be in a dialectical process with qualitative and theoretical approaches that help to understand the social factors promoting the evolution of economic complexity, as well as examining how the increasing complexity and interconnections affect the agency and well-being of people. Together these approaches are better than any single approach can be in developing effective policies that deliberately offer a positive feedback mechanism between structural economic transformations and human welfare, preventing negative effects (such as high levels of unemployment and social instability) and promoting the positive effects (such as the creation of valuable new choices).

A rapidly developing new methodology is agent-based (computational) modelling (Pyka and Fagiolo 2007; Tesfatsion and Judd 2006), which allows for the creation of simulation models to better understand the feedback mechanism of the capabilities and behaviour of bounded rational agents, the structure and dynamics of interaction, learning and innovation processes, agglomeration and diversification effects, and changes in the composition of the socioeconomic system. For example, the capabilities for entrepreneurship, networking and learning, or the reproduction of inequalities and the impact of different policy measures, can be studied within agent-based models (ABM) (e.g. Pyka *et al.* 1999; Cantner *et al.* 2001; Grebel *et al.* 2003; Morone and Taylor 2004, 2006; Pyka *et al.* 2007). ABM is a promising methodology which could have the ability to analyse the evolution of human capabilities in a complex evolving system. Nevertheless, from a qualitative perspective, the derivation of theoretical causalities and results from an agent-based simulation model should not stand alone, but must also be complemented by empirical data and case studies. Arguably the highest level of complexity emerges in qualitative case studies, where there are multiple factors and complex relations and an enormous level of diversity, all of which require great sensitivity and qualitative structuring skills from the researcher. Each individual or region is different, has different personal networks and experiences, and develops in different ways. For these reasons, case study research can provide rich insights into the qualitative reasons and complexity of human decision-making processes and behaviour in dynamic feedbacks within an evolutionary socioeconomic environment. The strong relations between social networks, learning processes and human capabilities in particular can become obvious through case studies.

In summary, this book illustrates that there are multiple new ways and methods to help understand the dynamic feedbacks between social networks, innovation, economic diversity, social choices and human agency. Examples of these new ways and methods can been seen in complexity research, as found in SNA, or big data methods, qualitative case studies and theoretical reasoning. The most recent scientific research provides a wide range of methodological means to take uncertainty into account and the complexity of human behaviour, overcoming static optimal solutions towards a more differentiated picture of the diversity, distribution and directions of development (e.g. Stirling 2010; STEPS Centre 2010). New access to data and information, new methods and the deliberate emphasis on diversity and cooperation allows us to benefit from the richness of socioeconomic complexity and to promote a pluralistic society and policy-making process. The emphasis on individual freedom and the promotion of collaborative actions in the information age is opening up many possibilities for interdisciplinary research and a better understanding and awareness of the complexity of socioeconomic development. The research presented here shows that the human development approach and Neo-Schumpeterian economics are compatible perspectives, which together can contribute to the development of a richer and deeper picture of the evolutionary dynamics of economic complexity and social welfare. Furthermore, various new methods can be applied to contribute to this emerging field of evolutionary welfare economics, taking simultaneously the structural and dynamic features of economic systems as well as the choices, well-being and agency of the people into account. This facilitates a better understanding of the complex relations between social networks, structural change and human development, and helps the design of economic policies that not only raise economic production and income, but also provide valuable new choices and promote social inclusion.

Bibliography

Abramowitz, M. 1956. 'Resource and Output Trends in the United States Since 1870'. *The American Economic Review*, 46(2): 5–23.

——1986. 'Catching Up, Forging Ahead, and Falling Behind'. *Journal of Economic History*, 46(2): 385–406.

Acemoglu, D. 2009. *Introduction to Modern Economic Growth*. Princeton, NJ: Princeton University Press.

Acs, Z. 2007. 'Schumpeterian Capitalism in Capitalist Development: Toward a Synthesis of Capitalist Development and the Economy as a Whole'. In *The Elgar Companion to Neo-Schumpeterian Economics*, edited by H. Hanusch and A. Pyka. Cheltenham: Edward Elgar.

Acs, Z. J. and Audretsch, D. B., eds. 2003. *Handbook of Entrepreneurship Research. An Interdisciplinary Survey and Introduction*. Boston, MA: Kluwer Academic Publishers.

Akçomak, I. S. and Weel, B. T. 2009. Social Capital, Innovation and Growth: Evidence from Europe. European Economic Review, 53(5): 544–67.

Albert, R. and Barabási, A.-L. 2002: 'Statistical Mechanics of Complex Networks'. *Reviews of Modern Physics*, 74: 47–97.

Albert, R., Jeong, H. and Barabási, A.-L. 1999. 'Diameter of the World Wide Web'. *Nature* (401), 130–1.

Aldrich, H. E. and Zimmer, C. 1986. 'Entrepreneurship through Social Networks'. In *The Art and Science of Entrepreneurship*, edited by D. L. Sexton and R. W. Wilson. Cambridge, MA: Ballinger.

Aldrich, H. E., Rosen, B. and Woodward, W. 1987. 'The Impact of Social Networks on Business Founding and Profit: A Longitudinal Study'. In *Frontiers of Entrepreneurship Research*, edited by N. C. Churchill, J. A Homaday, B. A. Kirchhoff, O. J. Krasner and K. H. Vesper. Wesley, MA: Babson College, pp. 154–68.

Alkire, S. 2010. 'Human Development: Definitions, Critiques and Related Concepts'. *Human Development Research Paper*, 2010/01.

Alkire, S. and Foster, J. 2007. 'Counting and Multidimensional Poverty Measures'. *OPHI Working Paper Series* (7).

Alkire, S. and Santos, M. E. 2010. 'Acute Multidimensional Poverty: A New Index for Developing Countries'. *Human Development Research Paper*, 2010/11.

Amsden, A. 2010. 'Say's Law, Poverty Persistence, and Employment Neglect'. *Journal of Human Development and Capabilities*, 11(1): 57–66.

Anand, P., Hunter, G., Carter, I., Dowding, K., Guala, F. and Van Hees, M. 2009. 'The Development of Capability Indicators'. *Journal of Human Development and Capabilities*, 10(1): 125–52.

Arata, A. 2007. 'Cautivos en su mercado. Pequeños productores de pisco y vino'. In *Perú Hoy. Mercados Globales y (des-)articulaciones internas*, edited by Desco, Centro de Estudios y Promoción del Desarrollo. Arequipa, Peru: Desco.

——2008. *Factores socioeconómicos en los niveles de innovación vitivinícola en pequeños agricultores en dos valles de la región Arequipa*. Masters thesis, Universidad Nacional Agraria La Molina.

Arata, A. and Toro, O. 2005. *Rumbo a la competitividad: aprendizajes de la promoción de la agroindustria rural en Caravelí*. Arequipa, Peru: Desco.

Arocena, R. and Sutz, J. 2005. 'Evolutionary Learning in Underdevelopment'. *International Journal of Technology and Globalisation,* 1(2): 209–24.

Arora, S. 2009. *Knowledge Flows and Social Capital – A Network Perspective on Rural Innovation*. Maastricht: Universitaire Pers.

Arrow, K. J. 1950. 'A Difficulty in the Concept of Social Welfare'. *Journal of Political Economy*, 58(4): 328–46.

——1951. *Social Choice and Individual Values*. New York: Wiley

——1963. *Social Choice and Individual Values*. New York: Wiley, second edition.

——1991. 'Highlights of the Discussion – the Dynamics of Technological Change'. In *Technology and Productivity The Challenge for Economic Policy*. Paris: OECD Publishing.

Arrow, K. J., Sen, A. and Suzumura, K. 1997. *Social Choice Re-examined*. New York: St. Martin's Press, 1 and 2.

——2008. *Handbook of Social Choice and Welfare.* Amsterdam: Elsevier, 2.

Arthur, W. B. 1994. *Increasing Returns and Path Dependence in the Economy*. Ann Arbor, MI: University of Michigan Press.

——1999. 'On the Evolution of Complexity'. In *Complexity: Metaphors, Models, and Reality*, edited by G. A. Cowan, D. Pines and D. Meltzer. Santa Fe, USA: Perseus Books.

Arumapperuma, S. 2006. 'Agricultural Innovation System in Australia'. *Journal of Business Systems, Governance and Ethics*, 1(4): 15–25.

Audretsch, D. B. and Thurik, A. R. 2000. 'Capitalism and Democracy in the 21st Century: from the Managed to the Entrepreneurial Economy'. *Journal of Evolutionary Economics*, 10: 17–34.

Backhaus, K., Erichson, B. Plinke, W. and Weiber, R. 2006. *Multivariate Analysemethoden – Eine anwendungsorientierte Einführung*. Berlin, Heidelberg, New York: Springer-Verlag.

Balassa, B. 1965. 'Trade Liberalization and "Revealed" Comparative Advantage'. *The Manchester School of Economics and Social Studies*, 33: 99–123.

Balzat, M. and Pyka, A. 2006. 'Mapping National Innovation Systems in the OECD Area'. *International Journal of Technology and Globalisation*, 2 (1/2): 158–76.

Banerjee, A. V. and Duflo, E. 2007. 'The Economic Lives of the Poor'. *Journal of Economic Perspectives*, 21(1): 141–67.

Banerjee, A. V. and Newman, A. F. 1993. 'Occupational Choice and the Process of Development'. *Journal of Political Economy*, 101(2): 274–98.

Barabasi, A.-L. and Albert, R. 1999. 'Emergence of Scaling in Random Networks'. *Science*, 286(5439): 509–12.

Barker, E. 1958. *The Politics of Aristotle*. London: Oxford University Press.

Barro, R. J. and Sala-i-Martin, X. 1991. 'Convergence Across States and Regions'. *Discussion Paper No. 629*. New Haven, CT: Economic Growth Center, Yale University.

Basu, K. 2009. The Mahbub ul Haq Lecture. [lecture] Human Development and Capability Association Conference, Lima, Peru, 10 September 2009. [unpublished].

Bauer, J. 2007. *Prinzip Menschlichkeit. Warum wir von Natur aus kooperiere.* Hamburg: Hoffman und Campe Verlag, third edition.

Baumol, W. J. 1990. 'Entrepreneurship: Productive, Unproductive, and Destructive'. *The Journal of Political Economy*, 98(5): 893–921.

Becattini, G. 1979. 'Dal settore industriale al distretto industriale: alcune considerazione sull'unitá di indagine dell'economia industrial'. *Rivista di Economia e Politica Industriale*, 1: 7–21.

Benkler, Y. 2006. *The Wealth of Networks. How Social Production Transforms Markets and Freedom.* New Haven and London: Yale University Press.

Binder, M. 2010. *Elements of an Evolutionary Theory of Welfare*. London: Routledge.

Binder, M. and Coad, A. 2010a. 'An Examination of the Dynamics of Well-being and Life Events Using Vector Autoregressions'. *Journal of Economic Behavior and Organization*, 76(2): 352–71.

——2010b. 'Disentangling the Circularity in Sen's Capability Approach: An Analysis of the Co-Evolution of Functioning Achievement and Resources'. *Social Indicators Research*, 103: 327–55.

Blau, P. M. 1964. *Exchange and Power in Social Life*. New York: John Wiley and Sons.

Boix Domenech, R. 2004. 'Redes de ciudades y externalidades'. *Investigaciones Regionales*, 4: 5–27.

Borgatti, S. P. 2009. Links Center Workshop. Advanced Session. *Working with Node Attributes*. [lecture] University of Kentucky, 2009. [unpublished].

Borgatti, S. P., Everett, M. G. and Freeman, L. 2002. *UCINET 6 for Windows. Software for Social Network Analysis. User's Guide, Analytic Technologies*. Lexington, KY: Analytic Technologies in cooperation with Harvard University, MA. Available at: http://www.soc.umn.edu/../UCINET_6_User's_Guide.doc [Accessed 30 June 2009].

Borgatti, S. P., Halgin, D. and De Jordy, R. 2008. NIPS UCINET & NetDraw Workshop. *An Introduction to UCINET and NetDraw*. [seminar] 2008. Boston: Carroll School of Management, Boston College. Available at: http://www.hks.harvard.edu/netgov/files/NIPS/Halgin_NIPS_2008.pdf [Acessed June 19 2010].

Borgatti, S. P,. Jones, C. and Everett, M. G. 1998. 'Network Measures of Social Capital'. *Connections,* 21(2): 27–36.

Borgatti, S. Mehra, A. Brass, D. J. and Labianca, G. 2009. 'Network Analysis in Social Sciences'. *Science*, 323: 892–5.

Bornstein, D. 2004. *How to Change the World – Social Entrepreneurs and the Power of New Ideas*. New York: Oxford University Press.

Boschma, R. 2004. 'Expert Group Meeting on Constructing Regional Advantage. Some Reflections on Regional Innovation Policy'. [Presentation.] 7 December. Brussels. [online] Available at: http://econ.geo.uu.nl/boschma/brusselmeetingpolicy.pdf [Accessed 31 January 2009].

Boschma, R. and Martin, R. 2010. *The Handbook of Evolutionary Economic Geography.* Cheltenham, UK: Edward Elgar.

Bosma, N. and Harding, R. 2006. *Global Entrepreneurship Monitor. GEM 2006 Summary Results*. Babson Park, MA and London, UK: Global Entrepreneurship Research Consortium (GERA) in cooperation with Babson College and London Business School.

Bosma, N., Jones, K., Autio, E. and Levie, J. 2008. *Global Entrepreneurship Monitor. 2007 Executive Report.* Babson Park, MA and London, UK: Global Entrepreneurship Research Consortium (GERA) in cooperation with Babson College and London Business School.

Bosma, N., Acs, Z. J., Autio, E., Coduras, A. and Levie, J. 2009. *Global Entrepreneurship Monitor. 2008 Executive Report.* Babson Park, MA; Santiago, Chile and London, UK: Global Entrepreneurship Research Consortium (GERA) in cooperation with Babson College, Universidad de Desarrollo and London Business School.

Bourdieu, P. 1983. Ökonomisches Kapital, kulturelles Kapital, soziales Kapital. In *Soziale Ungleichheiten, Soziale Welt, Sonderheft 2,* edited by R. Kreckel. Goettingen: Otto Schartz und Co.

Bourguignon, F., Ferreira, H. G. and Menéndez, M. 2005. 'Inequality of Opportunity in Brazil'. *Discussion Papers No. 133, Ibero-America Institute for Economic Research.* Göttingen: Georg-August-Universität.

Brenner, T. 2004. *Local Industrial Clusters, Existence, Emergence and Evolution.* London: Routledge.

Breschi, S. and Lissoni, F. 2001. 'Knowledge Spillovers and Local Innovation Systems: a Critical Survey'. *Industrial and Corporate Change*, 10(4): 975–1005.

Burt, R. S. 1992. *Structural Holes: The Structure of Competition.* Cambridge, MA: Harvard University Press.

Bustelo, P. 1999. *Teorías contemporáneas del desarrollo económico.* Madrid: Síntesis.

Campos, F. L. S., Moreira, I. T. and Moutinho, L. M. G., eds. 2010. *Economia Paraibana, estratégias competitivas e políticas públicas.* Joao Pessoa, Brasil: Editora UFPB.

Cantillon, R. [1755] 1959. *Essai sur la nature du commerce en generale,* edited with an English translation and other material by Henry Higgs, C.B. Reissued for The Royal Economic Society by Frank Cass and Co., Ltd., London..

Cantner, U. and Graf, H. 2006. 'The Network of Innovators in Jena: an Application of Social Network Analysis'. *Research Policy*, 35: 463–80.

Cantner, U., Ebersberger, B., Hanusch, H., Krüger, J. and Pyka, A. 2001. 'Empirically Based Simulation: The Case of Twin Peaks in National Income'. *Journal of Artificial Societies and Social Simulation*, 4(3).

Caplin, A. and Leahy, A. 1993. 'Miracle on Sixth Avenue: Information Externalities and Search'. *Columbia University Discussion Paper*, 681.

Capriati, M. 2013. 'Capabilities, Freedoms and Innovation: Exploring Connections'. *Innovation and Development*, 3(1): 1–17.

Cassiolato, J. and Lastres, H. 2008. 'Discussing Innovation and Development. Converging Points Between the Latin American School and the Innovation Systems Perspective'. *GLOBELICS Working Paper Series,* 08 (02).

Cassiolato, J., Lastres, H. and Maciel, M., eds. 2003. *Systems of Innovation and Development: Evidence from Brazil.* London: Edward Elgar Publishing.

Casson, M. and Della Giusta, M. 2007. 'Entrepreneurship and Social Capital'. *International Small Business Journal*, 25(3): 220–44.

Casson, M., Yeung, B., Basu, A. and Wadeson, N. 2006. *The Oxford Handbook of Entrepreneurship.* Oxford: Oxford University Press.

Castelacci, F. and Natera, J. M. 2011. 'A New Panel Dataset for Cross-country Analyses of National Systems, Growth and Development (CANA)'. *NUPI Working Paper, 783.*

Castells, M. 1996. *The Information Age: Economy, Society and Culture.* Oxford and Malden, MA: Blackwell Publishers.

Chen, D. H. C. and Dahlman, C. J. 2005. 'The Knowledge Economy, the KAM methodology and World Bank Operations'. *World Bank Institute Working Paper*, 37256 [online]. Available at: http://siteresources.worldbank.org/KFDLP/Resources/KAM_Paper_WP.pdf [Accessed April 2008].

Cimoli, M. 2005. *Structural Heterogeneity, Technological Asymmetries and Growth in Latin America*. MPRA Paper 3832 [online]. Munich, Germany: University Library of Munich. Available at: http://mpra.ub.uni-muenchen.de/3832/1/MPRA_paper_3832.pdf [Accessed 15 March 2008].

Coleman, J. 1988. 'Social Capital in the Creation of Human Capital.' *American Journal of Sociology*, 94: 95–120, Supplement: Organizations and Institutions: Sociological and Economic Approaches to the Analysis of Social Structure.

——1990. *Foundations of Social Theory*. Cambridge, MA: Harvard University Press.

Comim, M., Qizilbash, M. and Alkire, S. 2008. *The Capability Approach: Concepts, Measures and Applications*. Cambridge: Cambridge University Press.

Conley, T. G. and Udry, C. R. 2010. *Learning About a New Technology: Pineapple in Ghana*. American Economic Review, 100(1): 35–69.

Cooke, P. and Memedovic, O. 2003. *Strategies for Regional Innovation Systems, Learning Transfer and Application*. UNIDO Publication Policy Advice. [online] Available at: http://www.unido.org/resources/publications/publications-by-type/policy-advice/industrial-policies-and-strategies/strategies-for-regional-innovation-system-learning-tranfer-and-applications.html [Accessed 23 May 2006].

Couto Soares, M. C. and Cassiolato, J. E. 2008. 'Innovation Systems and Inequality: The Experience of Brazil'. [online] In: GLOBELICS 6th International Conference. Mexico City, Mexico, 22–24 September 2008. Available at: http://smartech.gatech.edu/handle/1853/39661 [Accessed 13 June 2009].

Cozzen, S. E. and Kaplinsky, R. 2009. 'Innovation, Poverty and Inequality. Cause, Coincidence, or Co-evolution?' In *Handbook of Innovation Systems and Developing Countries*, edited by Lundvall, Joseph, C. Chaminade and J. Vang-Lauridsen. London: Edward Elgar Publishing.

Dachs, B. and Pyka, A. 2009. 'What Drives the Internationalization of Innovation? Evidence from European Patent Data.' *Economics of Innovation and New Technology*, 19 (1): 71–86.

Dahl, M. S. and Sorenson, O. 2009. 'The Embedded Entrepreneur'. *European Management Review*, 6(3): 172–81.

——2010. 'Home Sweet Home: Entrepreneurs Location Choices and the Performance of Their Ventures'. *Management Science*, 58(6): 1059–71.

David, P. A. 1985. 'Clio and the Economics of QWERTY'. *American Economic Review*, 75(2): 332–37.

De Haas, H. and Rodriguez, F. eds. 2010. 'Special Issue: Mobility and Human Development'. *Journal of Human Development and Capabilities*, 11(2): 177–365.

De Herdt, T. and Deneulin, S., eds. 2007. 'Special Issue: Individual freedoms as relational experiences'. *Journal of Human Development and Capabilities*, 8(2): 179–84.

De Nooy, W., Mrvar, A. and Batagelj. 2005. *Exploratory Social Network Analysis with Pajek*. Cambridge: Cambridge University Press.

De Solla Price, D. J. 1965. 'Networks of Scientific Papers'. *Science*, 149 (3683): 510–15.

Deneulin, S. and Steward, F. 2002. 'Amartya Sen's Contribution to Development Thinking'. *Studies in Comparative International Development*, 37(2): 61–70.

Di Filippo, A. 1998. 'La visión centro-periferia hoy'. *Revista de la CEPAL*, October 1998: 175–85.

Diener, E. and Suh, E. 1999. 'National Differences in Subjective Wellbeing'. In *Well-Being: The Foundations of Hedonic Psychology*, edited by D. Kahneman, E. Diener and N. Schwarz. New York: Russel Sage Foundation.

Dixit, A. and Stiglitz, J. 1977. 'Monopolistic Competition and Optimum Product Diversity'. *American Economic Review*, 67(3): 297–308.

Dopfer, K., ed. 2005. *The Evolutionary Foundations of Economics*. Cambridge: Cambridge University Press.

Dopfer, K. Foster, J. and Potts, J. 2004. 'Micro-meso-macro'. *Journal of Evolutionary Economics*, 14: 263–79.

Dosi, G., Freeman, C., Nelson, R., Silverberg, G. and Soete, L., eds. 1988. *Technical Change and Economic Theory*. London: Pinter.

Dosi, G., Marengo, L. and Fagiolo, G. 2005. 'Learning in Evolutionary Environment'. In *Evolutionary Principles of Economics*, edited by K. Dopfer. Cambridge: Cambridge University Press.

Dreze, J. and Sen, A. 1989. *Hunger and Public Action*. Oxford: Clarendon Press.

Dreze, J. and Sen, A. 2002. *India: Development and Participation*. New Delhi: Oxford University Press.

Duarte, G. B., Sampaio, B. and Sampaio, Y. 2009. 'Programa Bolsa Família: impacto das transferências sobre os gastos com alimentos em famílias rurais'. *Revista de Econonomia e Sociologia Rural*, 47(4).

Durkheim, Emile. 1893. *The Division of Labor in Society.* New York: Free Press.

Eagle, N., Macy, M. and Claxton, R. 2010. 'Network Diversity and Economic Development'. *Science*, 328: 1029–31.

Easterly, W. 2001. *The Elusive Quest for Growth: Economists' Adventures and Misadventures in the Tropics*. Cambridge, MA: MIT Press.

——2006. *The White Man's Burden: Why the West's Efforts to Aid the Rest Have Done So Much Ill and So Little Good*. New York: Penguin Press.

ECLAC. 2008. *Structural Change and Productivity Growth. 20 Years Later. Old Problems, New Opportunities.* Santiago de Chile: ECLAC-United Nations.

Economist Intelligence Unit. 2005. [editorial] *The Economist Intelligence Unit's quality-of-life index 2005.*

——2008. [editorial] *Microscopio 2008 sobre el Entorno de Negocios para las Microfinanzas en América Latina y el Caribe.*

Edgeworth, F. T. 1881. *Mathematical Psychics: An Essay on the Application of Mathematics to the Moral Sciences.* London: Kegan Paul.

Edquist, C. 1997. *Systems of Innovation: Technologies, Institutions and Organizations*. London: Pinter Publishers.

Eliasson, G. 2000. *The Role of Knowledge in Economic Growth*. [online] Stockholm: Royal Institute of Technology in cooperation with OECD. Available at: http://oecd.org/innovation/research/1825633.pdf [Accessed 19 July 2009].

Esser, K., Hillebrand, W., Messner, D. and Meyer-Stamer, J. 1996. *Systemic Competitiveness. New Government Patterns for Industrial Development.* London: Frank Cass.

Eurostat. 2008. *Science, Technology and Innovation in Europe.* Luxembourg: Office for Official Publications of the European Communities.

Evans, P. 1995. *Embedded Autonomy: States and Industrial Transformation*. Princeton, NJ: Princeton University Press.

——1996. 'Government Action, Social Capital and Development: Reviewing the Evidence on Synergy'. *World Development*, 24(6): 1119–32.

——2002. Collective Capabilities, Culture, and Amartya Sen's 'Development as Freedom'. *Studies in Comparative International Development*, 37(2): 54–60.

Evers, H. D., Gerke, S. and Menkhoff, T. 2006. 'Little-understood Knowledge Trap'. *D+C Magazine for Development and Cooperation*, 2006 (6).

Fagerberg, J. and Srholec, M. 2006. 'The Role of "Capabilities" in Development: Why Some Countries Develop (While Other Stay Poor)'. *11th ISS Conference: Innovation, Competition and Growth: Schumpeterian Perspectives.* Université Nice/Sophia-Antipolis, France, 21–24 June.

Fagerberg, J., Mowery, D. C. and Nelson, R. R., eds. 2005. *The Oxford Handbook of Innovation.* Oxford, New York: Oxford University Press.

Fajnzylber. F. 1990. 'Industrialization in Latin America: from the 'Black Box' to the 'Empty Box': a Comparison of Contemporary Industrialization Patterns'. *Cuadernos de la CEPAL*, 60. Santiago, Chile: United Nations Publication.

Feenstra, R. C., Lipsey, R. E., Deng, H. Ma, A. C. and Mo, H. 2005. *World Trade Flows: 1962–2000.* NBER Working Paper Series, 11040 (January 2005) [online]. Cambridge, MA: National Bureau of Economic Research. Available at: http://m.nber.org//papers/w11040 [Accessed 12 March 2008].

Findeis, A. 2007. *Technologie- und Gründerzentren als Instrument zur Förderung der Regionalentwicklung – Eine regionalwirtschaftliche Erfolgsanalyse unter Berücksichtigung der Gründungsforschung.* Schriftenreihe Wirtschaftspolitik in Forschung und Praxis Band 31, Hamburg.

Foster, J. E. and Handy, C. 2008. *External Capabilities.* Oxford Poverty & Human Development Initiative, Working Paper, 8. [online] Oxford: Oxford University Press. Available at: http://www.ophi.org.uk/wp-content/../OPHI-wp08.pdf [Accessed 30 March 2009).

Foster, A. D. and Rosenzweig, M. R. 1995. 'Learning by Doing and Learning from Others: Human Capital and Technical Change in Agriculture'. *Journal of Political Economy*, 103(6): 1176–209.

Freeman, C. 1982. 'Innovation and Long Cycles of Economic Development'. Paper presented at the *International Seminar on Innovation and Development in the Industrial Sector*, University of Campinas, Campinas, Sao Paulo, 25–27 August 1982. Available at: http://www.globelicsacademy.org/pdf/JoseCassiolato_2.pdf [Accessed 30 June 2009].

——1987. *Technology Policy and Economic Performance: Lessons from Japan.* London, New York: Frances Printer Publishers.

Frenken, K. 2007. 'Entropy Statistics and Information Theory'. In *The Elgar Companion to Neo-Schumpeterian Economics*, edited by H. Hanusch and A. Pyka. Cheltenham, UK and Northampton MA: Edward Elgar, pp. 544–55.

Frenken, K. and Boschma, R. A. 2007. 'A Theoretical Framework for Evolutionary Economic Geography: Industrial Dynamics and Urban Growth As a Branching Process'. *Journal of Economic Geography*, 7(2007): 635–49.

Frenken, K., Saviotti, P. P. and Trommetter, M. 1999. 'Variety and Niche Creation in Aircraft, Helicopters, Motorcycles and Microcomputers'. *Research Policy*, 28: 469–88

Frenken K., Van Oort, F. and Verburg, T. 2007. 'Related Variety, Unrelated Variety and Regional Economic Growth'. *Regional Studies*, 41: 685–97.

Friedmann, J. R. P. 1972. 'A General Theory of Polarized Development'. In *Growth Centers in Regional Economic Development*, edited by N. M. Hansen. New York: The Free Press, pp. 82–107.

Funke, M. and Ruhwedel, R. 2001. 'Product Variety and Economic Growth: Empirical Evidence for the OECD Countries'. *IMF Staff Papers*, 48(2): 225–42.

Furtado, C. 1958. 'Capital Formation and Economic Development'. In *The Economics of Underdevelopment*, edited by A. N.Agarwala and S. P. Singh. Oxford: Oxford University Press.

——1961. *Desenvolvimento e subdesenvolvimento*. Rio de Janeiro: Fundo de Cultura.

GEM-Brazil. 2012. *Empreendedorismo no Brasil*. Curitiba: Global Entrepreneurship Research Association – GERA in cooperation with Instituto Brasileiro da Qualidade e Produtividade (IBQP), Serviço Brasileiro de Apoio às Micro e Pequenas Empresas (SEBRAE), Fundação Getulio Vargas (FGV-EAESP), Serviço Social da Indústria (SESI/PR), Universidade Federal do Paraná (UFPR) and Instituto de Tecnologia do Paraná (Tecpar).

Giuliani, E. and Bell, M. 2005. 'The Micro-determinants of Meso-level Learning and Innovation: Evidence from a Chilean Wine Cluster'. *Research Policy*, 34: 47–68.

Giuliani, E., Pietrobelli, C. and Rabellotti, R. 2005. 'Upgrading in Global Value Chains: Lessons from Latin American Clusters'. *World Development*, 33(4): 549–73.

Glaeser, E. L., Kallal, H. D., Scheinkman, J. A. and Shleifer, A. 1992. 'Growth in Cities'. *Journal of Political Economy*, 100(6): 1126–52.

Godinho, M. M., Mendonça, S. F. and Pereira, T. S. 2004. *Towards a taxonomy of innovation systems*. [online] Lisbon: Institute for Economics and Business Administration (ISEG), Technical University of Lisbon. Available at: http://www.repository.utl.pt/bitstream/..5/../wp132005.pdf [Accessed 30 July 2009].

Granovetter, M. 1973. 'The Strength of Weak Ties'. *American Journal of Sociology*, 78: 1360–80.

——1985. 'Economic Action and Social Structure – The problem of Embeddedness'. *American Journal of Sociology*, 91(3): 481–510.

Gray Molina, G. and Purser, M. 2010. 'Human Development Trends since 1970: A Social Convergence Story'. *Human Development Reports*. Research Paper 2010/02, United Nations Development Programme.

Grebel, T., Pyka, A. and Hanusch, H. 2003. 'An Evolutionary Approach to the Theory of Entrepreneurship'. *Industry and innovation*, 4: 493–514.

Gries, T. and Naude, W. 2010. *Entrepreneurship and Human Development. A Capability Approach*. UNU-WIDER Working Paper No. 2010/68 [online]. Helsinki, Finland: United Nations University. Available at: http://www.wider.unu.edu/..papers/../wp2010-68.pdf [Accessed 4 January 2011].

Grootaert, C., Narayan, D., Nyhan Jones, V. and Woolcock, M. 2004. *Measuring Social Capital. An Integrated Questionnaire*. World Bank Working Paper, 18. Washingon D.C.: The World Bank.

Gruber, M. 2007. 'Managing the Process of New Venture Creation: an Integrative Perspective'. In *The Elgar Companion to Neo-Schumpeterian Economics*, edited by H. Hanusch and A. Pyka. Cheltenham, UK: Eward Elgar, pp. 182–92.

Hair, J. F., Anderson, R. E., Tatham, R. L. and Black, W. C. 1995. *Multivariate Data Analysis with Readings*. New Jersey: Prentice-Hall International, fourth edition.

Hall, A., Mytelka, L. and Oyeyinka, B. 2006. *Concepts and guidelines for diagnostic assessment of agricultural innovation capacity*. UNU-MERIT Working Paper Series, 2006-017. Available at: http://www.merit.unu.edu/publications/../wp2006-017.pdf [Accessed 31 August 2008].

Hall, J., Giovannini, E., Morrone, A. and Ranuzzi, G. 2010. 'A Framework to Measure the Progress of Societies'. *OECD Statistics Working Papers*, 2010/05 [online]. France:

OECD in Cooperation with the Italian National Institute of Statistics, Italy. Available at: http://www.oecd-ilibrary.Org/Economics/a-framework-to-measure-the-progress-of-societies_5km4k7mnrkzw-en [Accessed 12 February 2011].

Hanneman, R. A. and Riddle, M. 2005. *Introduction to Social Network Methods*. Riverside, CA: University of California.

Hanusch, H. and Pyka, A. 2007a. 'The Principles of Neo-Schumpeterian Economics'. *Cambridge Journal of Economics*, 31: 275–89.

——eds. 2007b. *The Elgar Companion to Neo-Schumpeterian Economics*. Cheltenham, UK: Edward Elgar.

——2007c. The Troika of Economic Growth and Development. In *EU Economic Development and Employment in the Context of the Lisbon Strategy*. Warsaw: Editing Company of the F. Skarbek Graduate School of Business Economics.

——2007d. 'Applying a Comprehensive Neo-Schumpeterian Approach to Europe and its Lisbon Agenda'. In *50 years of EU Dynamics, Integration – Financial Markets and Innovation*, edited by R. Tilly, P. Welfens and M. Heise. Berlin, Heidelberg, New York: Springer, pp. 275–300.

Harris, R. I. D. 1988. 'Technological Change and Regional Development in the UK: Evidence from the SPRU Database on Innovations'. *Regional Studies*, 22(5): 361–74.

Hart, S. L. 2010. *Capitalism at the Crossroads: Next Generation Business Strategies for a Post-Crises World*. New Jersey: Wharton School Publishing, Pearson Education, third edition.

Hartmann, D. 2006. 'Ciencia, Tecnología, Innovación y el desarrollo sostenible en el Perú'. *Boletin Economía y Bienestar*, 2(9): 9–12.

——2011. 'Meaningful Help for Self-help'. *Development and Cooperation*, 52(2011/4): 162–3.

Hartmann, D., Pyka, A. and Hanusch, H. 2010. 'Applying Comprehensive Neo-Schumpeterian Economics to Latin American Economies'. *Structural Change and Economic Dynamics*, 21: 70–83.

Hartmann, D. and Arata, A. 2011. 'Measuring Social Capital and Innovation in Poor Agricultural Communities. the Case of Cháparra Peru'. *FZID Discussion Paper, 30-2011*. Stuttgart: Hohenheim University.

Hausmann, R. and Hidalgo, C. A. 2010. 'Country Diversification, Product Ubiquity and Economic Divergence'. *CID Working Paper*, 201.

Hausmann, R. and Rodrik, D. 2003. 'Economic Development as Self Discovery'. *Journal of Development Economics*, 72(2): 603–33.

Hausmann, R., Hidalgo, C. A., Bustos, S., Coscia, M., Chung, S., Jimenez, J., Simoes, A. and Yildirim, M. A. 2011. *The Atlas of Economic Complexity. Mapping paths to prosperity*. Research Report Online, Harvard University and MIT [online book]. Boston: Center for International Development at Harvard University in cooperation with MIT's Macro Connections at the Media Lab. Available at: http://www.hks.harvard.edu/centers/cid/publications/featured-books/atlas [Accessed 13 February 2012].

Hayek, F. A. von. 1937. 'Economics and Knowledge'. *Economica*, 4: 33.

Heidenreich, M. 2005. *Nationale Innovationssysteme*. [lecture] Bamberg: the University of Bamberg. [no date, unpublished].

Hernandez, I. and Dewick, P. 2011. 'Social Entrepreneurship for the Generation of Networking Capabilities'. In *Catching up, Spillovers and Innovation Networks in a Schumpeterian Perspective*, edited by A. Pyka and M. Derengowski Fonseca. Heidelberg, Berlin, New York: Springer.

Hidalgo, C. 2010. 'Graphical Statistical Methods for the Representation of the Human Development Index and its Components'. *Human Development Research Paper*, 2010/39.

Hidalgo, C. and Hausmann, R. 2009. 'The Building Blocks of Economic Complexity'. *PNAS*, 106(26) June 30: 10,570–5.

Hidalgo, C., Klinger, B., Barabasi, L. and Hausmann, R. 2007. 'The Product Space Conditions the Development of Nations'. *Science*, 317: 482–7.

Hirschman, A. 1958. *The Strategy of Economic Development*. New Haven: Yale University Press.

Hoang, H. and Antoncic, B. 2003. 'Network-based Research in Entrepreneurship. a Critical Review'. *Journal of Business Venturing*, 18: 165–87.

Hollanders, H., Tarantola S. and Loschky A. 2009. 'Regional Innovation Scoreboard (RIS) 2009 Methodology Report'. *Enterprise and Industrie Magazine, Pro Inno Europe Paper*, 14.

Human development data and charts. 2013. [online] Available at: http://hdr.undp.org/en/ [Accessed 4 January 2012].

Ibrahim, S. S. 2006. 'From Individual to Collective Capabilities: The Capability Approach as a Conceptual Framework for Self-help'. *Journal of Human Development*, 7(3): 397–416.

Imbs, J. and Wacziarg, R. 2003. 'Stages of Diversification'. *American Economic Review*, 93(1): 63–86.

Imbs, J., Wacziarg, R. and Montenegro, C. 2011. *Economic Integration and Structural Change*. [presentation] October 5 2011. World Bank. [online] Available at: http://siter-esources.worldbank.org [Accessed 18 November 2011].

Immelt, J. R., Govindarajan, V. and Timble, C. 2009. 'How GE is Disrupting Itself'. *Harvard Business Review*, October 2009.

INEI, Instituto Nacional de Estadística e Informática de Perú. 1993. *Censo Nacional Poblacional y de Vivienda*. [online] Lima: INEI. Available at: http:// www.inei.gob.pe [Accessed 15 February 2010].

——2005. *Censo Nacional Poblacional y de Vivienda.* [online] Lima: INEI. Available at: http://www.inei.gob.pe [Acessed 15 February 2010].

ILO, International Labour Organization. 1976. *Employment, Growth, and Basic Needs: A One World Problem*. Geneva: World Employment Programme, research in retrospect and prospect , International Labour Organization, p. 278.

——2008. *World of Work Report 2008: Income Inequalities in the Age of Financial Globalization*. Geneva: International Institute for Labour Studies.

——2009. *Yearbook of Labour Statistics*. Geneva: International Labour Office.

——2010. *International Labour Migration: A Rights-based Approach*. Geneva: International Labour Office.

IPEA. 2009. *Brasil em desenvolvimento: Estado, planejamento e políticas públicas*. Brasilia: Instituto de Pesquisa Economica Aplicada.

Jacobs, J. 1969. *The Economy of Cities*. New York: Random House.

Jacquemin, A. P. and Berry, C. H. 1979. 'Entropy Measure of Diversification and Corporate Growth'. *Journal of Industrial Economics*, 27(4): 359–69.

Jaramillo, H., Lugones, G. and Salazar, M., eds. 2001. *Manual de Bogotá. Normalización de Indicadores de Innovación Tecnológica en América Latina y el Caribe*. Bogotá and Buenos Aires: Red Iberoamericana de Indicadores de Ciencia y Tecnología (RICYT), Organización de Estados Americanos (OEA), Programa CYTED.

Jobson, J. D. 1992. *Applied Multivariate Data Analysis (II): Categorical and Multivariate Methods*. Berlin, Heidelberg, New York, Tokyo: Springer.

Johannison, B. 1988. 'Business Formation: A Network Approach'. *Scandinavian Journal of Management*, 4(3-4): 83–99.

Johnson, B., Edquist, C. and Lundvall, B.-A. 2003. 'Economic Development and the National System of Innovation Approach'. Presentation at *First Globelics Conference*, Rio de Janeiro, 3–6 November 2003. [online] Available at: https://smartech.gatech.edu/bitstream/handle/1853/43154/BengtAkeLundvall_2.pdf [Accessed 2 June 2004].

Juma, C., Fang, K., Honca, D., Huete-Perez, J., Konde, V., Lee, S. H., Ivinson, A., Robinson, H. and Singh, S. 2001. 'Global Governance of Technology: Meeting the Needs of Developing Countries'. *International Journal of Technology Management*, 22(7/8): 629–55.

Kagel, J. H. and Roth, A. E., eds. 1995. *The Handbook of Experimental Economics (I)*. Princeton, NJ: Princeton University Press.

Katz, J. 2007. 'Cambios estructurales y ciclos de destrucción y creación de capacidades productivas y technológicas en America Latina'. *Globelics Working Paper Series*, 2007 (06).

Kelley, D. J., Bosma, N. and Amorós, J. E. 2011. *Global Entrepreneurship Monitor 2010*. Global Report. Babson Park (USA), London (UK), Santiago (Chile): Global Entrepreneurship Research Association (GERA) in cooperation with Babson College, Universidad de Desarrollo and London Business School. Available at: http://www.gem-consortium.org/docs/266/gem-2010-global-report [Accessed 15 November 2011].

Kendall, M. G. and Gibbons, J. D. 1990. *Rank Correlation Methods*, fifth edition. London: Edward Arnold.

Kirzner, I. M. 1973. *Competition and Entrepreneurship*. Chicago: University of Chicago Press.

Klepper, S. 1997. 'Industry Life Cycles'. *Industrial and Corporate Change*, 6(1): 145–81.

Klinger, B. and Lederman, D. 2006. 'Diversification, Innovation, and Imitation inside the Global Technological Frontier'. *World Bank Policy Research Paper*, 3872.

Knight, F. H. 1921. *Risk, Uncertainty and Profit*. Boston: Houghton Mifflin.

Krueger, A. 1985. 'Import Substitution Versus Export Promotion'. *Finance and Development*, 22(2): 20–3.

Krugman, P. 1991a. *Geography and Trade*. Cambridge: MIT Press.

——1991b. 'Increasing Returns and Economic Geography'. *Journal of Political Economy*, 99: 483–99.

Kuklys, W. 2005. *Amartya Sen's Capability Approach: Theoretical Insights and Empirical Application*. Berlin: Springer-Verlag.

Kuznets, S. 1966. *Modern Economic Growth: Rate, Structure and Spread*. New Haven and London: Yale University Press.

——1971. 'Modern Economic Growth: Findings and Reflections'. Lecture to the memory of Alfred Nobel. [online]. 11 December 1971. Available at: http://www.nobelprize.org/nobel_prizes/economic-sciences/laureates/1971/kuznets-lecture.html [Accessed 1 June 2005].

Lancaster, K. 1966. 'A New Approach to Consumer Theory'. *Journal of Political Economy*, 74(2): 132–57.

Lasuén, J. R. 1973. 'Urbanisation and Development – The Temporal Interaction between Geographical and Sectoral Clusters'. *Urban Studies*, 10: 163–88.

Lewis, A. W. 1954. 'Economic Development with Unlimited Supplies of Labour'. *Manchester Scholl*, 22(2): 131–91.

Lin, N. 1999. 'Building a Network Theory of Social Capital'. *Connections*, 22(1): 28–51.

——2003. *Social Capital, a Theory of Social Structure and Action*. Cambridge: Cambridge University Press.

Lin, J. and Monga, C. 2011. 'Growth Identification and Facilitation: The Role of the State in the Dynamics of Structural Change'. *Development Policy Review*, 29 (3): 264–90.

Liñán, F. and Santos, F. J. 2007. 'Does Social Capital Affect Entrepreneurial Intentions?' *International Advances in Economic Research* [online], 13 (4) November: 443–53. Available at: http://link.springer.com/article/10.1007%2Fs11294-007-9109-8 [Accessed 23 August 2008].

Lipsey, R. G., Carlaw, K. I. and Bekar, C. T. 2005. *Economic Transformations: General Purpose Technologies and Long-Term Economic Growth*. Oxford: Oxford University Press.

List, F. 1841. *Das Nationale System der Politischen Ökonomie*. Basel: Kyklos.

López-Claros, A., Altinger, L., Blanke, J., Drezeniek, M. and Mia, I. 2006a. 'Assessing Latin American Competitiveness: Challenges and Opportunities'. In *The Latin America Competitiveness Review 2006 – Paving the Way for Regional Prosperity*, edited by K. Schwab, and A. Lopez-Claros. Geneva: World Economic Forum, pp. 1–36.

Lopez-Claros, A., Porter, M. E., Sala-i-Martin, X. and Schwab, K. 2006b. *The Global Competitiveness Report 2006–2007*. Navarra: World Economic Forum in cooperation with IESE Business School (University of Navarra) and the Anselmo Rubiralta Center for Globalization and Business Strategy.

Lu, Q. 2000. *China's Leap into the Information Age: Innovation and Organisation in the Computer Industry*. Oxford: Oxford University Press.

Lundvall, B.-Å. 1988. 'Innovation as Interactive Process: From User-Producer Interaction to the National System of Innovation'. In *Technical Change and Economic Theory*, edited by G. Dosi, C. Freeman, R. Nelson, G. Silverberg and L. Soete. London and New York: Pinter Publishers, pp. 349–69.

——1992. *National Systems of Innovation: Towards a Theory of Innovation and Interactive Learning*. London: Pinter.

——2007. 'Innovation System Research. Where it came from and where it might go'. *Globelics Working Paper Series*, 2007-01.

Lundvall, B-A., Joseph, K. J., Chaminade, C. and Vang, J., eds. 2011. *Handbook of Innovation Systems and Developing Countries: Building Domestic Capabilities in a Global Setting*. Cheltenham: Edward Elgar Publishing.

Maddison, A. 1991. *Dynamic Forces in Capitalist Development: A Long-Run Comparative View*. USA: Oxford University Press.

——2003. *The World Economy: Historical Statistics*. OECD Development Centre Studies, Paris: OECD.

Malerba, F. 2002. 'Sectoral Systems of Innovation and Production'. *Research Policy*, 31(2): 247–64

Malthus, T. R. [1803] 1989. 'An Essay on the Principle of Population: or a View of Its Past and Present Effects on Human Happiness: with an Inquiry into Our Prospects Respecting the Future Removal or Mitigation of the Evils Which it Occasions. In *An Essay on the Principle of Population: or a View of Its Past and Present Effects on Human Happiness: with an Inquiry into Our Prospects Respecting the Future Removal or Mitigation of the Evils Which it Occasions*, edited by P. James. Cambridge: Cambridge University Press.

Marshall, A. [1890] 1961. *Principles of Economics*. London: Macmillan, ninth edition.

Maskell, P., Eskelinen, H., Hannibalson, I., Malmberg, A. and Vatne, E. 1998. *Competitiveness, Localised Learning and Regional Development. Specialisation and Prosperity in Small Open Economies.* New York: Routledge.

Marx, K. 1867. *Das Kapital: Kritik Der Politischen Ökonomie. Buch I: Der Produktionsprocess Des Kapitals.* Hamburg: Verlag Otto Meissner.

Marx, K. and Engels, F. 1848. *Das Manifest Der Kommunistischen Partei.* London: Bildungs-gesellschaft Für Arbeiter.

Merton, R. K. 1968. 'The Mathew Effect in Science'. *Science*, 159 (3810): 56–83.

Metcalfe, S. 1995. 'The Economic Foundations of Technology Policy: Equilibrium and Evolutionary Perspectives'. In *Handbook of the Economics of Innovation and Technological Change*, edited by P. Stoneman. Oxford, UK and Cambridge, US: Blackwell Publishers.

Milanovic, B. 2007. *Worlds Apart: Measuring International and Global Inequality.* Princenton, NJ: Princeton University Press.

Mill, J. S. [1859] 1974. *On Liberty.* London: Parker [republished, 1974, London: Harmondsworth].

Miller, R., Marks, N. and Michaelson, J. 2008. 'Innovation and Well-Being'. *Innovation Index Working Paper*, September 2008. London: NESTA.

Ministerio de Agricultura de Perú (MINAG). 2007. Estadísticas Agrarias. [online] Available at: http:// www.minag.gob.pe [Accessed 3 February 2010].

Modern Times. 1936. Directed by Charles Chaplin. Beverly Hills, California: United Artists.

Monge, M., Hartwich, F. and Halgin, D. 2008. 'How Change Agents and Social Capital Influence the Adoption of Innovations among Small Farmers. Evidence from Social Networks in Rural Bolivia'. *International Food Policy Research Institute (IFPRI) Discussion Paper*, 761.

Morone, P. and Taylor, R. 2004. 'Small World Dynamics and the Process of Knowledge Diffusion. The Case of the Metropolitan Area of Greater Santiago De Chile'. *Journal of Artificial Societies and Social Simulation*, 7(2): 1–28.

Morone, P. and Taylor, R. 2006. 'Knowledge Diffusion with Complex Cognition'. In *Applied Evolutionary Economics and the Knowledge-based Economy*, edited by A. Pyka and H. Hanusch. Cheltenham: Edward Elgar.

Myrdal, G. 1957. *Economic Theory and Underdeveloped Regions.* London: Gerald Duckworth.

Mytelka, L. K. 2000. 'Local Systems of Innovation in a Globalised World'. *Industry and Innovation,* 7(1).

Neffke, F. and Svensson Henning, M. 2008. 'Revealed Relatedness: Mapping Industry Space'. Papers in Evolutionary Economic Geography (PEEG), 0819. Utrecht: Urban and Regional research centre Utrecht, Utrecht University.

Neffke, F., Svensson Henning, M., Boschma, R., Lundquist, K.-J. and Olander, L.-O. 2008. 'Who Needs Agglomeration? Varying Agglomeration Externalities and the Industry Life Cycle'. *Papers in Evolutionary Economic Geography (PEEG)*, 0808. Utrecht: Urban and Regional Research Centre Utrecht, Utrecht University.

Nelson, R. 1993. *National Innovation Systems: A Comparative Analysis.* New York: Oxford University Press.

Nelson, R. and Winter, S. 1982. *An Evolutionary Theory of Economic Change.* London: Belknap Press.

Neri, M. C., ed. 2009. *Pagando a Promessa do Microcrédito: Institucionalidade e Impactos Quantitativos e Qualitativos do CrediAmigo e do Comunidade*. Rio de Janeiro: FGV/IBRE, CPS.

North, D. 1990. *Institutions, Institutional Change and Economic Performance*. New York: Cambridge University Press.

Nurkse, R. 1953. *The Problem of Capital Formation in Underdeveloped Countries*. Oxford: Basil Blackwell.

Nussbaum, M. 2001. *Women and Human Development: The Capabilities Approach*. Cambridge: Cambridge University Press.

Nussbaum, M. and Sen, A. 1993. *The Quality of Life*. Oxford: Oxford University Press.

Ocampo, J. A. and Vallejo, J. 2012. 'Economic Growth, Equity and Human Development in Latin America'. *Journal of Human Development and Capabilities: A Multi-Disciplinary Journal for People-Centered Development*, 13(1): 107–33.

OECD. 1997. *National Innovation Systems*. Paris: OECD.

——2005. *Oslo Manual. Guidelines for Collecting and Interpreting Innovation Data*. Paris: OECD, third edition.

——2009. *OECD Patent Statistics Manual*. Paris: OECD publications.

Omamo, S. W. and Lynam, J. K. 2003. 'Agricultural Science and Technology Policy in Africa'. *Research Policy*, 32: 1681–94.

Oosterlaken, I. 2013. 'Taking a Capability Approach to Technology and Its Design. A Philosophical Exploration'. In *Simon Stevin Series in the Ethics of Technology*. The Netherlands: Technische Universiteit Delft, Technische Universiteit Eindhoven, University of Twente, pp. 1–263.

Oosterlaken, I. and Hoven, J., eds. 2012. *The Capability Approach, Technology and Design*. [online] Springer Series: Philosophy of Engineering and Technology, 5. Available at: http://www.springer.com/philosophy/epistemology+and+philosophy+of+science/book/978-94-007-3878-2 [Accessed 2 August 2013].

Oswald, A. J. 1997. 'Happiness and Economic Performance'. *The Economic Journal*, 107(445): 1815–31.

Parsons, T. and Smelser, N. J. 1956. *Economy and Society*. New York: Free Press.

Pasinetti, L. L. 1981. *Structural Change and Economic Growth*. Cambridge: Cambridge University Press.

——1983. *Structural Economic Dynamics*. Cambridge: Cambridge University Press.

Patel, S. J. 1974. 'The Technological Dependence of Developing Countries'. *Journal of Modern African Studies*, 12(1): 1–18.

Patel, P. and Pavitt, K. 1994. The Nature and Economic Importance of National Innovation Systems. *STI Review*, 14. Paris: OECD.

Perez, C. 1983. 'Structural Change and the Assimilation of New Technologies in the Economic and Social System'. *Futures*, 15(5): 357–75.

——2002. *Technological Revolutions and Financial Capital. The Dynamics of Bubbles and Golden Ages.* Cheltenham: Edward Elgar.

——2007. 'Great Surges of Development and Alternative Forms of Globalisation'. *Working Paper in Technology, Governance and Economic Dynamics*, 15. Tallin: The Other Canon Foundation in cooperation with Tallinn University of Technology.

——2011. IX International Symposium on Evolutionary Economics. 'Technological Revolutions, Major Financial Crashes and Implications'. [presentation] 8–10 September 2011. Pushchino, Russia: Moscow Center for Evolutionary Economics

Perroux, F. 1955. 'Notes sur la notion de 'pôle de croissance'. *Économie appliqué*, 7: 307–20.

Pigou, A. C. 1920. *The Economics of Welfare*. London: Macmillan.

Plott, C. R. and Smith, V. L., eds. 1998. *Handbook of Experimental Economics Results*. Amsterdam, New York: North-Holland.

Porter, M. E. 1990. *The Competitive Advantage of Nations*. New York: Free Press.

——1998. 'Clusters and the New Economics of Competition'. *Harvard Business Review*, 98609 (Nov-Dec): 77–90.

Portes, A. and Sensenbrenner, J. 1993. 'Embeddedness and Immigration: Notes on the Social Determinants of Economic Action'. *American Journal of Sociology*, 98(6): 1320–50.

Prahalad, C. K. 2004. *The Fortune at the Bottom of the Pyramid: Eradicating Poverty through Profits*. Upper Saddle River, NJ: Wharton School Publishing.

Prahalad, C. K. and Hart, S. L. 2002. 'The Fortune at the Bottom of the Pyramid'. *Strategy+Business*, 26: 54–67.

Prebisch, R. 1949. 'El desarrollo económico de la Améric aLatina y algunos de sus principales problemas'. *El Trimestre económico*, XVI(63): 347–431.

——1950. *The Economic Development of Latin America and Its Principal Problems*. New York: United Nations.

——1959. 'Commercial Policy in Underdeveloped Countries'. *American Economic Review*, 49(2): 251–73.

——1964. Planteamiento del comercio internacional y el desarrollo. In *Nueva política comercial para el desarrollo. Informe a la Conferencia de Naciones Unidas sobre Comercio y Desarrollo*. United Nations, Genebra, 23March 1964. México: FCE, pp. 9–37.

Programa de las Naciones Unidas para el Desarrollo en Peru, PNUD-Peru. 2006. *Índice de desarrollo humano a escala departamental, provincial y distrital – cuadros estadísticos*. Lima: PNUD-Peru.

Putnam, R. D. 1993. *Making Democracy Work: Civic Tradition in Modern Italy*. Princeton, NJ: Princeton University Press.

——2000. *Bowling Alone: The Collapse and Revival of American Community*. New York: Simon and Schuster.

Pyka, A. 1999. *Der kollektive Innovationsprozeß – Eine theoretische Analyse informeller Netzwerke und absorptiver Fähigkeiten*. Berlin: Duncker and Humblodt.

——2002. 'Innovation Networks in Economics: from Incentive-based to the Knowledge-based Approaches'. *European Journal of Innovation Management*, 5: 152–63.

——2011. *Social Innovations from a Neo-Schumpeterian Perspective*. [presentation] Lisbon Civic Forum 16 September 2011. Barcelona: University Abat Oliba CEU.

Pyka, A. and Fagiolo, G. 2007. 'Agent-based-modelling: a Methodology for Neo-schumpeterian Economics'. In *The Elgar Companion to Neo-Schumpeterian Economics*, edited by H. Hanusch and A. Pyka. Cheltenham, UK: Edward Elgar.

Pyka, A. and Scharnhorst, A., eds. 2009. *Innovation Networks – New Approaches in Modelling and Analysing*. Heidelberg, Berlin, New York: Springer.

Pyka, A., Cantner, U. and Krueger, J. J. 1999. 'Twin Peaks – what the Knowledge Based Approach Can Say about the Dynamics of World Income Distribution'. *Institute for Economics Discussion Paper Series 189*, Universität Augsburg.

Pyka, A., Gilbert, N. and Ahrweiler, P. 2007. 'Simulating Knowledge Generation and Distribution Processes in Innovation Collaborations and Networks'. *Cybernetics and Systems: An International Journal*, 38: 667–93.

Pyke, F., Becattini, G. and Sengenberger, W., eds. 1990. *Industrial Districts and Inter-firm Cooperation in Italy*. Geneva: International Institute for Labour Studies.

Rabellotti, R. and Schmitz, H. 1999. 'Internal Heterogeneity of Industrial Districts in Italy, Brazil and Mexico'. *Regional Studies*, 33(2): 97–108.

Raimondi, A. 1929. *El Perú. Itinerario de Viajes*. Primer fascículo: cuaderno VI viajes por el departamento de Arequipa 1863. Lima: Imprenta Torres Aguirre.

Ranis, G., Stewart, F. and Ramirez, A. 2000. 'Economic Growth and Human Development'. *World Development*, 28 (2): 197–219.

Rawls, J. 1971. *A Theory of Justice*. New York: Oxford University Press.

Ray, D. 1998. *Development Economics*. Princeton, NJ: Princeton University Press.

Rebelo, S. 1991. 'Long-Run Policy Analysis and Long-Run Growth'. *Journal of Political Economy*, 99: 500–21.

Reynolds, P. D., Camp, S. M., Bygrave, W. D., Autio, E. and Hay, M. 2001. *The Global Entrepreneurship Monitor 2001 Executive Report*. London, UK and Babson Park, MA: Global Entrepreneurship Research Consortium (GERA), United Nations Associations of the United States of America and The Business Council for the United Nations in cooperation with London Business School, Babson College, IBM and Kaufmann Center for Entrepreneurial Leadership.

Rickett, M. 2006. 'Theories of Entrepreneurship: Historical Development and Critical Assessment'. In *The Oxford Handbook of Entrepreneurship*, edited by M. Casson, B. Yeung, A. Basu, and N. Wadeson. Oxford: Oxford University Press, pp. 33–58.

Rist, G. 1996. *Le développement, Histoire d'une croyance occidentale*. Paris: Presses de Sciences Po.

Robbins, L. 1938. 'Interpersonal Comparisons of Utility: A Comment'. *Economic Journal*, 48(192):635–41.

Robeyns, I. 2005. 'The Capability Approach: A Theoretical survey'. *Journal of Human Development*, 6(1): 93–114.

Rodrik, D. 2004. *Industrial Policy for the 21st Century*. [online] Boston: Harvard University, John F. Kennedy School of Government. Available at: http:// http://www.hks.harvard.edu/fs/drodrik/Research%20papers/UNIDOSep.pdf [Accessed 12 June 2007].

Rogers, E. M. 1962. *Diffusion of Innovations*. Glencoe: Free Press

Romer, P. M. 1986. 'Increasing Returns and Long-Run Growth'. *Journal of Political Economy*, 94: 1002–37.

——1990. 'Endogenous Technological Change'. *The Journal of Political Economy*, 98 (5-2): S71-S102.

Rosenstein-Rodan, P. M. 1943. 'Problems of Industrialisation in Eastern and South-eastern Europe'. *Economic Journal*, 53: 202–11.

Sachs, J. D. 2005. *The End of Poverty: Economic Possibilities for Our Time*. New York: Penguin Books.

Sala-i-Martin, X. and Artadi, E. V. 2004. *The Global Competitiveness Index. Global Competitiveness Report*. Geneva: Global Economic Forum.

Santos, F. J. C. 2004. 'Convergencia, desarrollo y empresarialidad en el proceso de globalización económica'. *Revista de Economía Mundial*, 10(11): 171–202.

Santos Cumplido, F. J. and Guzmán, J. 1999. 'Hacia un modelo explicativo del empresario de calidad'. *Economia Industrial*, 325: 133–50.

Saviotti, P. P. 1996. *Technological Evolution, Variety and the Economy*. Cheltenham, UK: Edward Elgar.

——2000. 'On the Policy Implications of Variety Growth for Developing and Industrialising Countries'. *BNDES/FINEP/FUJB Project on Arranjos E Sistemas Produtivos Locais E*

210 Bibliography

As Novas Políticas De Desenvolvimento Industrial E Tecnológico, Nota Técnica 7. Rio De Janeiro: Instituto De Economia Da Universidade Federal Do Rio De Janeiro.

Saviotti, P. P. and Frenken, K. 2008. 'Export Variety and the Economic Performance of Countries'. *Journal of Evolutionary Economics*, 18(2): 201–18.

Saviotti, P. P. and Pyka, A. 2004. 'Economic Development by the Creation of New Sectors'. *Journal of Evolutionary Economics*, 14(1): 1–35.

Saxenian, A. L. 1994. *Regional Advantage: Culture and Competition in Silicon Valley and Route 128.* Cambridge, MA: Harvard University Press.

——2006. *The New Argonauts: Regional Advantage in a Global Economy*. Cambridge, MA: Harvard University Press.

Schmitz, H. 2004. *Local Enterprises in the Global Economy. Issues of Governance and Upgrading*. Northhampton, MA, USA and Cheltenham, UK: Edward Elgar.

Schnell, R., Hill, P. B. and Esser, E. 2005. *Methoden der empirischen Sozialforschung*. München and Wien: Oldenbourg Verlag, seventh edition.

Schubert, C. 2012. 'Is Novelty Always a Good Thing? Towards an Evolutionary Welfare Economics'. *Journal of Evolutionary Economics*, 22(3).

Schumpeter, J. A. 1912. *Theorie der wirtschaftlichen Entwicklung*. Berlin: Duncker and Humblodt.

——1939. *Business Cycles: a Theoretical, Historical and Statistical Analysis*. New York: McGraw Hill.

——1943. *Capitalism, Socialism and Democracy*. London: Allen and Unwin.

——1954. *History of Economic Analysis*. London: Routledge.

Schwartz, B. 2004. *The Paradox of Choice. Why More is Less*. New York: Harper Collins Publisher.

Sen, A. 1970a. *Collective Choice and Social Welfare*. San Francisco, CA: Holden-Day.

——1970b. Interpersonal Aggregation and Partial Comparability. *Econometrica*, 38(3): 393–409.

——1979. Tanner lectures on human values. *Equality of What?* [lecture] [online]. Salt Lake City, UT: University of Utah May 22. Available at: http://tannerlectures.utah.edu/_documents/a-to-z/s/sen80.pdf [Accessed 12 May 2007].

——1981. *Poverty and Famines: an Essay on Entitlement and Deprivation*. Oxford: Clarendon Press.

——1982. *Choice, Welfare and Measurement*. Oxford: Basil Blackwell.

——1985a. *Commodities and Capabilities*. Amsterdam: North-Holland.

——1985b. 'Well-being, Agency and Freedom: the Dewey Lectures 1984'. *The Journal of Philosophy*, 82(4): 169–221.

——1995. *Inequality Reexamined*. Oxford: Oxford University Press.

——1996. 'On the Foundations of Welfare Economics: Utility, Capability and Practical Reason'. In *Ethics, Rationality, and Economic Behaviour*, edited by F. Farina, F. Hahn and S. Vanucci. Oxford: Oxford University Press.

——1998a. Nobel Prize lecture. *The Possibility of Social Choice*. [lecture] [online] Cambridge UK: Trinity College 8 December 1998. Available at: http://www.nobelprize.org/nobel_prizes/economic-sciences/laureates/1998/sen-lecture.pdf [Accessed 29 January 2005].

——1998b. Amartya Sen – Biographical. [online] Available at: http://www.nobelprize.org/nobel_prizes/economics/laureates/1998/sen-autobio.html [Accessed 11 June 2011].

——1999. *Development as Freedom*. Oxford: Oxford University Press.

——2002. *Rationality and Freedom*. Cambridge and London: Harvard University Press.

——2006. *Identity and Violence. The Illusion of Destiny*. W. W. Norton & Company.

——2009. *The Idea of Justice*. London: Penguin.

Serageldin, I. 1996. 'Sustainability As Opportunity and the Problem of Social Capital'. *Brown Journal of World Affairs*, 3(2): 187–203.

Serida, J., Borda A. and Nakamatsu, K. 2007. *Global Entrepreneurship Monitor*. Perú, Lima: Global Entrepreneurship Research Consortium (GERA) in cooperation with Universidad ESAN.

Shannon, C. E. 1948. 'A Mathematical Theory of Communication'. *Bell System Technical Journal*, 27 (3): 379–423.

Sicsú, J. 2013. *Dez anos que abalaram o Brasil. Os resultados, as dificuldades e os desafios dos governos Lula e Dilma*. Rio de Janeiro: Geracao Editorial.

Simmel, G. [1908] 1955. Conflict and the Web of Group Affiliations. New York: Free Press.

Simon, A. 1947. *Administrative Behavior: a Study of Decision-Making Processes in Administrative Organization*. New York: Macmillan.

——1957. *Models of Man: Social and Rational*. New York: Wiley.

Singer, H. W. 1949. *Post-War Price Relations in Trade between Under-Developed and Industrialized Countries*. UN document no E/CN.1/Sub.2/W.5. Lake Success NY: UNDEA.

Smith, A. [1776] 1977. *An Inquiry into the Nature and Causes of the Wealth of Nations*. Chicago: University Of Chicago Press.

——[1759] 1982. 'The Theory of Moral Sentiments'. In *The Glasgow Edition of the Works and Correspondence of Adam Smith*, edited by D. D. Raphael and A. L. Macfie. Indianapolis: Liberty Fund.

Solow, R. 1956. 'A contribution to the Theory of Economic Growth'. *Quarterly Journal of Economics*, 70: 65–94.

——1957. 'Technical Change and the Aggregate Production Function'. *The Review of Economics and Statistics*, 39: 312–20.

Spielman, D. J., Davis, K., Negash, M. and Ayele, G. 2011. 'Rural Innovation Systems and Networks: Findings from a Study of Ethiopian Smallholders'. *Agriculture and Human Values*, 28: 195–212.

Srinivas, S. and Sutz, J. 2008. 'Developing Countries and Innovation: Searching for a New Analytical Approach'. *Technology in Society*, 30: 129–40.

STEPS Centre. 2010. *Innovation, Sustainability, Development: A New Manifesto*. Brighton: STEPS Centre.

Steward, F. 1979. 'Country Experience in Providing for Basic Needs'. *Finance and Development*, 16(4): 23–6.

——2005. 'Groups and Capabilities'. *Journal of Human Development*, 6(2): 185–204.

Stiglitz, J. E., Sen, A. and Fitoussi, J.-P. 2009. *Report by the Commission on the Measurement of Economic Performance and Social Progress*. [online] Available at: http://www.stiglitz-sen-fitoussi.fr/documents/rapport_anglais.pdf [Acessed 15 March 2011].

Stirling, A. 2007. 'A General Framework for Analysing Diversity in Science, Technology and Society'. *Journal of the Royal Society Interface*, 2007(4): 707–19.

——2010. 'Keep it Complex'. *Nature*, 468: 1029–31.

Streeten, P. 1979. 'From Growth to Basic Needs' *Finance and Development*, 16(3): 28–31.

Streeten, P., Burki, S. J., Ul Haq, M., Hicks, N. and Stewart, F. 1981. *First Things First: Meeting Basic Human Needs in Developing Countries*. Oxford: Oxford University Press for the World Bank.

Strogatz, S. 2003. *SYNC: The Emerging Science of Spontaneous Order*. New York: Hyperion.

Swann, P. G. M. 2009. *The Economics of Innovation: An Introduction*. Cheltenham, UK: Edward Elgar Publishing Company.

Swedberg, R. 1990. *Economics and Sociology. Redefining the boundaries: Conversations with Economists and Sociologists*. Princeton, NJ: Princeton University Press.

Szirmai, A., Naudé, W. and Goedhuys, M., eds. 2011. *Entrepreneurship, Innovation, and Economic Development*. Oxford: Oxford University Press.

Tesfatsion, L. and Judd, K. L., eds. 2006. *Handbook of Computational Economics*. Amsterdam: Elsevier, vol 2.

The Economist 2010. S*pecial Report: Innovation in Emerging Markets*. [online] Available at: http://www.economist.com/node/15879369 [Accessed 14 November 2011].

——2011. *The Magic of Diasporas*. [online] Available at: http://www.economist.com/node/21538742 [Accessed 21 December 2011].

Tödtling, F. and Trippl, M. 2005. 'One Size Fits All? Towards a Differentiated Regional Innovation Policy Approach'. *Research Policy*, 34: 1203–19.

Toye, J. 1987. *Dilemmas of Development – Reflections on the Counter Revolution in Development Theory and Policy*. Oxford: Blackwell.

UNDP-Brazil. 2013. *Atlas do desenvolvimento humano no Brasil 2013*. [online] Available at: http://www.pnud.org.br/IDH/Atlas2013.aspx?indiceAccordion=1&li=li_Atlas2013 [Accessed 31 July 2013].

UNDP. 1990. *Human Development Report 1990. Concept and Measurement of Human Development*. New York, Oxford: Oxford University Press.

——1991. *Human Development Report 1991: Financing Human Development*. New York, Oxford: Oxford University Press.

——2001. *Human Development Report 2001. Making New Technologies Work for Human Development*. New York, Oxford: Oxford University Press.

——2009. *Human Development Report 2009. Overcoming Barriers: Human Mobility and Development*. New York, Oxford: Oxford University Press.

——2010. *Human Development Report 2010. The Real Wealth of Nations: Pathways to Human Development*. New York, Oxford: Oxford University Press.

UNRISD. 2010. *Combating Poverty and Inequality*. Geneva: UNRISD – United Nations Research Institute for Social Development.

UNU-MERIT. 2010. European Innovation Scoreboard 2009. Comparative Analysis of innovation performance. Pro Inno Europe, InnoMetrics. [online] Available at: http://www.statistik.at/web_de/static/subdokumente/b_cis_bis_2004-06_eis_2009.pdf [Accessed 21 September 2010].

UNU-MERIT and the EC-JRC. 2006. European Innovation Scoreboard 2006. Comparative analysis of innovation performance. Pro Inno Europe, Innometrics. [online] Available at: http://www.berlin-partner.de/fileadmin/chefredaktion/pdf/studien-rankings/2006_en_European-Innovation-Scoreboard.pdf [Accessed 29 August 2008].

Valente, T. W. 2012. *Network Interventions*. Science, 337(6090): 49–53.

Van Zwanenberg, P., Ely, A. and Stirling, A. 2009. 'Emerging Technologies and Opportunities for International Science and Technology Foresight'. *STEPS Working Paper 30*. Brighton: STEPS Centre.

Vázquez-Barquero, A. 2002. *Endogenous Development. Networking Innovation, Institutions and Cities*. London and New York: Routledge Studies in Development Economics.

Veblen, T. 1898. *Why is Economics Not an Evolutionary Science?* The Quarterly Journal of Economics, 12.

——1899. *The Theory of the Leisure Class: An Economic Study of Institutions*. Macmillan Publishers.

Wallerstein, I. 1974. *The Modern World System*. New York, London: Academic Press.

Wasserman, S. and Faust, K. 1994. *Social Network Analysis: Methods and Applications*. Cambridge: Cambridge University Press.

Watts, D. J. and Strogatz, S. H. 1998. 'Collective Dynamics of "Small-world" Networks'. *Nature*, 393(6684): 409–10.

Weber, M. [1922] 1947. *The Theory of Social and Economic Organization*. New York: Free Press.

Weitzman, M. L. 1998. 'Recombinant Growth'. *Quarterly Journal of Economics*, 113: 331–60.

Williamson, J. 1989. 'What Washington Means by Policy Reform'. In *Latin American Readjustment: How Much has Happened*, edited by J. Williamson. Washington: Institute for International Economics.

Woolcock, M. and Narayan, D. 2000. 'Social Capital: Implications for Development Theory, Research, and Policy'. *The World Bank Research Observer*, 15(2).

World Bank. 2003. *World Development Report 2003: Sustainable Development in a Dynamic Economy*. New York: Oxford University Press.

——2006. *Enhancing Agricultural Innovation: How to Go Beyond the Strengthening of Research Systems*. Washington D.C.: The World Bank.

——2008. *World Development Report 2008: Agriculture for Development*. Washington D.C.: The World Bank.

——2013. PovcalNet: an online poverty analysis tool. [online] Available at: http://iresearch.worldbank.org/PovcalNet/index.htm [Accessed 31 January 2013].

Yunus, M. 2007. *Creating a World Without Poverty: Social Business and the Future of Capitalism*. New York: Public Affairs.

Ziegler, R. 2010. 'Innovations in Doing and Being: Capability Innovations at the Intersection of Schumpeterian Political Economy and Human Development'. *Journal of Social Entrepreneurship*, 1(2): 255–72.

Index

Note: Tables are indicated in bold; graphs in italics.